Philosophy, Public Policy, and Transnational Law

Series Editor
John Martin Gillroy
International Relations
Lehigh University
Bethlehem, PA, USA

Philosophy, Public Policy, and Transnational Law seeks, uniquely, to publish new and innovative arguments about global law and policy that transcend realist/positivist assumptions and the conventions of current legal/policy discourse. This series means to encourage the application of systematic philosophical and theoretical arguments to practical policy and legal issues that combine domestic, comparative or international law. We will pursue scholarship that integrates the superstructure of the positive law with its philosophical and public policy substructure, and which, in this way, produces a more three dimensional understanding of transnational law and its evolution, meaning, imperatives and future. We seek dissertations, solo and edited volumes, as well as innovative reports that integrate new methods, epistemologies and interdisciplinary perspectives with practical issues on the full range of policy and legal dilemmas challenging transnational relations.

More information about this series at
http://www.palgrave.com/gp/series/14550

Deepak Mawar

States Undermining International Law

The League of Nations, United Nations, and Failed Utopianism

palgrave
macmillan

Deepak Mawar
Dickson Poon School of Law
King's College London
London, UK

Philosophy, Public Policy, and Transnational Law
ISBN 978-3-030-64788-9 ISBN 978-3-030-64789-6 (eBook)
https://doi.org/10.1007/978-3-030-64789-6

This Palgrave Macmillan imprint is published by the registered company Springer Nature Switzerland AG
The registered company address is: Gewerbestrasse 11, 6330 Cham, Switzerland

For my family, Suchi, Nasib, Roshan & Diana

Series Editor's Preface

As series editor of Philosophy, Public Policy and Transnational Law I am happy to welcome *States Undermining International Law: The League of Nations, United Nations, and Failed Utopianism*, by Deepak Mawar. This unconventional book fits neatly into our effort to make the study and analysis of international law more interdisciplinary, philosophically sophisticated and in touch with the controversial connections between transnational law and public policy. This argument is a creative, unique and thought-provoking effort to understand both the history and policy process of the international legal system. It accomplishes what the tension between philosophical concepts, positive law and history ought to do: make the reader think in new ways about conventional assumptions and terminologies.

Superficially, this argument touches many familiar bases, including state sovereignty, philosophical idealism, utopianism, human rights and the degree to which international institutions like the United Nations and its predecessor, the League of Nations, affected rights as well as international peace and security. But fundamentally, the argument challenges the reader to see all of these concepts in a new, interdisciplinary and philosophically innovative light.

Specifically, instead of the conventional argument that idealism is primarily connected to individual human rights, this book makes the assertions, not only that idealism requires significant attention to the peace and security provided by states as 'social communities,' but that the stability of sovereign authority is necessary to any 'ideal' or utopian rights situation, if it is not to fail. Deepak Mawar's core idea of 'emancipatory idealism' is both unique and controversial. It is unique in that it focuses on 'communities of individuals' instead of separate persons and it is controversial in its effort to advance the peace and security of sovereign states not as a point of positivist legality but in philosophically idealistic terms as a basic imperative towards a more utopian future. No longer is peace and security the guarantee of the status-quo, but the basis for idealistic or real-utopian change.

The way in which this text changes the assumptive structure of international or transnational law engages the reader to reassess their assumptions about some of the basic principles of international law and what their expression in transnational policy means for individuals, nation-states and international organisations. On the last point, this book uniquely reconstructs the history of the League of Nations and the United Nations, and in this way presents an innovative picture of the international legal system. Through the lens of his core idea of 'emancipatory idealism,' the author moves the academic and legal debate on issues and institutions forward by shaking predispositions and challenging our expectations about the evolution of transnational law.

Overall, this is an important book, especially for a world caught up in a pandemic that different sovereign states have handled with varying degrees of success, but with no central coordination. The juxtaposition between individual rights, sovereignty and the welfare of transnational communities could not be more stark, and the failure of conventional approaches and assumptions about the role of the different agents of the international legal system, more acute.

It is clear that conventional assumptions and single discipline analysis are no longer adequate to the anticipation and regulation of threats to national and international 'peace and security.' The interdisciplinary and philosophical informed, non-traditional analysis of the human focus on 'utopia', presented in this book, is a necessary update to the literature of transnational law and an example of the kind of rethinking of ideas and facts, as well as their historical interrelationship, that will be necessary in the new world being created by the present crisis.

I welcome this fascinating, innovative and thought-provoking book into our series....

Fall 2020 J. M. Gillroy

Acknowledgements

This project has been a part of my life for almost six years and I am so proud of its final destination place. It started off as my doctoral thesis, which I defended at King's College London in 2019, and for it now to be published as a book is far beyond the hopes and aspirations I had when I first sat down in front of my laptop and began to type away in the university library one late night. I have toiled away at this subject, seeking to understand more about international law and this journey certainly had its fair share of ups and downs, so to see this book be released into the world in the way it has is a truly happy moment. But I couldn't have done this alone and I must thank a certain number of people for all their help.

First of all, I must thank my supervisors at King's College London, Philippa Webb and Thomas Schultz. Without their guidance and support, I would not have managed the calibre of work that I produced. Their help in writing this book has been invaluable. I must also thank my examiners, Gleider Hernandez and Patrick Capps for the way in which they challenged and drove me to produce a better piece of work. Their feedback has helped me to not only produce this book but has also helped me become a better academic. Their guidance has been so influential to my overall development, so for all this I thank them both greatly. A big thank you goes also to John Martin Gillroy who has supported this projected and gave me the opportunity to publish this monograph. His guidance and belief helped me to turn my thesis into a book.

I must also thank Palgrave Macmillan and the many people I have had the good fortune of working with to publish this book. Michelle Chen, Rebecca Roberts and Naveen Das, your efforts and support throughout the process has been nothing short of fantastic.

I must also thank a whole host of friends that have supported me throughout the years. I'm truly grateful for your friendship Luke Abbs, Michael Graschitz, Aniq Ahmed, James Fowler, Laurence Robinson, Anand Krishna, Aakash Dega, Mrug Upadhyay, Shaakir Salam, Musaab Kassim, Helen (Yunzi) Han, Jon Andvig, Tai Griffiths, Johnny Malynn, Kartar Ryatt, Danielle Belcher and Alex Finch.

A final thank you goes to my family for the countless years of support. An infinite number of words couldn't do enough to thank you for everything you have done for me. You have supported me through whatever path I have chosen, allowed me to grow and encouraged me to challenge myself always. So firstly I must thank my parents, Suchi and Nasib Mawar, my brother and my sister-in-law, Roshan and Gail Mawar, and finally my fiancée Diana Muñoz. I would not have reached the heights that I have were it not for you all.

Contents

CHAPTER 1

States Undermining International Law: An Introduction

In Robert Nozick's highly influential work, *Anarchy, State and Utopia*, whilst exploring utopianism, he cuts straight to the heart of all utopian theories. Nozick identified that utopian theories seek 'to realise all social and political goods.'[1] Inherent within all utopian theories is the desire to prevent suffering, and to guarantee that all individuals are provided a path to justice when required. Utopian theories ultimately seek social and political goods to trump possibilities of social and political ills. Given this understanding of utopianism, it becomes clear as to why such theories maintain relevance and influence in international law.

An illustration of such a claim is the development of international law following large-scale crisis, the formation of the United Nations after the Second World War being one such example. Creating an international organisation designed to maintain international peace and security was an attempt to remedy the social and political ills of the Second World War and achieve social and political goods by creating a process to deal with threats to the peace of the international community. It highlights a strong desire to overcome the destabilisation that was a result of the

[1] R. Nozick, *Anarchy, State and Utopia*, (2001) at 297.

D. Mawar, *States Undermining International Law*,
Philosophy, Public Policy, and Transnational Law,
https://doi.org/10.1007/978-3-030-64789-6_1

Second World War and to usher in a period of international peace.[2] The emergence of the human rights movement in 1948 is a further illustration of the influence of utopianism in international law. In Eleanor Roosevelt's famous speech, delivered at the University of Paris (at the Sorbonne), the push towards establishing human rights highlights the desire to realise all social and political goods:

> I have chosen to discuss [the preservation of human freedom] in the early days of the General Assembly because the issue of human liberty is decisive for the settlement of outstanding political differences and for the future of the United Nations. The decisive importance of this issue was fully recognized by the founders of the United Nations at San Francisco. Concern for the preservation and promotion of human rights and fundamental freedoms stands at the heart of the United Nations. Its Charter is distinguished by its preoccupation with the rights and welfare of individual men and women. The United Nations has made it clear that it intends to uphold human rights and to protect the dignity of the human personality. In the preamble to the Charter the keynote is set when it declares: "We the people of the United Nations determined...to reaffirm faith in fundamental human rights, in the dignity and worth of the human person, in the equal rights of men and women and of nations large and small, and... to promote social progress and better standards of life in larger freedom." This reflects the basic premise of the Charter that the peace and security of mankind are dependent on mutual respect for the rights and freedoms of all.[3]

Such utopian sentiments of ensuring the peace and security of mankind spurred the creation of the Universal Declaration of Human Rights,

[2] In fact, preparations for the creation of the United Nations date as far back as 1941, with the Atlantic Charter, as President Roosevelt and Prime Minister Churchill hoped to 'establish a peace which will afford to all nations the means of dwelling in safety within their own boundaries' and 'to bring about the fullest collaboration between all nations in the economic field with the object of securing, for all, improved labour standards, economic advancement and social security... after the destruction of the Nazi tyranny.' 'The Atlantic Charter- Declaration of Principles issued by the President of the United States and the Prime Minister of the United Kingdom' (August 14, 1941). https://www.nato.int/cps/en/natohq/official_texts_16912.htm?. Last accessed 1 July 2019. See also P. Malanczuk, *Akehurst's Modern Introduction to International Law*, (1997), 27.

[3] Eleanor Roosevelt, 'Struggle for Human Rights,' (University of Paris, September 28, 1948). https://erpapers.columbian.gwu.edu/struggle-human-rights-1948, Last accessed 19 June 2019.

and the subsequent international human rights instruments such as the International Covenant on Civil and Political Rights and the International Covenant on Economic, Social and Cultural Rights for example. Following the events of the Second World War, the human rights movement was a process of establishing a future where the realisation of social and political goods was at the forefront of international affairs. Ultimately, what these developments in the international legal system reveal is how utopianism has maintained an influential position in the development of international law when the international community is strongly focused on advancing positive change.

Indeed, when considering E. H. Carr and Ken Booth's support of a specific utopian theory—'utopian realism'—it becomes clear why there is reverence for utopianism in international law and international relations. Carr 'advocated a mature methodological approach situated between the naivety of the utopian and the sterility of the realist, one that has the ability to advance prescriptions that are not, at present, wholly attainable.'[4] Similarly, Booth 'advocated a "utopian realism" that navigates between the extremes of both utopianism and realism in an effort to effect positive change'.[5] Though the ideological foundations of Carr and Booth differ, they understood the ability utopianism possessed in pushing positive change on the international stage.

All three scholars—Nozick, Carr and Booth—regardless of their specific position on utopianism, emphasised the merits of such an ideology. It is the broader endeavour of this project to emphasise the merits of utopianism to international law. Such an ideology has been vitally important when attempting to recover from the international community's most testing periods, and it holds great potential to help structure the international legal system to realise all social and political goods.

However, E. H. Carr also noted how States, at times, have been a barrier to the achievement of utopian aspirations. Analysing the fall of the League of Nations and the collapse of utopian aspirations during the *interbellum* period, Carr asserted that States adopted a Darwinist doctrine

[4] A Hehir, '"Utopian in the Right Sense": The Responsibility to Protect and the Logical Necessity of Reform', (2017) 31.3 *Ethics & International Affairs* 335, at 337. See also E.H. Carr, *Twenty Years' Crisis*, (1964) at 10–12, 202.

[5] Ibid., at 337. See also K. Booth, 'Security in Anarchy: Utopian Realism in Theory and Practice', (1991) 67.3 *International Affairs* 531, 534.

where the utopian movement of the time 'became the tool of vested interests and was perverted into a bulwark of the *status quo*.'[6] Carr alludes to the State's tendency to forego utopian aspirations for the realisation of self-interested goals that solely advance their own position. In establishing the State's ability and past record of 'destroying utopian projects',[7] he emphasises the dangers of the primacy of States in international law for those seeking to realise utopian aspirations on the international stage.

Koskenniemi made similar claims, stating that a 'pure fact approach' to international law, where the State maintains its position as the primary object and subject of the international law, is problematic. The pure fact approach is based on the principle established in the *Lotus* case, where the Permanent Court of International Justice observed that there were no rules governing the exercise of jurisdiction by Turkey over foreign vessels in the High Seas.[8] To avoid a *non liquet*, the Court claimed that unless specific prohibiting rules exist, State sovereignty is unlimited.[9] In the absence of a positive prohibition, Turkey was presumed to possess jurisdiction. The concern for Koskenniemi was that with such an approach, 'it will do away with the law's binding force altogether. For if norms have no natural meaning but require interpretation and if the interpretative rule calls simply for respect to liberty, then hard cases can only be decided by letting each State do what it wishes.'[10] For those seeking to realise utopian aspirations, such a precedent lacks the balance between the individual liberties of the sovereign and the values of the collective community. States are thus in a position to bend the international legal system towards their vested interests and away from the utopian aspirations of the collective international community. Such a concern is evident in the *Nuclear Weapons* advisory opinion. When investigating whether the use of nuclear weapons would be a breach of international law, the International Court of Justice was unable to 'conclude definitively whether the threat or use of nuclear weapons would be unlawful,' when assessing 'the

[6] E.H. Carr, *Twenty Years' Crisis*, (1964) at 10–12, 225.

[7] Carr, *supra* note 6, at 224.

[8] PCIJ: Lotus Case, Ser. A 10 p. 30.

[9] Ibid., 18–19.

[10] M. Koskenniemi, *From Apology to Utopia*, (1989), 258.

current state of international law.'[11] The Court based its judgement on the fact that no legal precedent had been established by States expressly agreeing the prohibition of the threat or use of nuclear weapons. The Court's position on this specific issue of international law highlights the lack of balance between the sovereign's liberty and the collective values of the international community. Most importantly, it shows how dependent the realisation of utopian aspirations is upon the will of States. The realisation of utopian aspirations is wholly dependent on whether States are willing to construct the international legal system conducive for such outcomes.

Subsequently, the primary research aim of the project is to demonstrate that for those seeking to utilise international law to realise utopian aspirations, the primary position States enjoy in the international legal system is problematic. The research aim is analysed in a two-stage process. First, I assess the development and practice of international law from the perspective of utopianism. For the purposes of this project, and in the context of international law, such goods can be achieved through the protection of all individuals and communities of individuals from modes of oppression such as violations of human rights. I explain why the achievement of utopian goals should be encouraged. The first stage is to highlight the positive impact such an ideology has had on the development of international law. Second, I will argue that the primacy of the State in the international legal system is problematic from a utopian perspective. The key issue is that States tend to prioritise their domestic duties over the international duties, which has been to the detriment of achieving the international community's utopian aspirations.

In order to effectively survey these aspects of international law, the project rests predominantly on the analysis of the history of international law and the exploration of legal and political philosophy. The historical analysis of international law helps to identify the points of interest in regard to how utopianism has helped develop the international legal system, and when State primacy has been a barrier to the achievement of utopian goals of international law. Additionally, the examination of the relevant legal and political theories helps to explain the central arguments posed. Using the works of Hegel, Critical Theorists such as Habermas, Adorno and Linklater, and international lawyers such as Phillip Allott

[11] *Legality of the Threat or Use of Nuclear Weapons*, Advisory Opinion, ICJ Reports 1996, 226, 266.

and Anne Peters, I highlight the importance of utopianism to international law. Moreover, the theories of Thomas Franck, Abram Chayes and Antonia Handler Chayes, Jack Goldsmith and Eric Posner, Carl Schmitt, Michel Foucault and Hans Kelsen for example, assist in explaining the nature of the State and how its position as the primary object and subject of international law is problematic.

Chapters 2 and 3 outline the theoretical framework of the project. Chapter 2 addresses the important role utopianism plays in the international legal system by first introducing the concept, emancipatory idealism as a utopian focal goal of international law, to better explain and justify the importance of protecting individuals and communities of individuals from modes of oppression; and secondly, highlighting that utopianism is most likely to influence the international legal system following a large-scale crisis. Chapter 3 explores the nature of the State and the tensions that plague its dual duties: the first duty being to the State's domestic territory, the other duty being to the international community. By exploring the fact that the State is inherently designed to prioritise its domestic duty over its international duty, I argue that the primacy States enjoy in international law requires reassessment. Through setting up the theoretical framework, the two hypotheses of the project are established, reflecting the two-stage process of analysis. Hypothesis 1 is that the central aim of emancipatory idealism (which is to protect individuals and groups of individuals from modes of oppression) plays a significant role in the development of international law. Hypothesis 2 suggests that State primacy in the international legal system is problematic for those who seek to achieve emancipatory idealism.

Consequently, Chapters 4 and 5 seek to prove the hypotheses of the project by historically analysing the successes and failures of the League of Nations and the United Nations in achieving utopian goals of international law. Chapter 4 investigates the rise and fall of the League of Nations. By analysing the League's efforts to ensure international peace and security following the First World War, the chapter highlights the influential role utopianism has played in the development of international law following large-scale crisis. Chapter 4 also considers the League's failure to achieve the utopian goals of international law because of States, demonstrating how State primacy was a key factor to the collapse of the League. A similar approach is taken in Chapter 5, with the first part of the chapter analysing the influence of utopianism on the creation of the United Nations. The second part of Chapter 5 focuses on the

Security Council and the manner in which Member-States utilise the executive organ of the UN to further their own realist interests over the interests of the international community. The ramifications of such a phenomenon mean that the Security Council has at times failed to maintain international peace and security, leaving individuals and communities of individuals vulnerable to oppression.

In the last two centuries, international law's development has been in significant part a response to large-scale suffering and injustice. The desire to ensure that the international community is able to achieve social and political goods has been key during the establishment of an international legal framework. Revisiting the creation of the League of Nations and the United Nations supports the argument that utopianism has played a vital role in the development of international law. The history of international law suggests that when the international community has been destabilised by large-scale crisis such as the two World Wars, the appetite for achieving utopian goals is substantial. However, as the international community moves further away from such large-scale crisis, the State's appetite for achieving utopian goals that shall benefit the international community as a whole, is conditioned more so on whether it furthers the protection of their primary domestic duties. Thus, it becomes apparent that the power of utopianism has the ability to transform the international community to achieve social and political goods and help it recover from its most testing times. However, what also becomes clear is that States have and will continue to be a barrier to achieving utopian goals of international law, if it furthers their self-interest.

References

Booth, Ken. 'Security in Anarchy: Utopian Realism in Theory and Practice', (1991) 67.3 *International Affairs*, 527–545.

Carr, E.H. *The Twenty Years' Crisis 1919–1935: An Introduction to the Study of International Relations*, (1948).

Hehir, Aidan. '"Utopian in the Right Sense": The Responsibility to Protect and the Logical Necessity of Reform', (2017) 31.3 *Ethics & International Affairs*, 335–355.

Koskenniemi, Martti. *From Apology to Utopia: The Structure of International Legal Argument*, (2005).

Legality of the Threat or Use of Nuclear Weapons, Advisory Opinion of 8 July 1996, [1996], ICJ Rep. 226.

Malanczuk, Peter. *Akehurst's Modern Introduction to International Law*, (1997).

Nozick, Robert. *Anarchy, State and Utopia*, (2001).
Roosevelt, Eleanor. 'Struggle for Human Rights,' (University of Paris, September 28, 1948). https://erpapers.columbian.gwu.edu/struggle-human-rights-1948.
SS Lotus case (France v. Turkey), PCIJ Rep Series A No 10, at 18.
'The Atlantic Charter' Declaration of Principles issued by the President of the United States and the Prime Minister of the United Kingdom (August 14, 1941). https://www.nato.int/cps/en/natohq/official_texts_16912.htm?.
Wilde, Oscar. *The Soul of Man Under Socialism*, (1997).

CHAPTER 2

Emancipatory Idealism: A Utopian Focal Goal of International Law

2.1 Introduction

E. H Carr is most famously recognised for his critique of utopianism in his seminal work *The Twenty Years' Crisis 1919–1939*. He asserted that in the discipline of international relations the utopian 'believes in the possibility of more or less radically rejecting reality and substituting his utopia for it by an act of will.'[1] Carr went on further to claim that the 'complete utopian, by rejecting the causal sequence, deprives himself of the possibility of understanding either the reality which he is seeking to change or the processes by which it can be changed,'[2] and that 'the characteristic vice of the utopian is naivety.'[3] However, for all the scathing criticisms Carr directed towards utopianism, he saw value in such an ideology. When Carr critiqued realism he contended that the realist 'unconditionally accept[s] the causal sequence of events, depriv[ing] himself of the possibility of changing reality.'[4] Although utopianism may be naïve and

[1] E.H. Carr, *Twenty Years' Crisis, 1919–1939: An Introduction to the Study of International Relations*, (1964), 11.

[2] Ibid., at 11–12.

[3] Ibid., at 12.

[4] Ibid., at 11.

D. Mawar, *States Undermining International Law*, Philosophy, Public Policy, and Transnational Law, https://doi.org/10.1007/978-3-030-64789-6_2

not fully aware of reality, it is an important tool in advancing change in a way realists are unable to evoke.

It is this value of utopianism which is the integral focus of this chapter. Considering the ability of utopians to advance change in the realm of international relations, and indeed international law, the particular interest of this chapter is to highlight the important role utopianism plays in the international legal system. Subsequently, this chapter introduces the normative utopian concept 'emancipatory idealism' in order to advocate that the international legal system should be utilised to protect individuals and groups of individuals. Using a mixture of international lawyers, political scientists and philosophers, this chapter shall attempt to explain why international law's ultimate goal should be to protect individuals and groups of individuals on the basis that if such entities are not afforded the necessary protections, it is the technological and sociological advancement of human civilisation that is at risk. Furthermore, this chapter shall briefly critique the classical positivist tradition of international law in order to strengthen this chapter's central argument that international law should aim to protect individuals and groups of individuals for the sake of the survival and prosperity of the international community, and even human civilisation.

2.2 Human Dignity and Focal-Point Analysis

Before elucidating the value of utopianism in international law, the focal analysis theory requires clarification as it is an integral factor in examining the key questions of this chapter. Put simply, the focal analysis theory claims that specific focal goals or objectives outlined by social groups as a whole shape the manner in which a legal system—that such social groups shall be governed by—will develop.[5] Focal analysis gives social practices a sense of normativity for it helps characterise and organise the manner in which group activities are conducted.[6] Those engaged in a social practice justify their actions and undertake specific duties with the influence of norms and conceptions of how to conduct themselves towards achieving their purpose. The reasoning of any action is judged against this normative influence by which the social practice is defined. Such

[5] P. Capps, *Human Dignity and the Foundations of International Law*, (2009), 77.

[6] Ibid., at 77–78.

normative influences can be understood as part of its historic progression. 'The rationality, psychology and ideology of the individuals that comprise the practice drive its development, as does the sociological and physical environment within which it exists.'[7]

These complex normative influences are the crux of what is considered the subject of focal analysis. This methodological focus could be used to understand the international legal order as a normative practice and, in this way, could in fact help in understanding the manner in which the international legal system develops. The use of focal analysis legitimises the manner in which the international legal system develops by establishing such a methodological focus. 'If the purpose of the international legal order is to establish the conditions by which states can co-operate and co-exist, then we can begin to comprehend *prima facie*, the consent-based theory of international law—which clarifies the obligations states are under—is important and plays a vital role in the success of the international legal order as a practice.'[8] Considering it has a distinctive purpose of paramount importance to the international community and the international legal system is working towards such a purpose, the system is legitimised by this focal goal. The methodological focus therefore gives greater clarity as to the objective and nature of the international legal system. Furthermore, this legitimises the way in which the international community decides to develop the international legal system.

A prime example of the focal analysis theory being utilised is by the policy science school. McDougal and Lasswell employed the focal analysis methodology to legitimise the use of legal science in order to help focus the international legal system to achieve human dignity. McDougal asserted that legal science was a 'value-laden' form of inquiry directed towards reaching the goal of the protection of human dignity.[9] It is the assertion of an ideological conception that the community is encumbered with and consistently plays a role in determining the construction of a legal system. The point being here that legal orders can be developed with these values. This plays an important influence in the manner in which policies are shaped. Even the legal scientist who is on a journey

[7] Ibid., at 78.

[8] Ibid.

[9] Ibid., at 80.

of epistemological discovery in the field of law cannot help but to be influenced by this value or ideological standpoint:

> The Lasswell and McDougal version of policy science implies a distinction between institutional and ideological commitment: while the legal [scientist]... is supposedly able to view the mechanics of the legal process in a wholly dispassionate light—such detachment being the key to constructive legal critique— he or she cannot assume detachment from, and therefore cannot regard objectively, the social culture and values upon which the legal process is founded.[10]

For Lasswell and McDougal this central value or ideological standpoint is the concept of human dignity. The concept of human dignity focuses on the potential for a human being to live freely, independent of suffering and without any form of intrusion. For Laswell and McDougal, the intrinsic value of the concept of human dignity is not a debatable matter in a political or moral paradigm as it is the origin of all manners in which such debates move forward and consequently resulting in the shaping of legal structures. Moreover, such deviations from the values in normative practices can be subject to much criticism by the legal scientist. Furthermore, the legal official's actions are justified to the extent that practices implement the values in public decision-making.[11] Lasswell stresses this point further when critiquing McDougal's work with Florentino Feliciano, in *Law and Minimum Public Order*:

> They are explicitly cognizant of the fact that they occupy an observational vantage point. True what is said in a treatise of this kind flows into the stream of knowledge, prediction, and proposal reaching the decision-makers of many nations and associations. In the end, however, the decision-makers are the one who must expect to be better off—in terms of all their values—by following the lines of policy put forward in this book than by continuing to rely upon strategies that keep mankind at the brink.[12]

[10] N. Duxbury, *Patterns of American Jurisprudence*, (1995), 174.

[11] Capps, *supra* note 5, at 81.

[12] Ibid., 81. However to be more specific this argument is made in H Lasswell's introduction to M. McDougal and F. Feliciano, *Law and Minimum World Public Order: The Legal Regulation of International Coercion*, (1961).

The use of legal science in this particular paradigm is to promote the legal system to establish public order and peaceful relations for the community for which the system of law is presiding over. In this instance, human dignity is the central thrust to the conception of the normative practice. For the policy science school, the claim was that '[f]rom this man-centred, universalist and equalitarian perspective, the challenge is not merely to seek to resolve issues connected with law by "definition," but rather to relate authoritative decision to preferred public order.'[13] It seems that for the policy science school, legal scholarship can be used to direct law towards realising human dignity within the community it is governing and to have a transformative effect upon the community in a positive fashion. This influences their conduct to uphold such a value even on a non-coercive level. Laswell and McDougal stress such arguments for '[i]n any community, the legal system is but a part of a more inclusive system, the system of public order, which includes a preferred pattern for the distribution of values and a preferred pattern of basic institutions.'[14] Therefore, these normative practices are only the starting point, as the community's wider conception of this value is of primary importance for the successful operation of the system of law. 'This is why policy science reflects the strong claim made by versions of focal analysis: that all forms of law share a common practical purpose and actual normative practices called law can be criticised against this general concept.'[15]

2.3 Emancipatory Idealism

2.3.1 An Overarching Utopian Concept: Emancipatory Idealism

Though Capps, similar to Laswell and McDougal, suggested that human dignity may be a focal purpose of international law, this project seeks to utilise the focal analysis theory to explore how utopian focal goals have played an integral role in the development of international law. It is worth noting that human dignity is a focal goal that is in fact utopian in tradition. Human dignity as a focal goal of international law seeks to achieve some of the key goals for those focused on utilising international law for a

[13] H. Lasswell and M. McDougal, 'Criteria for a Theory about Law' (1970–71) 44 *S. Cal. L. Rev.* 362, at 374.

[14] Ibid., at 374–375.

[15] Capps, *supra* note 5, at 82.

utopian progression within the international community. The concept of human dignity focuses on the fact that the intrinsic worth of every person should always be respected, so that individuals 'are not to be perceived or treated merely as instruments or objects of the will of others,'[16] which is a utopian ideal. Therefore, advancing the concept of human dignity in the international legal system goes some way to ensuring international peace and security. However, human dignity is but a facet of an overarching utopian scheme to develop the international community positively and to maintain peaceful relations amongst states and the protection of every individual. Whilst the likes of Capps, Lasswell and McDougal have focused upon human dignity as a focal goal of international law, the aim of this project is to broaden the discourse. There are several primary goals of international law that differ in scope and objective but at times also correlate together to advance certain developments in the international legal system. Human dignity can be conceived as a focal goal of international law but not the only focal goal. Human dignity as one of the primary goals of international law has helped establish in some respect, the introduction of individual justice in international law, however it does not fully account for the most accelerated phases of development. As a focal goal of international law, its operation is somewhat limited. It is unable to wholly detail the most rapid phases of development the international legal system has undergone.

It would be more suitable to substitute human dignity with emancipatory idealism, as a heuristic model, in order to better account for the utopian development of international law. I believe that emancipatory idealism is a utopian focal goal of international law that's objective is larger in scope and for this reason explains the idealist progression of international law more broadly. It is one of the concepts that has driven the development of the legal system for the past four hundred years, and especially the last hundred years where we have seen two models of international law come into creation because of it. Put simply, emancipatory idealism is the idea that the protection of individuals and communities from wars and acts of oppression is of paramount importance in order to prevent the decline of civilisation and to ensure its development continues.

[16] O. Schacter, 'Human Dignity as a Normative Concept', (October 1983) 77.4 *American Journal of International Law* 848, at 849.

It is in postulating on human dignity, that it becomes clearer as to why such a heuristic model has been adopted in order to better account the significance utopian concepts have played in the development of international law. If human dignity is concerned with the protection of each individual's capacity to enjoy their liberties and to prosper independently from any forms of encroachment the question must be asked why is this so? Similarly, questions can be raised as to why every individual's human rights should be protected or even why is it that human security focuses on protecting the individual. These questions are answered by emancipatory idealists. Whilst concepts such as human dignity, human rights and human security establish safeguards for individuals or communities of individuals, emancipatory idealists give an explanation as to why safeguards are necessary for individuals or communities. Emancipatory idealists determine that every individual has an intrinsic worth to exist. They assert that every individual or community of individuals has the potential to contribute to the development of civilisation on either a technological or societal level. Therefore, if every individual has the potential to contribute to civilisational development, it is necessary to establish a stable political, economic and social environment for such persons to prosper. It is only under such stable conditions can individuals or communities successfully contribute. Conversely, modes of oppression such as war or genocide for example encroach upon the potential of individuals or communities of individuals and have an adverse effect, stunting civilisational development. With emancipatory idealism focusing on the protection of individuals or communities—whether they are the international community or regionalised communities—utopian developments in international law become more comprehendible. For example, the need to maintain international peace and security is justified as emancipatory idealists explain precisely why a stable political, economic and sociological environment is so vital. Revisiting the importance of concepts such as human rights and human dignity, emancipatory idealists assert the importance of such concepts as they are instrumental in ensuring the protection of individuals or communities. Such concepts ensure that such persons are able to operate in a stable political, economic and sociological environment in order to contribute to civilisational development on either a technological or societal level.

Therefore, the aim is not to replace human dignity with emancipatory idealism. Emancipatory idealism incorporates human dignity and its aims to ensure that all individuals are able to enjoy their liberties free from encroachment. In fact, those seeking to achieve emancipatory idealism naturally seek to achieve human dignity for such concepts ensure the protection of all individuals and groups of individuals. Emancipatory idealists encourage the achievement of human dignity, alongside the achievement of human security and the protection of every individual's human rights. The role emancipatory idealism plays is that it justifies the need to achieve human dignity by establishing every individual or community of individuals' potential to contribute to civilisational development on either a technological or sociological level. The shortcoming of human dignity is that its scope is somewhat limited for it does not fully justify why the intrinsic worth of every person should always be respected. Emancipatory idealists are able to justify the achievement of not just human dignity, but all utopian concepts. They are able to rationalise such a claim by asserting that the intrinsic worth of every individual or community of individuals lays in their capacity to contribute to civilisational development. It is in this desire to continue to see civilisation continue to advance that the aims of emancipatory idealism can be ascertained; which is to protect all individuals and communities of individuals from modes of oppression.

In order to further explore why emancipatory idealists place so much focus on protecting individuals and communities of individuals, German Idealism and Critical Theory play a key role. Such intellectual movements advance the argument that every individual has the capacity to contribute to civilisational development on both a technological and societal level. The foundations upon which emancipatory idealism is established are Georg Wilhelm Friedrich Hegel and Critical Theory. Such scholarly works provide the justification for emancipatory idealism, advocating that every individual or community of individual must be allowed a stable political, economic and societal environment. Whether it is exploring Hegel's *The Philosophy of History* or analysing Critical Theorist's work on emancipation, such sources nurture the argument that all individuals and communities have the potential to contribute to civilisational development and that all individuals or communities should be given the opportunity to do so.

2.3.2 *Hegel's Philosophy of History*

Hegel's work plays a significant role in strengthening the argument made by emancipatory idealists; that being that all individuals or communities must be provided a stable environment as they have the potential to contribute to civilisational development. His work supports such arguments when pronouncing his ethos of sociological and technological expansion in *The Philosophy of History*. This particular text is not merely a recollection of history, simply providing a surplus of information that is bare facts. Hegel himself said that 'philosophy of history means nothing but the thoughtful consideration of it.'[17] His work on history seeks to present the bare facts of history with thoughtful consideration and assumes that there is a rational process of development. He believed that history has some meaning and significance to the ontological scope of human beings. Human history is not a clutter of events void of purpose and conception. The course of history maintains significance in order to prelude to a better world still to come.[18] Hegel raised the notion that all facets of existence were part of history whether it is art, religion or science. They are all shaped by historical development and therefore every part of being is concerned with the notion of developing and realising freedom. 'It may unhesitatingly be granted that the philosophy of history should be placed at the close of the system.'[19] For those seeking to achieve emancipatory idealism, Hegel's position has value in advancing their central arguments. Hegel notes that such historical development has not exclusively occurred from one specific area, but from over a range of different communities of individuals.

Hegel took the example of the role and conception of the state to assert the notion that history is a process of development towards the realisation of freedom and knowledge. He treated history from the principle of the State. 'This followed Kant, who in 1784, in an original treatise, had apprehended the conception of the historical process from this point, because consciousness of freedom attained to objective distinctness in the State.'[20] Hegel ignored religion in his enquiry on the significance

[17] P. Singer, *Hegel: A Very Short Introduction*, (2001), 12.

[18] Ibid., at 15.

[19] Rosenkranz & Hall. 'Hegel's Philosophy of History', (October 1872) 6:4 *The Journal of Speculative Philosophy* 340, at 341.

[20] Ibid., at 341.

of history to development and furtherance. He instead focused on four particular ages of the world where the line of development can be plotted: '(1) the Oriental, (2) the Grecian, (3) the Roman, and (4) the German.'[21] Through this a dialectical process was identified, as Hegel believed the Greek and Roman age to be of the same ilk and essentially one. He thus listed the process of development that has occurred through the historical timeline as Johann Karl Friedrich Rosenkranz and G. S Hall suggest:

> Hegel gives this, therefore, in the form of the qualitative judgment, that in the Orient one is free; in the antique world, several; and in the modern world, all: or, in another form, (1) Despotism-Orient; (2) Republic-Greece and Rome; (3) Constitutional monarchy-the German State.[22]

Hegel thoroughly critiques and analyses how each age contributed to the development of civilisation. Whether it is the Oriental age of family preservation with the emphasis upon honour and obedience to one's family, Greek development of communitarian beliefs, Christian focus on the sanctity of the individual or German *synthesis*, all time periods were important to the overall historical development. Hegel adapts to the ethos that history should not be forgotten for civilisation is shaped by its history.

Moreover, such an example highlights how a stable political, economic and social environment can induce a contribution to civilisational development from any community of individuals. Such development in these specific ages has occurred when they were flourishing and void of modes of oppression. Thus, the acceleration in arts, technology, science, law, politics or philosophy for example depends on establishing a stable environment for individuals or communities. It supports the insistence of emancipatory idealists that every individual has an intrinsic worth to exist and why utopian developments in international law focus on maintaining international peace and security and preventing modes of oppression.

It is at this intersection that I believe it to be salient to discuss Hegel's perspectives on international law and relations. Although some scholars have pointed towards the fact that he treated both disciplines

[21] Ibid., at 344.

[22] Ibid., at 344.

with a certain level of 'indifference,'[23] Hegel's work nonetheless provides the strong backbone under which emancipatory idealism can be more extensively developed. Within Hegel's scholarly work, the international dimension is seen as a minor topic for he concentrated 'his attention on the social conflicts within the single political order.'[24] In fact, Hegel has often been seen as 'the ombudsman of that strand of political and legal thought that pleaded for moving away from the cosmopolitism of the enlightenment era and for endorsing the centrality of the nation State.'[25]

Hegel placed such importance upon the State, for the world of man becomes apparent for the first time in the State.[26] This is based on Hegel's insistence that the ethical community is the ultimate unit of social, political and moral life,[27] as the ethical life 'reconciles individuality and sociality, subjective self-consciousness and the social order, on the basis of intersubjective norms and customary rules and practices, which enable the individual to participate in social life.'[28] Moving deeper into the concept of ethical life, Hegel differentiates three components; the family, civil society and the State. Yet he regards the State as the most important component, for the State is 'the end and actuality of the substantial universal order and public life,'[29] for it 'constitutes the basis on which the family and civic society exist.'[30] Thus, for Hegel, the State is the actuality of the ethical idea,[31] for the State has been presented as the supreme embodiment of freedom, as 'freedom precisely consists in the membership of the individual in the community of the state.'[32]

[23] S. Dellavalle, 'The Plurality of States and the World Order of Reason: On Hegel's Understanding of International Law and Relations', in N. Bhuta, A. Pagden & B. Straumann (eds.), *System, Order and International Law: The Early History of International Legal Thought from Machiavelli to Hegel*, (2017), at 353.

[24] Ibid.

[25] Ibid., 352. See also Hermann Heller, *Hegel und der nationale Machtstaatsgedanke in Deutschland* (1921); Friedrich Meinecke, *Weltbürgertum und Nationalstaat*, (1922), 278.

[26] S. Avineri, *Hegel's Theory of the Modern State*, (2003), 178.

[27] G.W.F. Hegel, *Philosophy of Right*, trans. S.W Dyde, (2001), at 136, para 156.

[28] H. Jaeger, 'Hegel's Reluctant Realism and the Transnationalism of Civil Society', (2002) 28 *Review of International Studies* 497, at 502.

[29] Hegel, *supra* note 27, at 136, para 157.

[30] Jaeger, *supra* note 28, at 502.

[31] Hegel, *supra* note 27, at 194–195, para 257.

[32] Ibid., 195, at para 258.

It is the fundamental focus to realise the freedom of the individual that consequently pushes Hegel towards a state-centric theory, leading to some academics surmising that Hegel's theory of international law and relations is a realist theory.[33] For Hegel, a state-centric theory is based on the premise that individual freedoms are safeguarded:

> What is of the utmost importance is that the law of reason should be shot through and through by the law of particular freedom, and that my particular freedom should become identified with the universal end, or otherwise the state is left in the air. The state is actual only when its members have a feeling of their own self-hood and it is stable only when public and private ends are identical.[34]

Safeguarding individual freedom is of prime importance, for 'persons can be fully developed ethical individuals and full participants in community.'[35] Hegel was heavily focused on the vision of human self-realisation, for it serves as a 'basic material need for the preservation of humankind.'[36] He surmises that self-realisation can occur through '(1) the full development and expression of personality and subjectivity as free self-conscious individuals; (2) the full development and expression of citizenship, or our capability for free rational conduct at the level of social behaviour and interaction; and (3) the full cultivation and use of human intellectual powers in ways made possible by the unfettered flourishing of disciplines such as art, religion, science and philosophy.'[37] Subsequently, if individuals are able to reach such levels of self-realisation and additionally continue to contribute as a full participant in a community, it drives the development of humankind, expanding its limits and capabilities. Therefore, the individual and the community become invaluable, for it is the individual and the community they preside within that contribute to civilisational development on both a technological and societal level.

[33] T. Brooks, 'Between Statism and Cosmopolitanism: Hegel and the Possibility of Global Justice, in A. Buchwater (ed.), *Hegel and Global Justice*, (2012), at 66.

[34] Hegel, *supra* note 27, at 265.

[35] S.V. Hicks, *International Law and the Possibility of Just World Order*, (1999), 8.

[36] Ibid., at 8.

[37] Ibid., at 9. See also R. Schacht, 'Hegel, Marx, Nietzsche, and the Future of Self-Alienation', (April, 1991) 28.2 *American Philosophy Quarterly* 125, 131–132.

It is this intrinsic focus upon the value of the individual and the community to contribute to the realisation of the ethical life that urged Hegel to consider the positive nature of war. He deemed it 'a necessary step on the way to the higher self- realisation of the spirit.'[38] This was based upon the notion that 'almost every aspect of human experience—despite its limitedness—embodies a kind of partial truth on the way to the discovery of the absolute idea.'[39] War is not excluded from such a proposition, for 'in the state of war the independence of states is at stake,'[40] and precisely this frailty of the individual communities is what allows the spirit to develop further.[41] Ultimately, Hegel contends that war can help spur on the realisation of the ethical life and the progression of civilisation. However, the foundation upon which emancipatory idealism is established contradicts such assumptions on the positivity of war by returning to Hegel's *Philosophy of History* to negate such arguments. Hegel's selection of the four particular ages that contributed to civilisational development in a profound manner is all communities that were stable political, economic and social environments primed for technological and societal development. Such communities were able to safeguard the freedoms of individuals so that they could accomplish Hegel's vision of self-realisation in order to participate effectively within their community. Such accomplishments were therefore a direct result of the stable political, economic and sociological environment that they had maintained and established. Moreover, they were free from modes of oppression, thus becoming fertile ground for Hegel's vision of an ethical life.

A key feature of Hegel's work that plays significant importance to emancipatory idealism as a utopian focal goal of international law is the need to safeguard individuals and communities. It provides the justification for attempting to achieve the key aims of emancipatory idealism, as it explains the necessity of protecting individuals and communities

[38] Dellavalle, *supra* note 23, at 356.

[39] Ibid., at 355.

[40] G.W.F. Hegel, 'Vorlesungen über Naturrecht und Staatswissenschaft. Heidelberg 1817/18. Nachgeschrieben von P. Wannenmann', in Claudia Becker et al. (eds.), *Vorlesungen: Ausgewählte Nachschriften und Manuskripte*, vol. 1 (1983), 254; trans. G.W.F. Hegel, *Lectures on Natural Right and Political Science*, trans. J. Michael Steward and Peter C. Hodgson (1995).

[41] Dellavalle, *supra* note 23, at 356.

of individuals for the sake of contributing to civilisational development. Although Hegel imagined that the safeguards for individual freedom could also be realised through a state-centric theory, such goals can be translated within the framework of international law. It highlights a cosmopolitan interpretation of Hegel's work as 'he emerges as a visionary for a workable world order- an international order that can promote global peace, progress and human solidarity.'[42] Allen Wood asserts that:

> Hegel's historicised universalism that seeks to uncover, understand, further develop, and include whatever cultural and societal traditions have so far achieved the most adequate comprehension of the nature of reason and right, as well as the highest actualities of human potentialities, and the most comprehensive development of the human spirit in its moral, religious, aesthetic, and socio-political dimensions.[43]

This facet of Hegel's work provides the foundation upon which emancipatory idealism is established. Hegel's insistence on the principle of human universality being one of infinite importance[44] is a vital notion for it is the potential of individuals and communities of individuals to contribute to the developmental process of civilisation. For the capacity of the collective human spirit 'to raise itself from less adequate forms of self-comprehension and to conduct to more adequate ones'[45] establishes the necessity of protecting them from modes of oppression such as war, crimes against humanity or other violations to the freedoms of individuals.

2.3.3 Critical Theory's Principle of Emancipation

Similarly, critical theorists' principle of emancipation concurs with the desire and necessity for greater knowledge and epistemological strides forward. There is little surprise that critical theory and Hegelian philosophy do share such similarities in the desire for the expansion of

[42] Hicks, *supra* note 35 at 18. See also S. Avineri, *Hegel's Theory of the Modern State*, (2003), 194–207.

[43] Ibid., at 16. See also A.A. Wood, *Hegel's Ethical Thought*, (1990), 204.

[44] R. Fine, 'Contra Leviathan, Hegel's Contribution to Cosmopolitan Critique', in A. Buchwater(ed.), *Hegel and Global Justice*, (2012), at 50.

[45] Hicks, *supra* note 35, at 16.

civilisation for critical theory's origins come from the expansion and analysis of Marxist ideologies. Incidentally one of Hegel's most prominent students was Karl Marx, and he is very much considered to be a figure that advocated Hegelian philosophy in his writings. Thus, Hegel's work on the importance of history and its ability to progress civilisation draws parallels, in particular, with the earlier works of the Frankfurt School's most prominent figures such as Horkheimer and Adorno. Additionally, Habermas' work draws similar parallels to Hegel's philosophy. However, as the Frankfurt School and Critical Theory became more famed for the 'negative tendencies' in their later work,[46] 'Habermas diverged from the one contemporaneously developed by Adorno and Horkheimer, to the extent that Habermas recovered the research programme of the early critical theory.'[47] Additionally, Habermas' recovery of early critical theory does not correlate with the work of critical legal studies scholars who would deny that there is an ethical foundation to law. Scholars such as David Kennedy argue that 'legal principles, rules and policy arguments seem to dissolve far too easily into thin disguises for assertions of interests,'[48] for the 'normative moorings of the most basic doctrinal discourse by lawyers, scholars and judges seem infirm.'[49] Such a stance suggests that critical legal studies scholars hesitate to agree that the development of international law may contain an emancipatory project. Ultimately, this

[46] To analyse the turn of several prominent Critical Theorist to a more negative approach social philosophy see S. Brincat, 'On the Methods of Critical Theory: Advancing the Project of Emancipation beyond the Early Frankfurt School', at 219: 'While the early work of the Frankfurt School (FS) had expressed considerable hope for the eventual emancipation of humankind, the historical experiences of the defeat of the working class in Europe, the deformation of the Soviet Union, the rise of fascism, and the growth of the Western culture industry are all believed to have contributed to a brooding pessimism that ultimately culminated in a turn to religious metaphysics as a possible locus of negation (Horkheimer) or a retreat into aesthetics (Adorno). If one were to read isolated passages from the Adorno's *Minima Moralia*, Horkheimer's late essays, or even the whole text of *the Dialectic of Enlightenment*, one could be forgiven for assuming that society was perched on the edge of a precipice; like the sword of Damocles, hanging ever so precariously above society was the threat of totalitarian decay that seemed nigh inevitable.'

[47] L. Corchia, 'The Frankfurt School and the Young Habermas: Traces of an Intellectual Path (1956–1964)' (2015) 15.2 *Journal of Classical Sociology* 191, at 192.

[48] D. Kennedy, 'Critical Theory, Structuralism and Contemporary Legal Scholarship', (1985–1986) 21.2 *New England Law Review* 209, at 211.

[49] Ibid.

highlights the fragmented nature of critical theory and the scholars that operate under such a banner. It demonstrates the inherent nature of critical theory which is to analyse and critique the various aspects of society, leading various critical theorists to develop differing and unique avenues, perspectives and arguments. Although the potential for the emancipation of civilisation may not be a universally accepted by all critical theorists, there are those figures such as Jürgen Habermas and those that belong to the early critical theory wave that saw the possibility of the expansion of civilisation through emancipatory processes.

Such figures believed that the multidimensional methods of critical analysis through emancipation would lead to a progression in civilisation in all fields of existence. Horkheimer, in particular, was drawn towards the concern of human emancipation from suffering. With humankind buoyed by a drive towards achieving happiness, Horkheimer believed that this would help unfold all of humankind's capacities 'through the various materialist and humanist movements.'[50] He encouraged the practice of critical rationality, which would spur a 'revolution of consciousness,' as 'Horkheimer sought a critical theory to negate the "one-sidedness" in modern human society to point towards the future of a "rational organisation of human existence" and the "realisation of the good."'[51] Thus, the application of critical rationalism would help to advance the unfolding of humankind's capacities, as it would steer humankind's modes of development towards a 'reasonable organisation of society' and 'the abolition of social injustices.' Furthermore, Horkheimer placed the individual at the heart of such emancipatory advancements for 'when an active individual of sound common sense perceives the sordid state of the world, desire to change it becomes the guiding principle by which he organises given facts and shapes them into a theory.'[52] It asserts the notion that the individual

[50] Max Horkheimer, 'On the Concept of Philosophy', in W. Schirmacher (ed.), *German 20th Century Philosophy: The Frankfurt School*, (2000), at 7. See also S. Brincat, 'On the Methods of Critical Theory: Advancing the Project of Emancipation Beyond the Early Frankfurt School', (2011) 26.2 *International Relations* 218, at 220.

[51] S. Brincat, 'On the Methods of Critical Theory: Advancing the Project of Emancipation Beyond the Early Frankfurt School', (2011) 26.2 *International Relations* 218, at 221.

[52] M. Horkheimer, 'The Latest Attack on Metaphysics', in *Critical Theory: Selected Essays*, (1972), at 161–162.

has the potential to help emancipate humankind from suffering if the individual is provided with the suitable environment to do so. Moreover, it establishes the worth of every individual's existence for given the opportunity and correct tools they could help realise a 'reasonable organisation of society.'

Similarly, Adorno's work on the ethics of resistance nurtures ideals of emancipation and the belief in every individual's potential to contribute to the development of humankind. Adorno suggested that the ethics of resistance are an effective tool in dismantling social mechanisms of 'unfreedom,' which force subjects to 'adjust and accept socially given norms and pursue socially constituted ends.'[53] Subsequently, Adorno asserts that 'one is not living but only surviving in the late-capitalist world,'[54] and that 'worthwhile and valuable ends have been systematically removed and replaced by the means of self-preservation.'[55] Yet Adorno establishes that the ethics of resistance can overcome this if 'an autonomous (*mündig*) citizen' criticises and resists the administered world, the institutionalised bad, and the 'countless forms of morality imposed from outside' through 'the concrete denunciation of the inhuman.'[56] Adorno's ethics of resistance is somewhat analogous to Horkheimer's work on emancipation as it advances the ability of individuals to emancipate humankind from suffering towards Adorno's conception of a good life. Moreover, to effectively utilise the ethics of resistance, a key factor is the successful application of critical rationality for it uncovers the necessary means through which resistance should be conducted in order to dismantle social mechanisms of unfreedom. Nonetheless, Adorno establishes early Critical Theory ideals, supporting the intrinsic worth of every individual's existence, for they have the potential to contribute to humankind's development.

Emancipation is a central concern for Marxist thinkers, though the term comes with a great deal of ambiguity, so much so 'that the historical record is unfortunately replete with examples of unspeakably barbaric

[53] J.G. Finlayson, 'Adorno on the Ethical and Ineffable', (2002) 10.1 *European Journal of Philosophy* 1, at 2.

[54] C. Kaltofen, 'Engaging Adorno: Critical Security Studies After Emancipation', (2013) 44.1 *Security Dialogue* 37, at 43.

[55] Ibid.

[56] T.W. Adorno, *Probleme der Moralphilosophie*, (1963), 260.

behaviour being justified in the name of emancipation, of which imperialism and Stalinism are but two.'[57] Conventionally, Marxists have seen the belief in emancipation as a method of humanity mastering nature by developing on a technological level for its own benefit, fitting in with Hegel's belief in discovering freedom and knowledge. However, early critical theorists argued that humanity's increased domination over nature had been brought at too high a price, claiming that the mentality needed to conquer nature all to easily turn into the domination of other human beings.[58] Jürgen Habermas' central political point is that for emancipation to truly have a wider effect radical democracy is an absolute prerequisite. This establishes that the widest possible participation is invaluable and necessary. Effective radical democracy can successfully identify 'barriers to participation- be they social, economic or cultural.'[59] This in turn helps to understand how such barriers can be overcome, thus helping develop humanity in the correct direction for all.

Andrew Linklater followed Habermas' thesis on the potential of emancipation and for him such developments were a significant force in shaping international relations. Linklater believed in the inherent potential of critical theory and critical theorists' adoption of emancipation:

> No claim is made that critical theory is uniquely or lavishly endowed with the resources needed to flag the right course for the field. What is suggested is that critical theory possesses a vision of international relations which, when articulated more fully, can give direction to the field as a whole. While critical theory itself may not be the next stage, it can nevertheless shed light on what the ensuing phase should be. Critical theory can clarify the nature of the common scholarly enterprise to which different perspectives are related by setting out the particular strengths of different approaches and by showing how they can be drawn more closely together.[60]

[57] J. Bayliss, S. Smith, & P. Owens, *Globalisation of World Politics: An Introduction to International Relations*, (2011), 141.

[58] Ibid., at 141.

[59] Ibid.

[60] A. Linklater, 'The Question of the Next Stage in International Relations Theory: A Critical-Theoretical Point of View', (March 1992) 21 *Millennium: Journal of International Studies* 77, at 79.

Though Marxism (or possibly Hegel's work if one regards his work to have influenced Marx's writings) may have begun the devotion towards emancipation, it is critical theorists that identified a greater understanding of morality and that ethical behaviour is needed to efficiently undergo a process of emancipation. Cosmopolitan in nature, Habermas' argument raises the idea that human societies have evolved by learning how to utilise universal moral principles to resolve conflicting assertions about the organisation of social and political life. 'Modern challenges to class, ethnic, gender and racial forms of exclusion, challenges that stress the principle of self-determination, illustrate this social evolution.'[61] For these reasons, Habermas was greatly concerned with the ways in which human beings would include and exclude each other, and more specifically a central concern was that of the exclusion of particular individuals and groups. He conceived such exclusion a detriment to the development of societies and communities. This conception collaborates well with the particular idea of social human beings learning how to cope with the normative, sociological and praxeological facets of social life. The rationale of Habermas and Linklater is the use of more in-depth scrutiny using a wider variety of tools to conduct such a critique. Social and political inquiry is generally undertaken on the notion that the improvement upon the explanations and understandings of everyday life is a possibility and that it should be encouraged with the use of emancipatory methods. For Habermas and Linklater, there seems to exist a moral conviction that all individuals not only belong to their sovereign State but also to a wider stratosphere, which is in fact, the more inclusive community of humankind. This community that attempts to transcend the exclusionary trends of sovereign boundaries encourages cosmopolitan ideologies in order to form a world-unified order. Hence for critical theorists, the inclusion of all individuals and all communities is of the highest importance. This is because their particular normative, sociological and praxeological trend can contribute to the process of emancipation and for the development of human civilisation as a whole. This idea incidentally falls within the remit of emancipatory idealism. For each individual or collective of individuals (if given the freedom and liberty to flourish with the exclusion of oppression) can make a valid contribution to the development of the community of humankind.

[61] J. Habermas, *Communication and the Evolution of Society*, (1979), chapters 3–4.

Maintaining loyalty to the conception of emancipation, critical theorists such as Linklater and Habermas would object to intellectual dogmatism and disciplinary exclusiveness. Forgoing new paradigms of diverse academic points of view fuelled by a form of academic inquiry and movements that are in dissent with the more dogmatic intellectual strains is for such postmodern thinkers an unacceptable form of exclusiveness. Critical theorists have always remained a powerful advocate for 'explor[ing] new forms of community and different expressions of human identity.'[62] It follows in spirit the argument being brought forward about the reduction of exclusiveness in intellectual and social paradigms. Critical theory bears an essence of scepticism towards 'present orthodoxies and putative resolutions on the grounds that they depend on exclusionary practices.'[63] Deeply embedded in the composition of critical theory is the commitment towards human equality. There have been critical theorists such as Cos and Ashley who advocated for emancipation and the ascertainment of knowledge not just for technical interests, but also sought the use of emancipation for 'freeing human beings from unnecessary social constraints.'[64] Habermas concurs with such an argument for his claim was that advanced moral codes are committed to granting every human being an equal right to participate in open dialogue regarding societal and political arrangements of their community. This crucially substantiates that there is no ground for exclusiveness, apart from the justification that such inclusion is a substantial threat to the community. This also further questions the sovereign claim and its conduct if it is exclusionary directly or indirectly. Linklater delves into this issue even further, arguing that 'this enterprise of questioning traditional sovereign rights in light of the moral claims of the wider human community resembles the method of immanent critique used by the Frankfurt School.'[65] Instead of appealing to an ethical standard, which is external to the State, this method questions the practice of States and scrutinises their conduct as to whether they cause exclusionary implications. The anti-exclusionary dynamic has helped the evolution of modern citizenship by considering its ramifications for the domain of world politics and the international society. It has

[62] Linklater, *supra* note 60, at 89.

[63] Ibid., at 89.

[64] Ibid., at 90.

[65] Ibid., at 93.

also helped the emergence of human rights in this respect as such legal instruments are directly a result of preventing exclusionary implications upon an individual part of the community of humankind. The anti-exclusionary dynamic is fundamentally the attempt to lower barriers that do not allow an individual part of the community of mankind to participate in the community's development. This prevents the idea of excluded groups—such as subordinate classes, racial and national minorities, and women—from possessing 'the social and political rights monopolised by more powerful groups.'[66] This expounds on the fact that the nation-states' realist agendas and struggle for domination naturally make them one of the 'few bastions of exclusions, which has not had its rights and claims against the rest of the world seriously questioned.'[67]

The arguments posited by Habermas and Linklater further strengthen the position advanced by emancipatory idealists that all individuals or communities should be protected from modes of oppression and be given the opportunity to contribute to civilisational development. Focusing in on the fact that each individual or community's particular normative, sociological and praxeological trend can contribute to civilisational development in a unique manner grounds their intrinsic worth to exist and rationalises the utopian developments in international law. By substantiating emancipatory idealists' insistence that every individual or community has an intrinsic worth to exist and the focus on protecting such persons the overall significance of the utopian focal goals of international law can be analysed.

2.4 Emancipatory Idealism in International Law

2.4.1 Social Idealism

Emancipatory idealism, as a utopian focal goal of international law, is driven towards preventing any violation to the peaceful relations amongst members of the international community, which can cause political, economic and societal instability. By justifying the importance of protecting each and every individual and the communities in which these individuals reside, it establishes the normative framework within which the legal system is recomposed and legitimised. Through this utopian

[66] Ibid., at 93.

[67] Ibid., at 93.

perspective, international law is therefore a legal system that seeks to prevent a breakdown of the international community, whether it affects only a specific part or the whole composition. Seeing as every individual or collection of individuals consequently maintains the potential to play a significant role in the development of civilisation it is necessary to assure their protection and to provide a stable environment for this specific ambition to be achieved. Negative effects such as war, genocide or oppression for example are a detriment to such an objective of Hegel and critical theorists on two fronts. The first front is a more direct and simple reason being that the oppression or eradication of individuals or communities is an unacceptable violation. This is based on the suggestion that every individual's life must be protected on the basis that they have the potential and capacity to develop civilisation on a societal or technological level. For emancipatory idealism, such a capacity should not be delimited in any way.

The second reason is that for individuals or a community of individuals to be able to freely fulfil their potential, a stable economic, political and societal environment must be established. Under circumstances of war and oppression, such potential for a society to develop is stunted as the economic, political and societal upheaval that coincides with such a phenomenon of violence often leaves little possibility for the progression of civilisation both technologically and societally. Scientific, societal and moral progression cannot realistically take full effect as rights of individuals are usually curtailed and thus there is little scope for progression under such circumstances. More so, these events of conflict or oppression incur a decline in civilisation and depending on the extent of violence and disruption these events incur, the impact on the economic, political and societal equilibrium can be so monumental that it can lead to a significant breakdown and regression of development. Moral and sociological norms are in jeopardy and such instances can result in a scarcity of technological and economic resources. An inability for the specific society to expand and develop allows for regression. Fundamentally this sort of regression, depending on the scale of violence, can contribute to the destabilisation of a community. This may take a great period of time to recover from, unequivocally slowing the progress of the specific community and potentially overall civilisational development. To recover from such conflict or political upheaval takes a long period of time for it not only has the aforementioned sociological impact, but it also tends to impact the region economically. Recovery from such political and economic decline can take decades, possibly spanning several generations. Furthermore, such phases of economic, political and societal instability can allow for extremist political movements to take precedence, which has the danger of leaving the specific environment susceptible to greater decline. There is a cyclical pattern to the impact of violence and oppression. If there is no stable political, economic and societal environment, this limits the potential for progression. If progression is stunted then society tends to regress, this leads to greater instability and escalation of violence.

Incidentally, analysing the theoretical foundations and practical necessities of emancipatory idealism helps to identify what such a concept substantively requires. In fact, such analysis helps to order emancipatory idealism. For example, such analysis clarifies which human rights bear greater priority for emancipatory idealists in order to achieve the objectives set out in such a concept. Those seeking to achieve emancipatory idealism are able to develop a hierarchical ordering of human rights. By ordering human rights, emancipatory idealists clarify what is practically and theoretically required in order to achieve the central aims of emancipatory idealism. Such clarifications establish how the prioritisation of certain human rights shall ensure that all individuals or groups are able to contribute to civilisational development, whilst remaining free from modes of oppression. Those rights pertaining to the protection of life are at the top of hierarchical ordering of human rights, followed by the right to be free from discrimination and the right to education collectively ordered just below, and then finally those rights that effect economic, political and societal stability. Firstly, rights pertaining to the protection of life are at the top of the hierarchical order of human rights for emancipatory idealists. Without the protection of each individual or groups of individuals the main goals set out in emancipatory idealism cannot be achieved. Emancipatory idealism justifies why the existence of every individual or community of individuals is of paramount importance for the continued development of civilisation. As explored above, the fact that each individual or community of individuals can contribute to the technological or societal development of civilisation in a unique manner (based on their particular normative, sociological and praxeological trends), defends the insistence that each individual or groups of individuals should be protected from modes of oppression. The furtherance of civilisation would be detrimentally affected if any individual or group are prevented from contributing to its development. It is on this basis that rights pertaining to the protection of life supersede all other human rights for emancipatory idealists. Subsequently, international legal provisions (treaty or customary law) on genocide, war crimes or crimes against humanity for example are prioritised by those seeking to achieve emancipatory idealism as the role such provisions play in protecting the right to life are key.

The right to be free from discrimination and the right to education are then placed below rights pertaining to the protection of life by emancipatory idealists in the hierarchical ordering of human rights. Both these rights are on equal footing as they collectively ensure that individuals or groups of individuals are in a position to contribute to civilisational development on either a technological or societal level. The importance placed on the right to be free from discrimination coincides with the argument regarding the right to life because the circumvention of individuals or groups from contributing to civilisational development conflicts with the key tenets of emancipatory idealism. It is imperative that for the sake of civilisational development that all individuals and groups are provided the necessary stable political, economic and social environment. Discrimination, based on various grounds, has often been a reason for individuals or groups unable to contribute to civilisational development, be it the institutionalised or societal inequality such forms of discrimination may be responsible for.[68] The example of India's Dalits (Untouchables) community is a prime example for the 'age-old caste based discrimination' has prevented such a group from acquiring land, attending schools and fully accessing India's economic opportunities or safeguards for equal rights.[69] Dalits have also endured daily humiliation, assault, rape or murder from upper caste groups threatened by their rise.[70] Such levels of discrimination pose a 'direct challenge to a fundamental underpinning of the

[68] See E.T. Achiume, 'Putting Racial Equality into the Global Human Rights Agenda', (2018) 15 *International Journal on Human Rights* 141 & W.F. Felice, 'The UN Committee on the Elimination of all Forms of Racial Discrimination', (2002) 24.1 *Human Rights Quarterly* 205. These texts detail the impact of discrimination to the various groups in focus, demonstrating how such groups are restricted from a stable political, economic and social environment.

[69] C. Bob, '"Dalit Rights Are Human Rights": Caste Discrimination, International Activism, and the Construction of a New Human Rights Issue', (2007) 29 *Human Rights Quarterly* 167, at 173.

[70] See National Human Rights Commission, Central and State Authorities Urged to Prevent Atrocities against SCs: NHRC Releases Report on Atrocities Against SCs, available at http://www.nhrc.nic.in/disparchive.asp?fno=837 (2004).

human rights ideal—that all human beings are equal and deserve the same respect, dignity, and rights.[71]' For those seeking to achieve emancipatory idealism, the importance placed on the right to be free from discrimination are strengthened when assessing how Dalits have been prevented from contributing to civilisational development because of the unstable economic, political and social environment they have been forced into. Thus, international legal instruments such as the International Convention for the Elimination of all Forms of Racial Discrimination (1969), the International Convention on the Elimination of All Forms of Discrimination Against Women (1979) or the Convention on the Rights of Persons with Disabilities (2008) for example play an important role in achieving emancipatory idealism, for it paves the way for the eradication of economic and social deprivations and the opportunity for all individuals or groups to contribute to the civilisational development.

In accordance with the right to be free from discrimination is the right to education. This specific right is so intrinsic for the achievement of emancipatory idealism for technological and societal development of civilisation relies considerably upon all individuals or groups of individuals being provided the conditions to fulfil their potential through education. Joel Spring deftly argues the power of such a right as education 'is important for unlocking the social imagination of all people so that they can think about alternatives to current political, social, and economic systems.'[72] Likewise, 'education can provide citizens with the tools for resisting totalitarian and repressive governments and economic exploitation.'[73] This position can be pushed further to highlight that education can also play a vital role in unlocking important technological advancements that shall further the development of civilisation. In fact, the right to education is so vital in achieving emancipatory idealism that it supersedes rights that shall ensure a stable political, economic and social environment. This is because the transformative effects of education upon society, be it international or domestic, are so significant that the stable environment for civilisational development can be born out of individuals and groups of individuals who have access to education.

[71] Bob, *supra* note 69, at 169.

[72] J. Spring, *The Universal Right to Education: Justification, Definition, and Guidelines*, (2000), 2.

[73] Ibid., at 1.

Consequently, emancipatory idealists place social, political and economic rights below both the right to be free from discrimination and the right to education. Though they are vitally intrinsic in creating the stable environment for individuals or groups to contribute to civilisational development, they do depend on the existence of those rights that supersede them. However, it is important to stress the importance emancipatory idealists would place upon social, political and economic rights for they justify the importance of freedom of expression or the abolition of slavery for example. Such rights are justified on the basis of the value it has in creating the desired stable environment for civilisational development to take place. What becomes apparent here in analysing the substance of emancipatory idealism and how it should be ordered is that international law is being utilised for serving individuals and groups of individuals over States.

In fact, when assessing what emancipatory idealism requires substantively, it becomes clear that the theory of emancipatory idealism coincides with Phillip Allott's theory of Social Idealism. Similar to emancipatory idealism, Allott focuses on humanity, and in this sense also on individuals, and how law can help serve humanity's best interests. Allott in *Eunomia: A New Order for a New World*, criticised the model of international law in which international law was conceived as 'self-limiting of equal sovereigns in their externalised public realms.'[74] Allott suggested that 'it would have been possible for international society to develop a theory of representation, to articulate the way in which the state-societies aggregated the willing of citizens in order to will and act internationally as the representatives of their citizens.'[75] However, Allott contends that international law has failed to realise his theory of representation and instead, 'the consciousness-controlling activities of government, and their supporters, ensured that sovereignty should be externalised into a society which was conceived as being a society containing only sovereigns.'[76]

Ultimately, Allott felt that the aforementioned misuse of law in international society resulted in its 'stunted and primitive reality.'[77] This was problematic for Allott for he saw law's role not only in international

[74] P. Allott, *Eunomia: A New Order for a New World*, (2001), 304, para16.18.

[75] Ibid., at 303, para16.16.

[76] Ibid.

[77] Ibid.

society, but in all societies, as the means through which to 'discover the human potential of society.'[78] More specifically, 'through law, society is able to organise the reality of its words and ideas and theories and values, to organise its struggle with the perennial dilemmas of all society.'[79] For, Allott the ultimate goal of law is to serve the human race. His ambitions are to establish a world governed by the interests of humanity, rather than those interests of the State.[80] Indeed, Allott strongly advocates for international law to serve the interests of humanity when stating that:

> How can any morally sensitive person, knowing what happened in the twentieth century and seeing the prospects of the twenty-first century, fail to recognise a heavy burden of moral responsibility to do whatever can be done to improve human reality? Must we deny our feelings of righteous anger at the social evil that plagues the human world, of pity for the immeasurable suffering caused by the acts and omissions of holders of public power, of invincible hope that a better human world is possible?[81]

Allott focuses on international law servicing humanity and every individual that encompasses this group for there is the potential for 'the wonderful capacity of human consciousness to make the future other than it has been... to choose its future from all the possibilities which imagination can conceive and which reason can order.'[82] This subsequently requires humanity 'to take possession of the waste-land of international society in the name of the people and in the name of justice.'[83] Thus, the key commonality, for the purposes of the current discussion, of Allott's social idealism and emancipatory idealism is that both consider that the ultimate objective of international law should be to service the human components that are individuals or groups of individuals.

[78] Ibid., at 254, para14.1.

[79] Ibid., 254–255, at para14.3.

[80] I. Scobbie, 'Slouching Towards the Holy City: Some Weeds for Phillip Allott', (2005) 16.2 *EJIL* 299, at 300.

[81] P. Allott, *The Health of Nations: The Society and Law Beyond the State*, (2002), 33, para1.62.

[82] Allott, *supra* note 74, at 265, para15.13.

[83] Ibid., at 254, para14.1.

Consequently, in finding solidarity in such an ambition, emancipatory idealists similarly contend that international society—and in turn international law—should be ordered to service 'the total social process of international society, as all the people and the peoples of the world interacted with each other'[84] if the aim is to achieve utopian focal goals of international law. It is on this basis that Allott rues the current ordering of international law. By international law's perceived focus on the self-limiting of the equal sovereign, the legal system is being deprived of having a transformative effect upon international society:

> [International law] deprives itself of the wonderful power of legal relations to create an intensely dynamic human reality, matching the dynamic of the physical world, incorporating the dynamic of the physical world and of the world of human consciousness, creating the system by which the whole of reality, physical and human, may be transformed with a view to survival and prospering.[85]

It is in Allott's aspirations for the potential of law to transform humanity that links so acutely with the foundations of emancipatory idealism. As emancipatory idealists seek to ensure a stable economic, political and societal environment for all individuals so they can contribute to the technological and sociological advancements in civilisation, Allott argues for a similar proposition. His focus is on the 'natural human purpose of survival and prospering.'[86] Seeking technological and sociological advancements in civilisation is the same as Allott's focus. As Allott argues for international law to service humanity so it can survive and prosper,[87] emancipatory idealists seek to use international law to ensure that individuals and a community of individuals are protected from modes of oppression and that they are given a stable environment. This is so that they can contribute to civilisational development for the survival and prosperity of humanity.

Anne Peters' work also strengthens the argument made by those focused on achieving emancipatory idealism as a utopian focal goal of

[84] Ibid., at 303, para16.17.

[85] Ibid., at 304, para16.18.

[86] Ibid., at 387, para18.30.

[87] Ibid.

international law. Like Allott, Peters suggests that the role of the sovereign and the international legal system is to serve humanity:

> It has become clear that the normative status of sovereignty is derived from humanity, understood as the legal principle that human rights, interests, needs, and security must be respected and promoted, and that this humanistic principle is also the *telos* of the international legal system. Humanity is the A and Ω of sovereignty.[88]

Thus, for example, Peters contends that 'conflicts between state sovereignty and human rights should not be approached in a balancing process in which the former is played off against the latter on an equal footing, but should be tackled on the basis of a presumption in favour of humanity.'[89] Human needs are taken to be the starting point of international law,[90] which is similar to emancipatory idealism. Emancipatory idealists assert that the starting point of international law is indeed humanity, which is represented by individuals and communities of individuals. Therefore, to utilise international law in order to protect individuals and a community of individuals is to favour humanity.

Whereas Peters arguments are a descriptive claim, those focused on achieving emancipatory idealism explain why it is that international law should serve humanity. By using Hegel and the works of critical theorists it is better understood the potential every individual and communities of individuals has to advance human civilisation for its survival and prosperity. This potential to contribute to civilisational development justifies the argument that international law should focus on individuals or communities of individuals, or, as Peters and Allott would suggest, humanity.

[88] A. Peters, 'Humanity as the A and Ω of Sovereignty', (2009) 20.3 *EJIL* 513, at 514.

[89] Ibid.

[90] A. Peters, 'The Merits of Global Constitutionalism', (2009) 16 *Ind. J. Global Legal Studies* 397, at 399. See also, P. Allott, 'Intergovernmental Societies and the Idea of Constitutionalism', in Jean-Marc Coicaud & Veijo Heiskanen (eds.), *The Legitimacy of International Organisations*, (2001), at 92.

2.4.2 *Differing Visions for International Law*

The visions for international law that Allott, Peters and emancipatory idealists share differ in varying degrees to the more classical writers of international law such as Weil, Verdross and Oppenheim. For all three of these international lawyers, the focus of international law is States, and inter-State relations.

Prosper Weil suggests that the character of international law has not changed so drastically from the 'Romano-Germanic and Byzantine Christendoms and the world of Islam'[91] or the period which saw the 'collapse of Western Europe at the end of the Middle Ages of all higher... [which] resulted in the State entities that made their appearance in the Christian world.'[92] Weil states that international law gained its interstate character during these periods of history and 'despite the profound transformations that international society has undergone, especially since the end of the Second World War, the functions of international law have remained what they have always been since the outset.'[93] Citing the *Lotus* dictum, Weil asserts that 'international law governs relations between these co-existing independent communities or with a view to the achievement of common aims... in order to regulate the relations between these co-existing independent communities or with a view to the achievement of common aims.'[94] He justifies the focus of classical interpretations of international law on the State for the sake of the 'key concepts of "relations and coexistence" (now called respectively "friendly" and "peaceful")... and common aims (now translated into "cooperation")'[95] are achievable if international law's primary focus is on maintaining healthy relations amongst 'the equal sovereign States.'[96]

[91] P. Weil, 'Towards Relative Normativity in International Law?' (1983) 77.3 *The American Journal of International Law* 413, at 418. See also R. Ago, 'Pluralism and the Origins of the International Community', (1977) 3 *Italian Yearbook of International Law* 3; R. Ago, 'The First International Communities in the Mediterranean World', (1982) 53 *British Yearbook of International Law* 213; P. Weil, 'Le Judaïsme et le développement du droit international', (1975) 151 *Recueil de Cours* 253.

[92] Ibid.

[93] Ibid., at 419.

[94] SS Lotus case (France v. Turkey), PCIJ Rep Series A No 10, at 18.

[95] Weil, *supra* note 91, at 419.

[96] Ibid., at 418–419.

Alfred Von Verdross adopts a similar position to Weil, suggesting that 'the new term "International Law" has never completely replaced the old term "Law of Nations."'[97] He establishes that international law is 'the law of the community of States,'[98] for although there are subjects of international law other than States, they possess only a passive character,[99] 'as they do not participate in the making of these rules.'[100] Therefore, Verdross does admit that non-State actors do have a place in the international legal system, yet their role is a limited one. He argues that the original concept of international law, which sees 'international law as the norms stemming from a supra-Statal source and regulating relations between States'[101] remains the dominant conception of the legal system.

One of the most recognised positivist international lawyers, Lassa Oppenheim, contributes a conception of international law that corresponds with Weil and Verdross' critiques of the legal system. Oppenheim asserts that an international society of States is a necessary condition for the existence of international law.[102] Anthony Carty suggests that Oppenheim placed the State and its willingness to comply at the centre of international law.[103] Carty's summary of Oppenheim becomes all the more convincing when analysing the five morals set forth in the first edition of his famous textbook, *International Law*:

> The five morals set forth in the first edition of his textbook related to the necessity of international law of a balance of power, the importance of States basing their military interventions and political behaviour only on real State interests (as opposed to dynamic interests), the inevitability of

[97] A.V. Verdross, 'On the Concept of International Law', (1949) 43.3 *American Journal of International Law* 435, at 437.

[98] Ibid., at 439.

[99] Ibid.

[100] Ibid.

[101] Ibid., at 436.

[102] L. Oppenheim, 'The Science of International Law: Its Task and Method', (1908) 2.2 *American Journal of International Law* 313, at 316. See also B. Kingsbury, 'Legal Positivism as Normative Politics: International Society, Balance and Power', (2002) 13 *EJIL* 401, at 402.

[103] A. Carty, 'Why Theory? The Implications for International Law Teaching', in P. Allott, A. Carty, M. Koskenniemi, & C. Warbrick (eds.), *Theory and International Law: An Introduction*, (1991) 75, at 80.

> nationalist State formation and the need for minority rights, the prudential counsel to make haste slowly, and the interdependence between international law, international economic interests and public morality.[104]

This typifies Oppenheim's conception of international law. It was a conception that firmly saw the role of international law to service States and inter-State relations. His 'most basic idea was that international law is the law of an international society of mutually recognised States, which he called the Family of Nations.'[105] This was because Oppenheim held a narrowly statist conception of the international society and 'broadly pluralist with regard to the pursuit of diverging State interests and values.'[106]

Additionally, Oppenheim did not believe that an international community of individuals was plausible, 'as he regarded the *civitas gentium maxima* as a strained (by which he meant untenable) conception.'[107] Subsequently, unlike Verdross' arguments that international law is the law of the community of States, Oppenheim's view of international law consisted exclusively of States. The State, which for Oppenheim meant the government, was the source of sovereignty.[108] He paid little regard for the relationship between government and people when analysing international law and international society. What this ultimately showed about Oppenheim's conception of the international sphere was that it belonged to States, and that international law was to be utilised to ensure healthy relations amongst those that belonged to the Family of Nations.[109]

However, it is important to note the problematic nature of some of Oppenheim's views. He considered only States in Europe and the Americas, plus a few others States that met the standards of civilisation, part of the international society.[110] People outside the recognised States were not

[104] L. Oppenheim, *International Law*, vol. 1 (1st ed., 1905), 73–75. See also Kingsbury, *supra* note 94, at 407.

[105] Kingsbury, *supra* note 102, at 409.

[106] Ibid., at 409.

[107] Ibid. See also L. Oppenheim, *International Law*, vol.1 (2nd ed. 1911), 93.

[108] Ibid., at 217.

[109] Oppenheim, *supra* note 104, at 34.

[110] Ibid.

protected and constrained under international law.[111] For example, 'he did not believe that native tribes were legally capable of any transactions governed by the law of nations.'[112] Consequently, Oppenheim omitted them from the international society and the constrains of international law.

On this level, Oppenheim's arguments can easily be rejected by emancipatory idealists. The exclusionary dynamic of Oppenheim's work in this regard is problematic for those seeking to achieve emancipatory idealism as civilisational development would suffer. If all individuals and communities of individuals are not protected from modes of oppression, this is detrimental to the sociological and technological advancements that civilisation could undergo. Yet his positivist conception of international law that parallels Weil and Verdross cannot be dismissed so easily and requires greater counter-argumentation. All three international lawyers seek to argue that the focus of international law should be States, yet it is in returning to Allott where emancipatory idealism's focus on the individual or communities of individuals can be justified.

Referring to Allott, Iain Scobbie argues that the centrality of the State in international relations (and also international law) should be considered 'a tragedy, because it encapsulates a fundamental misconception about what matters: it authorises the pursuit of specifically State interests to the detriment of those of humanity.'[113] This State-centric conception:

> is not merely a tradition of international law. It implies a pure theory of the whole nature of international society and hence of the whole nature of the human social condition; and it generates practical theories which rule the lives of all societies, of the whole human race. It is nothing but mere words, mere ideas, mere theory, mere values- and yet war and peace, human happiness and human misery, human wealth and human want, human lives and human life have depended on the for two centuries and more.[114]

[111] Ibid., at 269.

[112] Ibid.

[113] I. Scobbie, 'A View of Delft: Some Thought About Thinking About International Law', in M. Evans (ed.), *International Law*, (2018), at 75.

[114] Allott, *supra* note 74, at 243, para13.105.

Moreover, focusing on the interests of States does not ensure the survival and prosperity of human civilisation.[115] Thus, for those focused on achieving emancipatory idealism as a utopian focal goal of international law, Weil, Verdross and Oppenheim's accounts of international law are unsatisfactory. The central goal for those seeking to achieve emancipatory idealism is for human civilisation to continue to advance technologically and sociologically. Within this advancement is also the ambition to see the whole of human civilisation survive and prosper, which includes every individual and community of individuals. Therefore, if human civilisation is to continue advancing, and if human civilisation is to survive and prosper the focus of international law must be every individual and community of individual that comprise human civilisation.

2.5 Conclusion

The intrinsic focus of emancipatory idealism as a utopian focal goal of international law is the individuals and groups of individuals that encompass human civilisation. The argument being made is that by turning the attention on individuals and groups of individuals rather than States, the international community is more likely to achieve international peace and security and overcome the modes of oppression that destabilise it. Using Hegel and critical theory, the focus on individuals and communities of individuals has greater resonance. Their works acutely articulate the potential that each individual or community of individuals possess for contributing to the advancement of civilisational development. Their works subsequently help to justify the need to ensure fundamental rights and other such safeguards are afforded to all individuals and communities of individuals.

Incidentally, when pondering upon such justifications, it becomes apparent that emancipatory idealism is not solely applicable to international law or the international community but can also be utilised in a domestic setting. Such a utopian focal goal can significantly influence the drafting of legislation that may reshape society within a State. Emancipatory idealism is not a concept exclusive to the international level, which highlights its universal characteristic, indicating that such a concept can influence several vertical levels of society. Therefore, the protection of

[115] Ibid., at 247, para13.105(13).

individuals and communities of individuals and the justifications asserted by those seeking to achieve emancipatory idealism must be accomplished on all levels of human civilisation for it to continue to advance.

This universal element of emancipatory idealism demonstrates how integral such utopian focal goals are to the development of international law. In fact, when looking at the development of international law, some of the most accelerated phases of development the legal system has undergone can be attributed to the focus of protecting all individuals and communities of individuals. The development of the League of Nations following the First World War is a prime example. This period saw international law transition from the Westphalian non-institutionalist model to the institutionalist model which was introduced with the formation of the League in order to better prevent large-scale crisis from reoccurring. Alfred Zimmern discusses at length the reasoning behind creating the League, from the fact that the war had somewhat of an educational value as to why peace is so important for the international community:

> War' said a Greek historian over two thousand years ago, 'is a forcible teacher'. The Great War taught the world the lesson of interdependence. It taught it by two methods at once. By its destructiveness, by its overthrow of all that had hitherto been regarded as stable in international politics, it compelled men to seek for new and surer forms of organisation. And at the same time by its own purposes it provided working models for the peacetime machinery of the future.[116]

The war maintained its influence upon the construction of the League and the drafting of the Covenant, for 'it must never be forgotten that the Covenant was drawn up by men filled with the recent experience of the war. It affected different minds in different ways, but it deeply affected them all.'[117] The developments following the Second World War similarly prove that some of the most significant developments in international law have occurred when the focus has been on protecting individuals and communities of individuals. This is illustrated with the creation of the Genocide Convention, the further developments in international humanitarian law with the Geneva Conventions and the human rights movement

[116] A. Zimmern, *The League of Nations and the Rule of Law*, (1998), 137.
[117] Ibid., at 137–138.

which was sparked by the Universal Declaration of Human Rights in 1948.

These developments briefly listed above highlight that international law has been influenced by what social idealists or utopians have been advocating for. Emancipatory idealism's contribution to this debate is that it justifies international law's focus on individuals and communities of individuals in a way that Allott and Peters have not. Indeed, Allott exposes that prosperity and survival depends on international law refocusing on humanity rather than States. However, emancipatory idealism explains why this refocus should happen with greater detail. Emancipatory idealists align with Allott's arguments, yet there is a greater explanation as to why protecting individuals and communities of individuals from modes of oppression will ensure prosperity and survival of human civilisation. By outlining the potential all individuals and communities of individuals possess in advancing civilisation on a technological and sociological level, emancipatory idealists validate the importance of refocusing international law towards achieving such a utopian focal goal.

CHAPTER 3

States and Utopian Goals of International Law

3.1 Introduction

The previous chapter demonstrates that making emancipatory idealism one of the focal goals of international law would be fundamentally instrumental to making the system of international law develop in a utopian way. When emancipatory idealism is left out as a focal goal of international law, modes of oppression follow and the international community experiences significant detrimental effects. The importance of ensuring emancipatory idealism cannot be over-emphasised, especially considering the influence it has played in this legal system's most accelerated phases of development, i.e. after the First World War and the Second World War. Sadly, however, there have been periods in history when utopian goals of international law were not given adequate attention or were undermined. Given the significance of emancipatory idealism as a focal goal of international law, it is important to understand the main reasons why this focal goal has been undermined and what can be done to remedy the failures to achieve this focal goal. This lack of attention to emancipatory idealism is, arguably, a consequence of the State's position in international law as its primary object and subject.

This chapter will explain why, from the perspective of those seeking to achieve emancipatory idealism, the position of States in international law as the primary objects and subjects of the legal system is problematic. I

D. Mawar, *States Undermining International Law*, Philosophy, Public Policy, and Transnational Law, https://doi.org/10.1007/978-3-030-64789-6_3

will argue that an international legal system based so strongly on States tends to lean towards achieving realist goals instead of utopian goals. This is due, as I will explain, to the inherent nature of States, which is to be focused primarily on their territory and populace. This puts the State in a difficult situation: on the one hand, it is expected to ensure peace and security within its territory and, on the other hand, to ensure international peace and security—to aim for both simultaneously has the potential to be rife with issues. I will thus explain what exactly the inherent nature of States is in this regard and how this inherent nature has undermined utopian goals of international law and will continue to do so. It would follow that, as I will explain, moving away from the Westphalian model that supports an international community over 'an international society of States' is conducive to achieving emancipatory idealism.

To build my argument, I will use the works of legal as well as political thinkers. This will allow me to explain why the dual duties of States (peace and security within, but also international peace and security) is at odds with the State's primacy in international law, resulting in a failure to achieve utopian focal goals of international law. I will base my arguments on the writings of international lawyers such as Jack Goldsmith, Eric Posner, Abram and Antonia Chayes, and Thomas Franck. These authors help develop the descriptive claim that States tend to interact or comply with international law primarily for the sake of their realist agendas. Then, I will turn to the works of political thinkers Carl Schmitt and Michel Foucault and legal philosopher Hans Kelsen. Their ideas help explain the reasons for the behaviour of States described by the international lawyers from above, i.e. that they tend to prioritise their domestic duties over their international duties. This, I recall, is problematic for those seeking to achieve emancipatory idealism. The mixture of legal and political writings collectively helps to develop the main argument of this chapter that State primacy in international law requires re-assessment.

3.2 The State and International Law

3.2.1 Why Do States Interact with International Law?

'At least by the nineteenth century, international law was generally conceived as a body of rules and forms of conduct applicable to States in their relations with each other.'[1] The traditional positivist conception of international law places an emphasis on the will of States, for 'in the absence of central authority, law can only be based on the consent of States.'[2] This conception of international law is heavily influenced by eighteenth-century international legal thinker Emer de Vattel. He asserted that the law of nations is primarily the law of States, ultimately defining the law of nations as 'the science which teaches the rights subsisting between nations or states, and the obligations correspondent to those rights.'[3] It is through this positivist conception of international law that the position of States in international law as the primary objects and subjects of the legal can be identified. This is additionally substantiated by the fact that customary international law is developed by States, as well as the fact that the legally binding nature of international treaties is affirmed once States sign and ratify such documents.

Establishing State primacy in international law highlights the influential position States enjoy in the international legal system. What is perhaps of greater interest is investigating how States utilise not only the position they enjoy in the international legal system, but the legal system itself. Goldsmith and Posner posit the claim that States use international law to justify their actions 'no matter how transparently self-interested their actions are.'[4] 'Their legal or moral justifications cleave to their interests, and so when interests change, so do the rationalisations.'[5] Citing the major realist writings of Niebuhr, Carr and Morgenthau,[6] Goldsmith and Posner contend that States' legal and moral rhetoric are 'disguises' or

[1] K. Parlett, *The Individual in the International Legal System: Continuity and Change in International Law*, (2011), 3. See also H. Grotius, *The Rights of War and Peace*, (1625), chapter 1.

[2] Ibid., 7. See also G. Jellinek, *Die Rechtliche Natur der Staatenvertrage*, (1880), 2, 42–49, 56–58; S.R. Ratner and A.-M. Slaughter, 'Appraising the Methods of International Law: A Prospectus for Readers', (1999) 93 *AJIL* 291, at 293.

[3] E. Vattel, *The Law of Nations*, (1758), introduction, para 3, p. 67.

[4] J. Goldsmith & E. Posner, *The Limits of International Law*, (2005), 169.

[5] Ibid.

[6] R. Niebuhr, *Moral Man and the Immoral Society*, (1946); E.H. Carr, *The Twentieth Century Crisis 1919–1935: An Introduction to the Study of International Relations*, (1948); H. Morgenthau, *Politics Among Nations* (1948) & *In Defence of the National Interests*, (1951).

'pretexts' for actions motivated by a desire for power.[7] Such 'pretexts' are aimed at domestic constituents, whom leaders persuade to support the State's foreign policy.[8]

Thus, Goldsmith and Posner's position on States utilising international law is that it is a means to an end. It is a thinly veiled tool to pursue self-interested ambitions. The allure of international law is 'because it is purely formal, is particularly convenient. The appeal to law is simply the denial of self-interest.'[9] The formalist nature of law that Goldsmith and Posner allude to gives legitimacy to actions that use legal rhetoric to pursue their goals. For the law is the making of States. States are considered the agreed normative conduct that has been translated in to law, whether it be in treaty form or custom. Therefore, States using such legal rhetoric gives the impression of conduct that is accepted by the international community, in part or in whole, thus legitimising such conduct. Whether in fact such legal rhetoric is truly in accordance with international law or even legitimate is up for debate but using the formalist characteristic of law still gives States a sense of legitimacy in their actions.

For those focused on the utopian goals of international law this is problematic. If States are interacting with international law to justify the fulfilment of a self-interest, as Goldsmith and Posner suggest, this leaves emancipatory idealism vulnerable. Their example of Hitler utilising international law to justify 'his invasions of Austria, Czechoslovakia, Poland, Denmark, Norway, Belgium, Holland, France, Yugoslavia, and Russia and for his declaration of war against the United States'[10] typifies this concern. Hitler used the argument that there was 'the need for humanitarian intervention in other countries to halt mistreatment of German-speaking populations,'[11] in order to sway the German people to support his expansionist policies. This subsequently resulted in several groups of individuals vulnerable to modes of oppression. This indicates the problematic nature of State primacy in international law for those focused on utopian focal goals of international law, as the State's use of the legal system will not always ensure achievement of emancipatory idealism.

[7] H. Morgenthau, *Politics Among Nations* (1948), at 61–62.

[8] Goldsmith & Posner, *supra* 4, at 170.

[9] Ibid., at 184.

[10] Ibid., at 168.

[11] Ibid.

3.2.2 Why Do States Obey International Law?

It is also perhaps pertinent to explore the nature of the State with the question of why it is that States obey international law. Being able to answer such a question clarifies the problems those focused on achieving utopian goals of international law may have with the States' position as the primary subject and object of the international legal system. The compliance question is long standing and it has been analysed through various paradigms such as 'religious, moral, philosophical, political science, process and empirical.'[12] Many international law and international relations scholars have attempted to articulate why States obey international law. This has resulted in numerous propositions from both disciplines, each garnering legitimate explanations and moreover representing how answers to such a question have developed over the last three centuries.[13]

Harold Koh stated that the two texts that provide the most 'comprehensive and sophisticated efforts to date' in addressing the demanding question of compliance are *The New Sovereign* by Abram and Antonia Chayes, and *Fairness in International Law and Institutions* by Thomas Franck.[14] It is because their accounts of why States obey international law have been so influential in the debate surrounding the topic that dissecting their arguments is the most appropriate way to further explore the nature of States.

Beginning with Antonia and Abram Chayes' text *The New Sovereign*, their claims are that States would more likely obey international law on the basis of preventing a 'diminution of status through loss of reputation.'[15] The Chayeses contended that States are inclined to obey treaty rules because of three factors: efficiency, national interest and regime

[12] H.H. Koh, 'Why Do Nations Obey International Law?' (1997) *The Yale Law Journal* 2599, at 2604.

[13] For a comprehensive account of how the question of why States obey international law has developed over time, see H.H. Koh, 'Why Do Nations Obey International Law?' (1997) *The Yale Law Journal* 2599, at 2604–2634. This section of the article starts from ancient and primitive international law right up to the theory of the New Haven School and International Legal Process, to provide a somewhat comprehensive account of how the compliance question has been tackled in international law and international relations.

[14] Ibid., at 2601.

[15] Ibid., at 2636.

norms,[16] however noncompliance still remained a problem. This was due to the ambiguity and indeterminate nature of treaties, and what the Chayeses termed 'the temporal dimension' which are avoidable and unavoidable time lags between a State's undertaking and its performance.[17] In order to promote treaty compliance, they suggested two strategies. Firstly, the enforcement model, which utilises various coercive devices such as treaty-based military or economic sanctions, membership and unilateral sanctions, was considered ineffective. They argued that 'sanctioning authority is rarely granted by treaty, rarely used when granted, and likely to be ineffective when used.'[18] Repeated use of sanctions entails high costs to those that impose the sanctions and can raise serious problems of legitimacy.[19]

However, the second strategy the Chayeses suggested was considered a more effective incentive of ensuring that States obey international law. This was the 'managerial' model, whereby national actors seek to promote compliance not through coercion, but rather through a cooperative model of compliance, which seeks to induce compliance through interactive processes of justification, discourse and persuasion.[20] They argue that the prospect of losing 'status- the vindication of the State's existence as a member of the international system,'[21] encourages States to obey international law for the repercussions of losing such status is significant in the State's ability to conduct relations with other States.

The Chayeses argued that treaty regimes would be able to manage compliance through an iterative process of justificatory discourse.[22] Through various tools that they termed as 'instruments of active management,' such as transparency, reporting and data collection, verification and

[16] A. Chayes & A.H. Chayes, *The New Sovereign*, (1995), 1–28.

[17] Ibid., at 15.

[18] Ibid., at 32–33.

[19] Ibid., at 54.

[20] Ibid., at 109–111.

[21] Ibid., at 190. '[F]or all but a few self-isolated nations, sovereignty no longer consists in the freedom of states to act independently, in their perceived self-interest, but in membership in reasonably good standing in the regimes that make up the substance of international life .... In today's setting, the only way most states can realize and express their sovereignty is through participation in the various regimes that regulate and order the international system.'.

[22] Ibid., at 25.

monitoring, dispute settlement, capacity-building, and strategic review and assessment,[23] the Chayeses argued that non-governmental and inter-governmental institutions can be revitalised as instruments of managing treaty compliance.

The New Sovereign was a consolidation of Abram Chayes' previous work with Thomas Ehrlich and Andreas Lowenfeld in developing the international legal process theory[24] (ILP). ILP 'concentrates not so much on the exposition of rules and their content as on how international legal rules are actually used by the makers of foreign policy.'[25] They concluded that whilst law was not normally decisive, it was usually important to international affairs, and 'like Hart and Sacks, [they] posited that legal issues mainly arise not before courts, but in the process of making policy decisions, with lawyers playing a more important role than judges, and consent playing a greater role than command.'[26] Ultimately, Chayes, Ehrlich and Lowenfeld suggested that international law served as justification, constraint and an organising device for activity in foreign affairs.[27] Thus, the Chayeses' managerial model advanced in *The New Sovereign* more concisely articulates the suggestions made by ILP for it is under the pressure of not losing its status in the international community, that States use international law to justify conduct, or that treaty regimes restrain and organise State conduct in the international sphere.

Turning to Thomas Franck's *Fairness in International Law and Institutions*, the question of prime interest is not 'why do nations obey international law?' but 'is international law fair?'[28] Franck attempts to answer this question with the assumption that 'nations have little incentive or obligation to obey rules that fail his fairness criteria. In his universe, illegitimate rules have little compliance pull.'[29] Ultimately, Franck suggests that State perceptions regarding the legitimacy of rules are dependent upon

[23] Koh, *supra* note 12, at 2637.

[24] A. Chayes, T. Ehrlich & A. Lowenfeld, *International Legal Process*, (2 Vols. 1968).

[25] M.E. O'Connell, 'New International Legal Process', (April, 1999) 93.2 *AJIL* 334, at 334.

[26] H.H. Koh, 'Transnational Legal Process', (1996) 75 *Nebraska Law Review* 181, at 189.

[27] O'Connell, *supra* note 25, at 337.

[28] T. Franck, *Fairness in International Law and Institutions*, (1995) at 6.

[29] Koh, *supra* note 12, at 2641–2642.

whether they fall in line with principles of fair process.[30] It is on this basis that Franck agrees that States obey rules of international law when the benefits of complying exceed the costs.[31] If international rules fulfil the fairness criteria for a particular State, regardless of the subjective nature of such criteria fulfilment,[32] such compliance will more than likely incur benefits in terms of national interest. Moreover, 'he sees a transnational actor's impulse to comply as deriving not from a multitude of cost–benefit calculations regarding particular rules, but as more broadly rooted in the solidaristic, "communitarian peer pressure" that nations feel as members of a club.'[33] This bears similarity to the Chayeses´ argument, for the pressure from the international community and its key members create the expectancy of compliance. However, unlike the Chayeses' managerial model, Franck's propositions apply not only to treaties but also to customary international law.

These two seminal texts taken together complement each other's approaches and 'give cogent modern expression to two prominent intellectual traditions in international legal scholarship.'[34] The first tradition is the realist argument that international law is not really law because of a lack of enforceability,[35] and the second tradition is the 'rationalistic claim,' which is that States obey international law only to the extent that it serves national interest. For the purposes of outlining the problematic

[30] Franck, *supra* note 28, at 7.

[31] Ibid., at 7.

[32] The subjectivity of the fairness criteria fulfilment is worth elucidating. What may be perceived as fair for one particular State for the sake of their national interests, may not be the same for another State, or even the international community as a whole. As States seek to comply with rules of international law on the basis of Franck's fairness criteria, there is a strong correlation with the perceived fairness of rules and the benefit to national interest.

[33] Koh, *supra* note 12, at 2642. See also Franck, *supra* note 28, at 196. ('Nations, or those who govern them, recognize that the obligation to comply is owed by them to the community of states as the reciprocal of that community's validation of their nations' statehood.').

[34] Ibid., at 2602.

[35] See T. Nardin, 'Ethical Traditions in International Affairs', in T. Nardin & D.R. Mapel (eds.), *Traditions of International Ethics*, (1992), 1, at 13. ('Every student of international affairs has encountered the view that international law is 'not really law' because it lacks effective institutions for making and applying laws, and that it is therefore of negligible importance in international affairs.').

nature of States being the primary object and subjects, the focus shall be on the second tradition. Louis Henkin labelled the rationalistic claim as the 'cynics formula,' suggesting 'since there is no body to enforce the law, nations will comply with international law only if it is in their interest to do so; they will disregard law or obligation if the advantages of violation outweigh the advantages of observance.'[36] By initially assuming 'that nations act deliberately and rationally, after mustering carefully and weighing precisely all the relevant facts and factors,[37]' Henkin suggested 'that barring an infrequent non-rational act, nations will observe international obligations unless violation promises an important balance of advantage over cost.'[38]

Other scholars agree with Henkin's arguments regarding State compliance with international law. Kenneth Abbott depicts States as egoistic, establishing that 'their preferences are based on assessments of their own well-being.'[39] Moreover, States 'consistently order [their] preferences and choose among alternative courses of action so as to further those preferences.'[40] Ultimately, their interactions with international law are to obtain either short- or long-term domestic benefits, although Abbott suggests that States are more likely 'to pursue a complex, multifaceted long-run national interest, in which compliance with negotiated legal norms serves as a winning long-term strategy in a reiterated "prisoner's dilemma" game.'[41] Regardless of State preferences to either short- or long-term goals for national interests, what becomes clear is that their interactions with the international legal system are often inspired by goals of domestic self-interest.

This phenomenon of self-interest is prevalent in both the Chayeses' and Franck's work. Pressurising voluntary compliance through the prospect of losing status is rooted in ensuring that the State in question maintains its position in the international community for the sake of its

[36] L. Henkin, *How Nations Behave*, (1979), 49.

[37] Ibid., at 47.

[38] Ibid., at 47.

[39] K.W. Abbott, 'Modern International Relations Theory: A Prospectus for International Lawyers', (1989) 14.2 *The Yale Journal of International Law* 335, at 349. See also R. Keohane, *After Hegemony*, (1984), 66–67.

[40] Ibid. at 350. See also R. Keohane, *After Hegemony*, (1984), 111–116; E. Mackay, *Economics of Information and Law*, (1980), 135–143.

[41] Koh, *supra* note 12, at 2632. See also Abbott, *supra* note 39.

domestic situation. The State is pressurised in voluntary compliance to treaties in fear of losing its political influence on the international community or protecting its domestic situation from economic damage for example. Thus, the Chayeses′ 'managerial model' is dependent upon the fact that States take the necessary measures to ensure their domestic self-interests are protected. Moreover, with Franck's principles of fairness, a key component for States is whether compliance serves national self-interest.

However, although several international legal theories show that States obey international law on the basis of self-interest, international legal theories do not perhaps explain why it is that States prioritise their national self-interest over utopian focal goals of international law if there is a tension between the two. It is here that turning to political philosophy seems more appropriate. Where international law can identify the motives of States, the work of political philosophers such as Carl Schmitt and Michel Foucault is able to explain the reasoning behind such motives. Their works identify the ontology of States, revealing that their very existence is predicated on maintaining peace and order in the territory that they possess sole authority over. International legal scholars have undergone the task of showing that States' tendency to interact with international law is based on self-interest, and political philosophers have undergone the task of explaining why it is that States have a tendency to interact with international law based on the objective of self-interest. Thus, a combination of international law and political philosophy helps to show the problematic nature of State primacy in international law, if the aim is to achieve emancipatory idealism.

3.3 Carl Schmitt

3.3.1 The Power of Exception

Carl Schmitt's influential political writings are a suitable position to embark upon the exploration of why it is that States prioritise their domestic duties over their international duties for his dissection of the State remains as relevant as ever in understanding the landscape of international relations and international law. His theoretical postulations identify some of the key reasons as to why States undermine utopian goals of international law and why their position as the primary subject and object of the legal system is problematic.

There is the recurrent focus upon Carl Schmitt's affiliations with the Nazi movement that saw him expelled from academic circles. Yet to dispel Schmitt and his work in such a manner, brandishing him merely as a supporter of a Fascist movement is to the detriment of the wider discourse that is occurring in international relations and international law forums. His work can 'provide scholars of both international relations and international law with a new common multidisciplinary research platform that helps the thinking on the present international predicament of crisis in international order and legitimacy, of contested liberal hegemony, and of the issue of unipolarity and the emergence of new forms of warfare, such as terrorism and the "global war on terror".'[42] No more is such an importance on the focus placed upon Carl Schmitt's work on the sovereign evident than when assessing the undermining of utopian goals. His work goes some way to explaining why the international community continues to witness the undermining of emancipatory idealism as a utopian focal goal of international law.

Schmitt saw the role of the State as one of ensuring the security of its populace, and by acknowledging the constant state of war; he believed the State's role to be of paramount importance. In fact, Schmitt contended that only the State held the true power to ensure the security of its populace, for 'absolute internal sovereignty implied absolute external independence.'[43] He agreed with Hobbes' exercising of the *autoritas, non veritas facit legem* mantra. The one with authority can demand obedience, and the authority of the sovereign does not necessarily have to attain legitimacy so long as it seeks to exercise the primary role of protecting its populous.[44] All that mattered for Schmitt was that the State's raison d'être- to 'maintain its integrity in order to ensure order and stability'[45] was realised. Similar to Hobbes, Schmitt had opted for a strong State that would ensure order, peace and security, for they both gave in to the

[42] L. Odysseos & F. Petto, 'Introducing the International Theory of Carl Schmitt: International Law, International Relations, and the Present Global Predicament(s)', (2006) 19 *LJIL* 1, at 2.

[43] F.H. Hinsley, *Sovereignty*, (1986), 158.

[44] G. Schwab, 'Introduction' in C. Schmitt, *Political Theology: Four Chapters on the Concept of Sovereignty*, (2005) at xxxix.

[45] Ibid., at xlii.

idea that 'man is basically dangerous and that his primary goal is physical security.'[46]

In fact, when analysing Schmitt's text *Political Theology*, immediately he establishes his leanings with the concept of a strong State:

> Sovereign is he who decides on the exception.[47]

Schmitt did not define the sovereign through 'an abstract scheme advanced to define sovereignty (namely, that sovereignty is the highest power, not a derived power).'[48] Instead, he defined the sovereign by the ability to exercise the exception 'in a situation of conflict what constitutes the public interest or interests of the state, public safety and order, *le salut public*, and so on.'[49] The power of exception is a vital tool in dealing with the constant state of conflict that is prevalent in human existence. With such states of emergencies emerging sporadically and in an unprecedented manner, the power of exception is an integral instrument to counter such states of emergencies and to maintain order, peace and security.

Schmitt contested the liberal constitutional development that sought to eliminate powers of exception for extreme cases of emergencies. The forging of checks and balances within the constitutional framework of a territory was seen as merely hampering the sovereign's ability to exercise its main role when a strong authoritative entity is most needed. Thus, it would seem that Schmitt would contest the rule of law principle. He felt that the sovereign should be presented with unlimited jurisdictional competence. He suggested that 'although [the sovereign] stands outside the normally valid legal system, [the sovereign] nevertheless belongs to it, for it is he who must decide whether the constitution needs to be suspended in its entirety.'[50] Michael Walzer adopts a similar position when exploring the concept of 'supreme emergencies,' which would exempt States from the standard restraints of *ius in bello*. Walzer argued for such 'supreme emergencies' on the basis that:

[46] Ibid., at xlix.

[47] C. Schmitt, *Political Theology: Four Chapters on the Concept of Sovereignty*, (2005) at 5.

[48] Ibid., at 6.

[49] Ibid., at 6.

[50] Ibid., at 7.

> We might better say that it is possible to live in a world where individuals are sometimes murdered, but a world where entire peoples are enslaved or massacred is literally unbearable. For the survival and freedom of political communities-whose members share a way of life, developed by their ancestors, to be passed on to their children-are the highest values of international society. Nazism challenged these values on a grand scale, but challenges more narrowly conceived, if they are of the same kind, have similar moral consequences. They bring us under the rule of necessity.[51]

Along similar lines to Schmitt, Walzer supports the idea that the State should be able to stand outside of the law in times of absolute necessity. In order to protect the values and livelihood of a populace, there may be the need to override the law, and both Schmitt and Walzer suggest that the State is best suited to do this. In times of war, responsibility falls upon the State on how to appropriately use the military force it possesses, and 'faced with some ultimate horror, their options' exhausted, they will do what they must to save their own people.'[52]

Schmitt embraced the concept of a strong State for he placed all his faith in the State to ensure order, peace and security within its territory. He had no qualms with awarding the sovereign with unlimited jurisdictional competence as Schmitt saw the sovereign as the only suitable entity to ensure order, peace and security within its territory. From this standpoint, liberal constitutionalist attempts to apply the rule of law and hamper the sovereign would be incompatible with Schmitt's postulations. For Schmitt, the validity of the legal order is determined by the sovereign, for 'order must be established for juridical order to make sense. A regular situation must be created, and sovereign is he who definitely decides if this situation is actually effective.'[53] Moreover, rather than seeing the power of the exception as an external factor to the legal system, Schmitt saw 'exceptional practices... [as] constitutive of sovereignty, modern law, and political communities.'[54]

[51] M. Walzer, *Just and Unjust Wars-A Moral Argument with Historical Illustrations*, (2015) at 254.

[52] Ibid.

[53] C. Schmitt, *The Crisis of Parliamentary Democracy*, (1985) at 13.

[54] C. Aradau & R. Van Munster, 'Exceptionalism and the War on Terror', (2009) 49 *British Journal of Criminology* 686, at 689.

Schmitt consolidated such argumentation by asserting that the sovereign is the only entity to ensure order, peace and security, and thus limits to its powers in times of emergencies would be counterintuitive. For this reason, Schmitt reiterates Bodin's argument that 'the prince is duty bound toward the estates or the people only to the extent of fulfilling his promise in the interest of the people; he is not so bound under conditions of urgent necessity.'[55] Schmitt agreed with the indivisibility of the sovereign, as the repercussions of dissolving its powers were potentially too severe to be risked. Schmitt put forward the question that if the sovereign is too concerned with justifying its actions of emergencies to the populous, how much destabilisation would occur to the territory's order, peace and security? For him, to slow down the sovereign's response to instances of emergencies is far more detrimental to a State or a community than failing to achieve liberal constitutionalist goals.

It is probably most apt here to stipulate that Schmitt is not anti-democratic when arguing the indivisibility of the sovereign's power. It is in his aim of protecting the rights of the citizens within the sovereign's territory that he advocates and justifies the indivisibility of the sovereign's power. The sovereign should normally follow the law, it is only in the unique times of emergencies should the sovereign flex its ability to exercise the power of exception. The sovereign must operate outside of the law to preserve the democratic order in the face of an attack on a territory's order, peace and security. Schmitt would advocate the suspension of the entire existing order 'on the basis of its right of self-preservation.'[56]

Schmitt seeks to prioritise the exception over the existing legal order, stating that:

> The exception is more interesting than the rule. The rule proves nothing; the exception proves everything: It confirms not only the rule but also its existence, which derives only from the exception. In the exception the power of real life breaks through the crust of a mechanism that has become torpid by repetition.[57]

This prioritisation plays two important roles in the overall analysis of the position of the State in international law. First of all, it grounds the notion

[55] Schmitt, *supra* note 47, at 8.

[56] Ibid., at 12.

[57] Ibid., at 15.

that the entity with the greatest power is the sovereign. The power of the State is absolute and no other can supersede its authority, however much liberal constitutionalist advocates the adoption of the rule of law. Subsequently, and moving on to the second role such a prioritisation plays, the legal order itself plays second fiddle to the power of the State. No matter how robust and exhaustive the legal order may be, if the State sees fit to exercise the power of exception for instances of emergency, for Schmitt the power of the State would rightfully supersede the legal order.

Having established absolute sovereignty in the domestic realm, Koskenniemi highlights that for Schmitt this in turn defined the limits of the State on an international level as well. 'Absolute internal sovereignty implied absolute external independence.'[58] Schmitt's view was that the State maintained absolute sovereignty in both the domestic and international realm.[59] 'The essence of sovereignty – against the liberal "neutralisers and depoliticisers" – is that it is the highest, legally independent, underived power.'[60] Schmitt's vision of the domestic and international realm is both 'state-centric and absolutist.'[61]

3.3.2 Friend and Enemy

Schmitt established the absolute authority of the sovereign, justifying the State's unlimited jurisdictional competence in the text, *Political Theology*. This compliments much of what international lawyers posit regarding the reasons why States obey and interact with international law. Yet in *Concept of the Political,* he seeks to stretch this idea even further and expands upon his theories, establishing the friend and enemy dichotomy to justify actions the State may take for the sake of establishing order, peace and security. He synthesises his work on the exception with the friend/enemy dichotomy to further strengthen his 'state-centric and absolutists' vision. Huysmans argues that exceptional policies:

[58] M. Koskenniemi, 'International Law as Political Theology: How to Read Nomos der Erde', (2004) 11.4 *Constellations* 492, at 499.

[59] Ibid.

[60] Ibid. See also C. Schmitt, *supra* note 47, at 17.

[61] Ibid., at 500.

> ...are not simply about civil liberties, the legality of going to war, and the constitutional limits to strengthening executive-centred government. Since these political, legal and social contests strongly reiterate fear of the enemy they directly bear upon the extent to which one is structuring and possibly institutionalizing fear of the enemy as the organizing principle of politics in both national and international society.[62]

For Schmitt, the friend and enemy distinction is explained by 'the utmost degree of intensity of a union or separation, of an association or disassociation.'[63] The enemy is considered to be 'the other, the strange' that is 'in a specially intense way, existentially something different and alien, so that in the extreme case conflicts are possible.'[64] Schmitt creates lines of differentiation, noting the enemy could endanger the life of the entity in question and one that is 'not merely any competitor or just any partner of a conflict in general.' The political enemy is the most intense and extreme form of antagonism.

Such a specific enemy works outside of a theological tradition, and in assessing this facet of Schmitt's work in conjunction with his work on the exception it becomes apparent why he makes such a distinction of the political enemy. Schmitt is creating such an enemy, generating strong levels of animosity and segregation, to justify the subsequent methods of quelling the danger of the enemy. It justifies the taking up of arms and the physical killing of the enemy, the removal of their rights, or even treating them in a manner that would be considered inhumane. If this political enemy can destabilise the order, peace and security of the sovereign's territory, the sovereign must be able to deal with such matters in whichever manner they deem fit. Thus, such measures to kill, remove rights or implement inhumane measures are legitimised by the sovereign's primary goal. In fact, Schmitt insisted that '[t]he enemy in the political sense need not be hated personally; for that is irrelevant to whether we will kill him if necessary.'[65] The elimination of the enemy is not motivated by personal hatred but because the enemy is a threat to one's own way of life. Luban stated that 'if such physical destruction of human life

[62] J. Huysmans, 'Minding Exceptions: Politics of Insecurity and Liberal Democracy', (2004) 3 *Contemporary Political Theory* 321, at 338.

[63] C. Schmitt, *Concept of the Political*, (2007), at 27.

[64] Ibid., at 27.

[65] Schmitt, *supra* note 63, at 29.

is not motivated by an existential threat to one's own way of life, then it cannot be justified. Just as little can war be justified by ethical and juristic norms.'[66] By painting the political enemy in such a light that they are in no circumstances redeemable, the actions the sovereign may take to neutralise such political enemies are not as difficult to implement on an ethical basis.

Schmitt makes it clear that the 'State as an organised political enemy decides for itself the friend and enemy distinction.'[67] This is because it is up to the State to eradicate the danger of the enemy who can potentially threaten the order, peace and security of the State's territory. This gives greater legitimacy as to why the State does maintain the power of the exception. If the State is the one to decide who is the political enemy or friend, then it must be up to the State to choose how to appropriately deal with such groups. The friend and enemy groups can potentially coexist within a territory, and it is up to the State to consequently decide whether actions are required immediately, eventually or not at all, to deal with the enemy.

It is worth considering Giorgio Agamben's work which explores the implications of Schmitt's work in the *Concept of the Political*. In Agamben's text *Homo Sacer-Sovereign Power and Bare Life*, he assesses the sovereign power to decide on bare life. He suggests that:

> The sovereign who, insofar as he decides on the state of exception, has the power to decide which life may be killed without the commission of homicide, in the age of biopolitics this power becomes emancipated from the state of exception and transformed into the power to decide the point at which life ceases to be politically relevant.[68]

Agamben establishes the extent of the powers the sovereign maintains when dealing with the political enemy. He states that 'what lies at its basis is not man as a free and conscious political subject but, above all, man's bare life, the simple birth chart as such is, in the passage from subject to citizen, invested with the principle of sovereignty.'[69] Thus, this

[66] D. Luban, 'Carl Schmitt and the Critique of Lawfare', (2010) 43 *Case Western Reserve Journal of International Law* 457, at 464.

[67] Schmitt, *supra* note 63, at 29–30.

[68] G. Agamben, *Homo Sacer: Sovereign Power and Bare Life*, (1998), at 142.

[69] Ibid., at 128.

separation of bare life and citizenry rights awards the State the power to take away the rights of a citizen, leaving them with nothing more than bare life.[70] When citizens are left in such a state, the sovereign can treat them in any way they deem fit, thus potentially incurring the loss of life or inhumane treatment. Schmitt also strengthens the assertion that the State maintains the capacity to decide when to strip away the rights of a citizen for 'he who determines a value, *eo ipso* always fixes a non-value.'[71] Indeed, Schmitt advocates that the State must be allowed to exercise the decision to strip away all rights leaving citizens with merely bare life. If such citizens are the political enemies of the State, such measures are integral for the overall order, peace and security of the State's territory.[72] The State must exercise its power of exception to the existing legal order, for the repercussions to the territory overall are far too detrimental according to Schmitt.

Schmitt further strengthens the position of the State so that it can exercise its primary role more effectively. With the work in the *Concept of the Political*, he broadens the concept of a strong State justifying the measures it may have to take to ensure order, peace and security within its territory, for 'the sense of this determination of a non-value is the annihilation of the non-value.'[73] However, Agamben's critiques of the concept of bare life and Schmitt's development of a strong State being able to decide its political enemy raise concerns of the repercussions such sovereign powers may inflict upon groups or individuals. Especially for the liberal constitutionalists, such unchecked powers are troublesome if in the wrong hands.

Agamben highlights such concerns when analysing the Nazi regime's euthanasia programme. One of the principal reasons for/of the Nazi euthanasia programme was based on eugenics, and the idea of 'racial hygiene.' There was the staunch belief that the German people needed to be cleansed of the racial enemies, in this case primarily the Jewish population. Thus, the sovereign's decision on bare life in this instance 'comes to be displaced from strictly political motivations and areas to a

[70] Ibid.

[71] C. Schmitt, *Theorie des Partisanen, Zwischenbemerkung zum Begriff des Politischen*, (1963) at 80.

[72] Agamben, *supra* note 68, at 142.

[73] Schmitt, *supra* note 71, at 80.

more ambiguous terrain in which the physician and the sovereign seem to exchange roles.'[74] Agamben here reveals the fundamental flaw in Schmitt's adherence to a strong State with unlimited jurisdictional competence. Awarding such level of unchecked power to the sovereign can incur severe detrimental effects, where unethical practices are justified for the sake of the State ensuring order, peace and justice within its territory.

3.3.3 Carl Schmitt in International Law

The two propositions that sprout out of Schmitt's prioritisation of the sovereign over the legal order, coupled with the importance of the friend and enemy dichotomy, are some of the reasons as to why Schmitt did not believe that an international legal order, that was liberal in tradition, could be established. If the power of the sovereign was absolute and unlimited in terms of jurisdictional competence over its territory, the idea of a supranational order would not be possible. The sovereign would be unable to exercise the power of exception or do what is necessary to ensure the order, peace and security of its territory if a higher order superseded its authority. Moreover, for Schmitt, in order for the effective operation of an international legal order to be established, States must sacrifice their sovereignty. Through Schmitt's paradigm such a sacrifice is not possible, for then the State would put its territory potentially at risk, hindering the ability to exercise its primary duty. Thus, no State would willingly transfer its sovereignty if a strong State were required for the maintenance of order, peace and security of its territory. Furthermore, in regard to an international legal order, Schmitt argued that even if such a legal order was established and the sovereign State is still able to exercise the power of the exception, the legal order would be superseded by any State on any occasion that it saw fit. The international legal order would be untenable as compliance would be an issue on some of its most fundamental principles. Put simply, the system would become redundant if its main subjects were violating the order for the sake of ensuring their own territorial order, peace and security.

As Koskenniemi critiques Schmitt's *The Nomos of the Earth*, what becomes apparent is that Schmitt's admiration for *jus publicum*

[74] Agamben, *supra* note 68, at 143.

europaeum highlighted that '*Nomos der Erde* is less a history of international law than a political manifesto against the moralization of warfare that Schmitt saw as a cynical instrument to justify the enormous destruction Western technological superiority was inflicting on its adversaries.'[75] Schmitt advocated 'the European order on the emergence of the State as the political form that regulated the occupation and administration of land inside and outside Europe from the late fifteenth until the late nineteenth century.'[76] He argued in favour of such an order for the State was unrestrained and free to act in order to amass the necessary levels of protection of its populace and—in the case of the European powers—beyond. It is on this basis that he argued against the current form of international law, for 'this new, state-centric system of public order had had the extraordinary merit of limiting and channelling inter-European warfare.'[77]

What is intriguing is that however much Schmitt was a fervent critic of the liberal concept of international law, much of his writing can be identified in the international legal order in theory and practice. States continue to have the power of exception. The PCIJ *Lotus* case asserts the primacy of the State in international law, with judges holding that:

> International law governs relations between independent States. The rules of law binding upon States therefore emanate from their own free will as expressed in conventions or by usages generally accepted as expressing principles of law and established in order to regulate the relations between these co-existing independent communities or with a view to the achievement of common aims. Restrictions upon the independence of States cannot therefore be presumed.[78]

Establishing such jurisprudence emphasises that States are the primary subject and object of the international legal order. Yet such jurisprudence comes with concerning repercussions. Stipulating that the binding nature of international law is dependent upon the free will of States asserts that they would still be able to exercise the power of exception when required

[75] Koskenniemi, *supra* note 58, at 495.

[76] Ibid., at 496.

[77] Ibid. See also C. Schmitt, *The Nomos of the Earth: in the International Law of the Jus Publicum Europaeum*, (2006).

[78] *SS Lotus case* (France v. Turkey), PCIJ Rep Series A No 10, at 18.

to ensure order, peace and security within its own territory. J.L Brierly was a strong critic of such jurisprudence, advancing the argument that the majority opinion:

> Was based on the highly contentious metaphysical proposition of the extreme positivist school that the law emanates from the free will of sovereign independent States, and from this premise... that restrictions on the independence of States cannot be presumed. Neither... can the absence of restrictions; for we are not able to deduce the law applicable to a specific state of facts from the mere fact of sovereignty or independence.[79]

Brierly's criticisms continue to maintain relevance as depending upon the nature of the State; compliance to even fundamental international legal norms may become an issue.

Take for example the Bush administration's actions after the 9/11 attacks that were a direct violation of *ius cogens* norms prohibiting the use of torture. Bearing in mind Bush's speech on 26 June 2004, on the UN International Day in Support of Victims of Torture, where he asserted that 'the United States reaffirms its commitment to the worldwide elimination of torture' and that 'Freedom from torture is an inalienable human right, and we are committed to building a world where human rights are respected and protected by the rule of law,'[80] evidence of the violation of such provisions appear hypocritical. When the Bush Administration was forced to face the evidence of the use of torture mechanisms, US Attorney General Jay Bybee argued that 'the relevant legal treaties (such as the Geneva Conventions, the Convention Against Torture and the ICCPR) do not apply to these detainees; what the US interrogators want to do or are doing does not constitute torture (i.e. the pain inflicted has to be as great as that associated with organ failure or even death); and, moreover, international law is not directly enforceable in US courts.' Moreover, Bybee affirmed the President's 'Commander in Chief role,'[81] claiming that it provided him with overriding power to 'ensure the security of the

[79] J.L. Brierly, The 'Lotus' Case, (1928) 44 *Law Quarterly Review* 154, at 155. Reprinted in *The Basis of Obligation in International Law and other papers* 143–144 (Sir Hersch Lauterpacht ed., 1958).

[80] Annex 2 to the 'Second Periodic Report of the United States of America to the Committee Against Torture', submitted 6 May 2005, US Department of State.

[81] R. Foot, 'Torture: The Struggle over a Peremptory Norm in a Counter-Terrorist Era', July (2006) 20.2 *International Relations Issue* 131, at 133.

United States in situations of grave and unforeseen emergencies' by means that he sees fit.'[82] Considering how the legal repercussions for the US' violation of peremptory norms of international law were so limited, this example supports how much of Schmitt's theories are prevalent within international law. The United States exercised its power of exception to the legal order citing the need to ensure the security of its territory. Little could be done to curtail the action of the State within the international legal framework to ensure compliance. The United States identified its political enemy and superseded the international legal order, for the suspects who had been tortured posed a threat to the territorial order, peace and security of the State, and such threats had to be quelled. The United States implemented torture techniques upon terrorist suspects in question in Guantanamo Bay, regardless of the fundamental nature of the norms being overridden.

Furthermore, it also typifies Schmitt's argument of the primacy of the State. Regardless of the plethora of legal sources prohibiting the use of torture, if the legal order is contending with the primacy of the State, it is the latter that seems to come out as the victor. It is intriguing to analyse international law alongside Schmitt's theories and his view on the international legal order. For as much as he refuted the idea of international law, the international legal system that is in place is operating with much of his theories imbedded in the functioning of the international legal order. The international legal system has been designed in such a manner that would see Schmitt's theories be realised, as the primacy of the State has persisted regardless of the inclusion of non-State actors, such as non-governmental organisations or the inclusion of individuals. Regardless of the disdainful treatment Schmitt and his work has received, his theories resonate deeply in the current international legal system. Fundamentally, it appears that it is indeed the State running the show.

[82] Memorandum for Alberto R. Gonzales, Counsel to the President, from Jay S. Bybee, Assistant Attorney General, 1 August 2002, reprinted in full in M. Danner, Torture and Truth, (2004), 115–166; see also 146–149 for the Commander in Chief argument. Sir N. Rodley, Torture in the 21st Century, see also the William J. Butler Lecture on International Law, given to the Urban Morgan Institute for Human Rights at the University of Cincinnati College of Law, 23 September 2004.

3.3.4 Carl Schmitt and the Utopian Goals of International Law

For those focused on emancipatory idealism as a focal goal of international law, Schmitt's influence is indeed a concerning disposition for the legal system. Analysis of the history of international law highlights how the resonance of Schmitt's theories on the international stage is detrimental to achieving utopian goals of international law. When both the League of Nations and the United Nations failed in achieving utopian goals (which shall be more thoroughly covered in Chapters 4 and 5), on many occasions it has been a result of the will of States. The furtherance of such goals is reliant firstly upon how willing States are to contribute to the effectiveness of international law and secondly if States' realist interests fall in line with achieving such focal goals.

History thus underlines two key postulations. Firstly, the primary position States enjoy in international law has led to the undermining of emancipatory idealism, with many failures of the international legal system resulting in a lack of either State compliance or contribution. With Schmitt's argument—justifying States conducting themselves in whichever manner in order to ensure the order, peace and security of its territory—being a prevalent occurrence within the international community, the potential to undermine the protection of all individuals or a community of individuals is not at all surprising. Secondly, international law has persisted with protecting the primacy of the State, regardless of however much evidence there is to suggest that this is a flaw in the international legal framework. Schmitt himself brings this argument forward when discussing 'that the whole normative structure of international law, based upon treaties, is emptied of content because of the reservations which States make.'[83] The nature of having reservations of States within treaties,[84] expresses a return of the hard and repressed fact that law can only be based on the concrete lives of States.[85] It is on this basis that the debate returns to Schmitt's insistence that the State would not hand over sovereignty to a supranational order, as such a transferal would be in tension with its primary objective. The nature of the international legal

[83] A. Carty, 'Carl Schmitt's Critique of Liberal International Legal Order Between 1933 and 1945', (2001) 14.1 *LJIL* 25, at 33.

[84] In this instance, Schmitt was particularly referring to the Geneva (Draft Protocol), the Locarno Treaties and the Kellogg-Briand Pact.

[85] C. Schmitt, *Nationalsozialismus und Völkerrecht*, (1934), at 23–25.

order allows for States to embark upon their realist goals and it is on this basis States are less inclined to loosen their advantageous position within international law.

This argument is proven by the calls for Security Council reform by both previous UN Secretary-Generals Kofi Annan and Ban Ki-Moon, with the former stating: 'I firmly believe that the Council should be reformed. It cannot continue as it is. The world has changed, and the UN should change and adapt.'[86] When delving deeper into this specific matter, it becomes apparent that Annan and Moon are not the sole voices advocating Security Council reform. There are those, both in the professional and academic forum of international law, who are pushing for such reform to go forward.[87] However, falling in line with Schmitt's arguments, the p-5 would not be so inclined for such reform and weaken the advantageous position they have within the legal framework of the UN.[88] When States have a primary obligation to ensure the order, peace and security of their own territory, the responsibility to ensure international peace and security or the achievement of emancipatory idealism falls to the wayside when these two focal goals do not align. Yet the Security Council has been set up in a manner that is dependent upon the contribution of States, and more particular the p-5 members. This only strengthens Schmitt's argument that the State is the most influential entity in international law. Therefore, for those seeking to achieve emancipatory idealism as a focal goal of international law, this facet of the legal system has proven to be problematic.

Several legal scholars have similarly advanced the argument that State interaction with international law is mostly predicated on maintaining peace and order within its own territory. When Eric Posner analysed whether States have a moral obligation to obey international law, he surmised that there is no moral obligation, but a State's drive to best

[86] https://www.theguardian.com/world/video/2015/sep/23/kofi-annan-un-security-council-expand-reform-video, (last accessed 14 May 2019).

[87] See Nadin, *supra* note 23, at 47–48; A. Roberts, 'The United Nations and International Security', (2008) 35.2 *Global Politics and Strategy* 3, at 5; S. Tharoor, 'Security Council Reform: Past, Present and Future', (2011) 25.4 *Ethics & International Affairs* 397; I. Hurd, 'Legitimacy, Power, and the Symbolic Life of the UN Security Council', (2002) *Global Governance* 35, at 47.

[88] M. Glennon, 'Why the Security Council Failed', (2003) 82.3 *Foreign Affairs* 16, at 25.

serve its own citizens. 'When people argue that States should comply with international law, they always appeal to the rights or welfare of individuals. Individuals would be better off in a world in which States had an obligation to comply with international law.'[89] Posner contended that international lawyers often confuse two separate ideas, that States have a moral obligation to promote the good of all individuals in the world, regardless of their citizenship, and a moral obligation to comply with international law.[90] These ideas are not the same, 'they are in tension as long as governments focus their efforts on helping their own.'[91] Posner suggested that even the most liberal democratic States are imbued with the same characteristic for 'they never attach as much weight to the well-being of foreigners as they do their own citizens... the democratic institutions of such States drive them towards [certain] results as long as the interest groups or publics in those States care more about their own well-being than that of the population of the third State.'[92]

Additionally, Koskenniemi argued that States interact with international law adopting a pragmatic-instrumentalist approach.[93] He contends that it is difficult to refute the significant realist undercurrent in the international legal system.[94] This asserts that the legal system is determined by the power of States, and that their interactions are driven by nationalist impulses. Thus, when States utilise a pragmatic-instrumentalist approach they do so with the objective of fulfilling certain domestic purposes, even if it undermines certain international legal principles.[95]

What becomes clear is that the two concepts underlined by the historical analysis of international law promote the argument that the legal

[89] E. Posner, 'Do States Have a Moral Obligation to Obey International Law?' (2003) 55 *Stanford Law Review* 1901, at 1912.

[90] Ibid., at 1914.

[91] Ibid., at 1914–1915.

[92] Ibid., at 1913.

[93] M. Koskenniemi, 'What Is International Law For?' in M.D. Evans (ed.), *International Law*, (2018), at 34.

[94] Ibid.

[95] Koskenniemi suggests that 'Much instrumentalist thinking about international law today adopts the point of view of the decision-maker in a relatively prosperous State or transnational network, in possession of resources and policy options and seeking guidance on how to fit their objectives within international legality- or to overrule the legality with minimal costs' in ibid., at 34.

system is full of contradictions. On one side, there is the disdainful treatment of Schmitt's work and the figure himself. Moreover, there is the encouragement within the international community to achieve emancipatory idealism with the idealist developments in the international legal system. Such progressions can be identified with the rise of individual justice in international law post-Second World War and the focus on ensuring international peace and security. Yet on the other side, it is apparent that Schmitt's central concepts are imbedded so strongly in the way in which the international community operates and interacts with the international legal system. There is the constant focus to ensure the primacy of the State, which does not work for a legal system where the primary creator of the system is also the primary subject. It becomes problematic when attempting to ensure compliance and to establish the rule of law. This position that States enjoy within the confines of the legal system undermines not only the potential to achieve emancipatory idealism, but also the legitimacy of the legal system itself when compliance is dependent upon the willingness of States.

3.4 Hans Kelsen

3.4.1 Attempts to Overcome the Primacy of the State

Analysing Carl Schmitt is valuable in exploring the position of the State in international law. His work details why it is that States enjoy a dominant position in the international legal system as the primary object and subject. In the light of this, it is an interesting proposition to explore the work of Hans Kelsen in conjunction with Carl Schmitt, considering they were intellectual and ideological opponents, in the *interbellum* period especially.

Where Schmitt advocated the idea of a strong State that could not be governed by a supranational order, Kelsen pushed for an international legal system that would establish the successful rule of law and limit the position States enjoy in the legal system. Kelsen sought to thus establish 'the traditional doctrine of State and international law on a new methodological foundation,'[96] one that was more objective and scientific in tradition.[97] He identified that the main issue international law suffered

[96] J. Von Bernstorff, *The Public International Law Theory of Hans Kelsen*, (2010), 44.
[97] Ibid.

from was the inclusion of the political dimension. He proposed a different approach to international law as the idealist effort failed to achieve international peace and security. Kelsen was highly critical of the model of international law that emerged after the First World War, and the establishment of the primacy of the State within the legal system. He advocated the separation of the League from the Peace Treaties, criticising the lack of legislative powers within the League and the supremacy of the Council over the Permanent Court of International Justice. He was also critical of the absence of a provision for the PCIJ to have competences to order sanctions.[98] The system was far too political and Kelsen argued that this led lawyers to become 'amateur sociologist or a dilettante moralist.'[99]

In order to escape such a weakness, the only legal question that required assessment was whether 'this or that normative proposition was "law,"'[100] and consequently if it is necessarily required to be applied to a specific legal issue. That question was answered on the basis that it was part of the system, the chain of validity, for if 'law' had been rightfully passed in accordance with the relevant statute; and if that statute was 'law' enacted in accordance with the constitution and the constitution was 'law' that had entered into force in accordance with the first constitution, its validity grew from this notion. What closed the ascending chain of delegations was the famous *Grundnorm*, the basic norm that provided for the validity of the whole system. Kelsen interpreted such a norm that one needed to believe valid in order for everything that one already knew about the legal system should be true.[101] What his system advocated did not require political or sociological evaluation, however Kelsen believed such an approach to law would still accommodate for extra evaluations:

> The Pure Theory of Law exposes once and for all the attempt to use the concept of sovereignty to lend a purely political argument – which is always vulnerable to a comparable counter-argument – the appearance of a logical argument, which would by its very nature be irrefutable. And precisely by exposing the argument as political, the Pure Theory of Law facilitates

[98] H. Kelsen, *Völkerrechstslehre*, (1995), 278–283.

[99] Published in English as H. Kelsen, *Introduction to the Problems of Legal Theory. A Translation of the First Edition of the Reine Rechtslehre or Pure Theory of Law*, (1992).

[100] M. Koskenniemi, *The Gentle Civilizer of Nations: The Rise and Fall of International Law 1870–1960*, (2004), 241.

[101] Kelsen, *supra* note 98, at 55–76.

> development that has been stunted by mistaken notions, development in terms of legal policy – facilitates such development.[102]

This method of legality, moreover, created a formalist structure that held within it far more validity and substance than the first phase of international law and operated, in Kelsen's opinion at least, on the basis of pure logic.

Kelsen advocated for this method of legality for international law not only to protect the system from unwanted political arguments but also in order to assert that the 'sovereignty is a systemic concept; not something external to but determined within the law.'[103] Through this mechanism, Kelsen attempted to create an international rule of law. The origin of this argument is cemented in Kelsen's ambition to drive non-legal (particularly political) dimensions out of the international law framework. In order to 'rid law of apologism, a higher normative code needs to be assumed.'[104] For Kelsen and other legalists who advocated the purely legal approach, the belief was that the legal order pre-existed the sovereignty of the State and remains in control thereof. The State therefore derives its authority from a superior normative code. Hence, for the likes of Kelsen and H.L.A Hart international law 'allocates competences and legitimate spheres of action to entities it chooses to regard as legal subjects. No subjects, no sets of rights, competences or liberties are externally given. They are constituted by the law itself.'[105] In such an international legal system, the State cannot justify action solely based on its own sovereignty, but rather a 'rule of law, which has given it the right, liberty or competence to act in a certain way.'[106]

For Kelsen, this pure theory of law was intended to solve many of the weaknesses the first model of international law had suffered from. Firstly, by eradicating the political, moral and sociological dilemmas from the legal system, legal processes would be driven by a pure path of logic. He intended to tighten the international legal system, ensuring that the

[102] H. Kelsen, *Das Problem der Souveränität*, (1960), at 134–139.

[103] M. Koskenniemi, *From Apology to Utopia: The Structure of International Legal Argument*, (2005), at 228.

[104] Ibid., at 231.

[105] Ibid., at 230.

[106] Ibid., at 231.

law was free from all those 'elements foreign to the specific methods of a science whose only purpose is the cognition of law.'[107] For him, the idealist hope of creating international peace and justice would be achieved through a purely technical positivist mechanism.

Furthermore, through such a mechanism, Kelsen intended to create legal obligations upon States to adhere to their new international responsibility, and in the instance where a conflict between international and national responsibility ensued, the international rule of law would ensure the primacy of the international legal system over all other system of law. Kelsen envisaged a monistic construction of international law, where international and domestic legal systems existed simultaneously without contradictions. Therefore, depending on which legal system one is operating within, different legal norms are valid, for 'norms of the State legal system that are created by "violating" international law remain valid, even from the standpoint of international law, because international law makes no provision for a procedure whereby norms of the state legal system "contrary to international law" can be invalidated.'[108] It can be argued that Kelsen's monist conception of international law allows States to supersede international law, drawing parallels with Schmitt's argumentation. By the fact that State legal norms that violate international law cannot be invalidated, States can argue circumvention of international law. However, there is a marked difference between what Kelsen and Schmitt argue for. Schmitt would support the violation of international law on the basis of political necessity which drives the State to act in any manner that shall protect its territory, regardless of legal validity, whereas Kelsen's monist conception sees the possibility of States circumventing international law on the basis of its own domestic law. The rule of law—international or domestic—still exists in this prism, for States are not justifying their actions on the basis political variables, but the legal norms established by the State's legal system.

Moreover, Kelsen insists upon the primacy of the international legal system over the domestic legal system. Unlike a pluralist conception of international law, which would see international law being recognised by

[107] Kelsen, *supra* note 98, at xiv. See also J. Kammerhofer, 'Hans Kelsen in Today's International Legal Scholarship' in J. Kammerhofer & J. D'Aspremont (ed.), *International Legal Positivism in a Post-Modern World*, (2014), at 83.

[108] H. Kelsen, *Introduction to the Problems of Legal Theory*, (1997), at 119.

the State legal system,[109] Kelsen's monist conception asserts that it is the international legal system that 'determines the spatial and temporal sphere of validity of the State legal system formed thereby.'[110] This proposition is supported by Kelsen's insistence that it is the international legal system that allows for State legal systems to generate norms that violate international law. This compliments Kelsen's ambition for an international rule of law, for this further strengthens the perspective that sovereignty is a systemic concept, determined by the international legal system. Therefore State actions cannot be argued for by political justifications, but instead, either by the legal norms established by international law, or the contradictory legal norms of States that have been permitted by the international legal system.

Kelsen believed such a model of international law would not be marred by self-interest due to the strict confines of a purely legal structure. 'He wanted to get beyond the logic of power in international relations so that "the particular states could be regarded juridically as entities of equal rank" and thus a "world and universal state" could be formed, organized as a "universal community superior to the particular states, enveloping them all within itself."'.[111]

When the second stage of development occurred at the creation of the United Nations in San Francisco in 1945, positivism was the prevalent influence during the construction of the international law framework. Similar to Kelsen's support for an international rule of law, the UN Charter created a more centralised system with the Security Council taking a more dynamic executive role than the previous Council in the League, as it possessed legal powers to 'maintain or restore international peace and security,'[112] as inscribed in Chapter VII of the Charter. Furthermore, as Kelsen had further encouraged a legal system born out of positivism, the second model of international law revelled within the confines of formalism. An indication of such formalism can be identified in the International Court of Justice and its statute. Article 38(1) establishes

[109] Ibid., at 117.

[110] Ibid., at 120.

[111] M. Hardt & A. Negri, *Empire*, (2000), at 5. See also Kelsen, *supra* note 102, at 205 and H. Kelsen, *Principles of International Law*, (1952), 586.

[112] *UN Charter*, (1945), Article 40.

the sources of international law, and some writers have argued that international conventions, custom and general principles of law are considered as the three-exclusive law-creating processes that are regarded as formal sources that confer upon the rules an obligatory character.[113] However, judicial decisions and academic writings are regarded as law-determining agencies, dealing with the verification of alleged rules,[114] comprising the content of the rules.[115] There was also Article 38(2) which gave the 'power of the Court to decide a case *ex aequo et bono*, if the parties agree thereto.'[116] The Statute has adopted a positivist approach, as purely legal sources took greater precedence, whereas the possibility of equity, which would potentially allow non-legal dimensions to be utilised in order to make judgements, can only be used when both parties agree that is shall be utilised.

Even though Kelsen attempted to propose a formalist model of international law, this approach has done little to counteract the problems pertaining to State primacy. In order for such a model to work, the legal system must be exhaustive and extensive in dealing with issues that may arise in the territory that its jurisdiction presides over. This has been a central criticism directed towards international law for there are several gaps apparent in the system. This is a significant issue because there have been many occasions in which international law has not developed sufficiently in order to effectively deal with problems that have arisen within the international community.

An example that illustrates this criticism is the lack of clarity in the relevant legality in relation to the US operation that led to the killing of Osama Bin Laden in Pakistani territory. Former US Secretary of State George Schultz stated that international law does not prohibit a State from 'attacking [terrorists] on the soil of other nations... or using force against States that support, train, and harbour terrorists or guerrillas.'[117] The United States contended such an operation was an act of self-defence

[113] M. Shaw, *International Law*, (2011), 71.

[114] G. Schwarzenberger, *International Law*, (1957), 26–27.

[115] Shaw, *supra* note 113, at 71.

[116] *Statute of the International Court of Justice*, (1945), Article 38(2).

[117] See, 'Shultz Urges Limited Attack on Terrorists', Hous. Chron., (16 January 1986), at 6, col. 3; 'Shultz Supports Armed Reprisals', *N.Y. Times*, (16 January 1986), at AI, col. 5. The entire speech is now reprinted in 'Documents Showing the Evolution of Sanctions Against Libya', (1986) 25 *International Legal Materials* 174, at 204.

in accordance with Article 51 of the UN Charter. However, invoking self-defence to justify cross-border operations—where the legitimate mandate for US troops to enter Pakistani territory is already in question—requires several controversial doctrinal leaps. 'These include: that a terrorist act can constitute an "armed attack"; that in the face of multiple attacks, self-defence applies on a continuous basis and not only in the immediate aftermath of any one attack; that self-defence can be exercised in the territory of a state that is not acting in collusion with the menace; that self-defence can be exercised against a single individual in keeping with the principle of necessity; and—most importantly—that the law supports a form of anticipatory self-defence that can be exercised in the absence of a concrete threat of future attack.'[118] It is worth noting that before 9/11 such cross-border operations were widely condemned by the international community for violating the sovereignty of an independent State. For example, in 1988, the Security Council asserted that Israel's 'assassination' in Tunisia of an alleged Palestine Liberation Organisation leader, Khalil El Wazir, was an act of aggression. Similarly, States condemned Colombian Operation Phoenix, which took place in Ecuador to pursue Raul Reyes and other Revolutionary Armed Forces of Colombia guerrillas. However, Colombia was not sanctioned in any meaningful way for its actions. Yet the responses that emerged from the execution of such operations sent a clear message that this was not normative behaviour within the international community or international law.

Yet in a post-9/11 world, hegemonic States have sought to alter such a perception. Such States affirm that there should be greater tolerance towards States conducting such cross-border operations as these States are merely taking 'defensive action within territories of other States that are unable or unwilling to repress irregular fighters in their midst, even if the territorial State could not be held responsible for the acts of those militants. The theory is that such States forfeit their right to non-interference when they fail to deal with such transnational security threats.'[119] Regardless, of such justifications, this position is based on doctrinal leaps in the law as there is no international law stipulating what is acceptable conduct

[118] B. Van Schaak, 'The Killing of Osama Bin Laden and Anwar Al-Aulaqi: Uncharted Legal Territory', (2011) 14 *Yearbook of International Humanitarian Law* 255, at 280.

[119] Ibid., at 272.

when dealing with cross-border operations to terminate threats to international peace and security that are non-State actors. It is important to note that such doctrinal leaps are only possible when there are gaps in the law allowing States to utilise the law—or lack of law—to justify the furtherance of their realist interest. Considering that the repercussions of establishing such doctrinal leaps as legal norms would be problematic for the international community, for States could violate the sovereignty of any State on any occasion for the sake of territorial order, peace and security. Thus, Kelsen's formalist model of international law is only effective if the system of law is robust. Given that international law is not at this stage just yet it allows States to dominate the legal system. Consequently, States can manipulate and bend the laws to suit their interest, which is problematic for those seeking to achieve emancipatory idealism.

The failing of Kelsen's model of international law is all the more concerning for those focused on achieving utopian focal goals of international law when bearing in mind the primacy of the State. This issue is increasingly perturbing for the State exists in an international legal system where a global police is not present. Consequently, the State thrives in an environment where they can avoid punishment for severe violations of international legal norms. If rules are broken, States can—and have—avoided punishment for exercising the power of exception and superseding the international legal order. Therefore, a disregard of the rules laid down by international law can potentially face no drastic repercussions, especially if a State has an influential position in the international community.

3.5 Michel Foucault

3.5.1 Understanding the State

It seems that as much as Kelsen sought to overcome the issue of realism in international law with an objective approach to law, the primacy of the State continues to be the dominating factor in the international legal system. Moreover, within such a formalist model, States continue to undermine utopian goals of international law. With an international legal system where the State and its interest takes centre stage, the international community has witnessed individuals and communities of individuals be subjugated to modes of oppression without any form of protection or recourse to justice for such wrongdoing. Precisely for this inability to realise utopian focal goals of international law, further analysis of the State is required as to exactly why it chooses its own preservation over the preservation of the international community as a whole. The question must be raised as to whether the international community asks too much of the State to simultaneously ensure order, peace and justice within its own territory and international peace and security.

Analysing Schmitt's work addresses some of the reasons for why the heavy responsibility placed upon States to ensure international peace and security is so troublesome, yet further exploration by the analysis of other scholarly sources is necessary. For example, Michel Foucault's work on biopolitics helps to highlight the nature of the State and why its primacy in the international legal system is therefore such an issue. Though Foucault did not coin the term, what he made of biopolitics is a fascinating reflection upon the nature of the State. His work on this topic gives context as to why the State responds in the manner it does in the international community in a post-Enlightenment era. There are two sources that are of particular interest in regard to Foucault's work on biopolitics, firstly his series of lectures published in *Society Must be Defended* and his popular text *History of Sexuality.* Both sources will be analysed collectively in order to understand the importance Foucault's work on biopolitics bears on assessing the problems inherent in the primacy of the State in the international legal system.

Foucault analyses the effect the enlightenment era had upon the sovereign and its exercise of power. He suggests that before the nineteenth century, the classical theory of sovereignty was the prominent conception of the State. Foucault suggested that the 'the right of life and death was one of sovereignty's basic attributes.'[120] Ultimately, the classic theory of sovereignty establishes the right the sovereign has to decide the life and death of its subjects, meaning 'that he can, basically, either have people put to death or let them live, or in any case that life and death are not natural or immediate phenomena which are primal or radical, and which fall outside the field of power.'[121] Foucault asserted that 'in a formal sense, it derived no doubt from the ancient *patria patestas* that granted the father of the Roman family the right to "dispose" of the life of his children and his slaves; just as he had given them life, so he could take

[120] M. Foucault, *Society Must be Defended*, (2003), at 240.

[121] Ibid., at Pg240.

it away.'[122] This right the sovereign possesses therefore would have practical implications as it would in the instance of war for example. Thus, if the sovereign was in danger from an external threat, its right would allow him to legitimately wage war, 'and require [the sovereign's] subjects to take part in the defence of the state; without 'directly proposing their death,' the sovereign was empowered to 'expose their life': in this sense, he wielded an 'indirect' power over them of life and death.'[123] In fact, it seemed that the power of the sovereign was not an absolute privilege over life and death; rather it was the power of the sovereign to use this right for his own defence.

Foucault suggests in *Society Must be Defended* that the sovereign's right to decide the life and death of its subjects in fact is exercised in an unbalanced manner for the sovereign cannot 'grant life in the same way that he can inflict death.'[124] Ultimately:

> The sovereign exercised his right of life only by exercising his right to kill, or by refraining from killing; he evidenced his power over life only through the death he was capable of requiring. The right which was formulated as the "power of life and death" was in reality the right to take life or let live.[125]

Foucault thus contends that the sovereign's right is essentially the right of the sword. With such a classic theory of sovereignty, the focus of society is not the subjects, but rather the defence of the sovereign from external, or even internal strength. The sovereign ultimately focuses on the idea of punishment, harking back to the ecclesiastical influences in regard to the conception of the State. The classical conception of the State did not possess the capacity to prolong life, only to punish, consequently maintaining the power to end life and bring about death. The sovereign focused on the 'life after death' ideal, emphasising the concept of punishment for those who have committed sinful acts. Attention was driven towards more theological adaptations of sovereignty for such means of governance was based on a 'specific system bearing salvation, obedience, and truth… more precisely, it meant that the things of the world were

122 M. Foucault, *History of Sexuality*, (1978), at 135.

123 Ibid., at Pg135.

124 Foucault, *supra* note 120, at 240.

125 Foucault, *supra* note 122, at 136.

made for man and that man was not made to live in this world, at any rate not definitively, but only in order to pass into another world.'[126] Therefore, the right of life and death the sovereign possesses is intrinsically to maintain its own life and preservation. In this concept of the sovereign, the populace is at the will of the sovereign for the sake of its own preservation, thus if the sovereign seeks to wage war, it can utilise its populace for its own preservation. Also, if a citizen has been sinful and requires punishment, it is for the sovereign to decide whether or not their life should be taken away to ensure its own order and peace. In such a circumstance, it is the populace that is serving the sovereign for the sake of its preservation.

Yet this model underwent a dramatic reworking come the nineteenth century. There are several reasons for this. Firstly, seventeenth- and eighteenth-century jurists explored the sovereign's right of life and death, questioning the classical theory. Foucault outlines some of the questions that were being surveyed by the jurists during that period:

> When we enter into a contract, what are individuals doing at the level of the social contract, when they come together to constitute a sovereign, to delegate absolute power over them to a sovereign? They do so because they are forced to by some threat or by need. They therefore do so in order to protect their lives. It is in order to live that they constitute a sovereign. To the extent that this is the case, can life actually become one of the rights of the sovereign? Isn't life the foundation of the sovereign's right, and can the sovereign actually demand that his subjects grant him the right to exercise the power of life and death over them, or in other words, simply the power to kill them? Mustn't life remain outside the contract to the extent that it was the first, initial, and foundational reason for the contract itself?.[127]

This examination led to a rethinking of the role of the government. It pushed forward the argument that it is not the sovereign utilising its populace for its own preservation, but the sovereign exercising its authority to preserve the life of the populace.[128] The imbalance had been

[126] M. Foucault, *Security, Territory, Population*, (2007), at 87.

[127] Foucault, *supra* note 120, at 241.

[128] M. De Larrinaga & M.G. Doucet, 'Sovereign Power and the Biopolitics of Human Security', (2008) 39 *Security Dialogue* 517, at 520.

shifted with the questions seventeenth- and eighteenth-century jurists were advancing. Rather than the weight being placed upon death, the focus would be rather placed on the sovereign's right of life.[129] This shift would turn the sovereign from a sword into a shield.

However, for this reimagining to take place the sovereign would have the capacity to ensure life and prolong the life of its citizens. This is exactly what the enlightenment period had done. With the emergence of science into the mainstream, the sovereign was able to prolong the life of its populace. Scientific development birthed biopolitical structures of governance focused upon the life of its citizens, using any methods to do so. With medical advancements emerging, this provided the capability for humans to live longer. This is where Foucault's concept of biopolitics emerged with the shift in the conception of the sovereign. The State would now justify its actions not for its own preservation but to ensure that the life of its populace would not be endangered, for:

> Wars are no longer waged in the name of a sovereign who must be defended; they are waged on behalf of the existence of everyone; entire populations are mobilized for the purpose of wholesale slaughter in the name of life necessity: massacres have become vital. It is as managers of life and survival, of bodies and the race, that so many regimes have been able to wage so many wars, causing so many men to be killed. And through a turn that closes the circle, as the technology of wars has caused them to tend increasingly toward all-out destruction, the decision that initiates them and the one that terminates them are in fact increasingly informed by the naked question of survival.[130]

The primary objective of the State thus became the life of its citizens and to enact any measures or mechanisms to ensure this goal. Subsequently, 'there was a rapid development of various disciplines -universities, secondary schools, barracks, workshops; there was also the emergence, in the field of political practices and economic observation, of the problems of birth-rate, longevity, public health, housing, and migration.'[131] Inevitably, 'deduction' was no longer the primary source of sovereign power, as the focus shifted away from a commanding 'body impeding

[129] Ibid.

[130] Foucault, *supra* note 120, at 137.

[131] Ibid., at 140.

[the populace], making them submit, or destroying them'[132] to 'working to incite, reinforce, control, monitor, optimize, and organize the forces under it: a power bent on generating forces, making them grow, and ordering them.'[133]

Foucault also pondered upon the detrimental nature such a shift in the perception of the sovereign had. Pausing upon the issue of genocide, he surmounted that such conduct could be legitimised or at least justified for the sake of the sovereign protecting its populace. He first asserts that 'the principle underlying the tactics of battle- that was one has to be capable of killing in order to go on living- has become the principle that defines the strategy of States. But the existence in question is no longer the juridical one of the sovereignty; at stake is the biological existence of a population.'[134] He subsequently touches upon the issue of genocide stating that, 'if genocide is indeed the dream of modern powers, this is not because of a recent return to the right to kill; it is because power is situated and exercised at the level of life, the species, the race, and the large scale phenomena of population.'[135] Now that the role of the State was no longer focused upon exercising the right of life and death, but rather focusing on 'fostering life' or disallowing life to the point of death, this opened up the possibility of State conduct carrying through with acts such as genocide.

Biopolitics has a strong connection with Schmitt's concept of the State, as much of what justified Schmitt's inclination for a strong State revolves around the need for the State to protect its populace. Whereas Schmitt administers the need for a strong State to ensure order, peace and security within its region, Foucault gives an explanation of why such a phenomenon has become so prevalent. His work on biopolitics goes some way to understanding the nature of the State, highlighting the effects that scientific development has had upon the role of the State. Biopolitics delineates why States favour Schmittian ideologies when interacting with international law, for such an ideology allows the State to ensure the fostering of life that it is in control of most effectively. Ultimately, State interaction in international law has become the pursuance of 'the

[132] Ibid., at 136.

[133] Ibid., at 136.

[134] Ibid., at 137.

[135] Ibid., at 137.

administration of life and the management of populations through the deployment of biopolitical techniques of power'.[136]

Biopolitics also helps explain the instances where States take an interest in utopian concepts. Utopian developments within the international community do assist in ensuring that States do lengthen the life of its populace. When assessing the development of the League of Nations or the United Nations for example, these idealist projects have been successful in also achieving State-centric aims. Creating these international organisations assist the most powerful States at the time to ensure the life of its populace or be in a position to help exercise such a role of the sovereign. Yet the State is selective in its focus upon utopian goals of international law. The complete achievement of emancipatory idealism as a focal goal does not always help the State in exercising its primary goal. Consequently, there is not as much interest in States dedicating themselves completely to the utopian project. Exploring the post-First World War events and the emergence of the League exemplifies this argument accurately. A central reason States showed such dedication to utopian goals of international law during this period was because they believed at the time this was the only way in which a second large-scale crisis would be prevented from reoccurring. States had occupied themselves with a form of governmentality that 'operates on populations and seeks to promote life.'[137]

When we assess State behaviour towards utopian focal goals of international law, the tendency is for States to only support such goals if it helps ensure order, peace and the security of its territory. This is indicative when assessing the instruments that have been developed to ensure that States—more specifically the most influential States in the international community—can protect their populaces, or in the last three decades, when humanitarian intervention has taken place, for example. When analysing State conduct when interacting with international law, it becomes all the more apparent that States are not necessarily interested in the full utopian project. Instead, States are more concerned with how much international law—and the pursuance of utopian goals of international law—can help serve their biopolitical and realist agenda.

[136] M. Dillon & J. Reid, 'Global Liberal Governance: Biopolitics, Security and War', (2001) 30.1 *Millennium* 41, at 46.

[137] Ibid., at 47. See also Foucault, *supra* note 122, at 139.

It is because, 'biopolitical governance is less concerned with States and non-governmental organisations as pre-formed political subjects, than it is concerned with the detailed knowledgeable strategies and tactics that affect the constitution of life and the regulation of the affairs of populations, no matter how these are specified.'[138] It is rare for States to partake in international law with the general aim of ensuring utopian goals of international law in a selfless manner. There must be an interest for States to commit to such utopian goals, which highlights why States have tended to undermine such goals of international law. It indicates that all aspects of governmentality are primarily based on the biopolitical agenda, so that 'all the processes of re-productive circulation that impinge upon species existence'[139] within their jurisdiction is secured. Therefore, this subsequently highlights that for States, achieving utopian focal goals of international law is a secondary and optional focus.

Take for instance, the issue of Statehood and the recognition of new emerging States. As much as the declaratory theory establishes a guideline to validate a claim for statehood, 'the legal theory of statehood remains inconsistently applied in practice, and often the geo-political reality of a given region dictates whether an entity is treated as a state by the international community.'[140] It becomes apparent that the constitutive theory—a theory asserting that statehood is dependent upon recognition by external actors—is a more prevalent phenomenon within international law. It seems that 'an entity will be recognised as a new state only if it garners the support of the most powerful states in the international legal system.'[141] The recognition of statehood is a utopian project falling in line with emancipatory idealism as it protects communities of individuals from modes of oppression. For a new State can overcome economic and trade issues, developmental concerns, and monetary hurdles in a globalised world if it is recognised by the international community. By overcoming such concerns, the new State can successfully establish a stable political, economic and societal environment for such a community to be able to contribute to civilisational development. Yet the most

[138] Ibid., at 48.

[139] M. Dillon, 'Governing Terror: The State of Emergency of Biopolitical Emergence', (2007) 1 *International Political Sociology* 7, at 9.

[140] M. Sterio, 'On the Right to Self-Determination: 'Selfistans', Secessions and the Great Power's Rule' (2010) 19.1 *Minnesota Journal of International Law* 137, at 149.

[141] Ibid., at 150.

powerful States in the international legal system seem to only recognise new States when they have an invested interest in the matter.[142] Also, the opposite seems to occur when these States see a realist benefit to not recognise a new State. Such decisions are made regardless of the legitimacy of such claims for statehood or how such recognition would further emancipatory idealism within the international community.

Such an argument is strengthened when analysing the levels of legitimacy Kosovo and Palestine both claim to possess for statehood. Zohar Nevo and Tamar Megiddo contend that the 'examination factors of the Kosovo case shows that, in some regards, the Palestinian case is in a more favourable position.'[143] However, recognition seems more plausible for Kosovo, as it has the support of UK, France, eighteen other EU Member-States, and the United States. On the other hand, Palestine have struggled in their claim for recognition, as the greater focus on the US' position on the matter has proven to be an obstacle.[144] Ultimately, the unequal approach to statehood recognition highlights that the decisive factor for States is not to help achieve emancipatory idealism. Instead, it is to fulfil their biopolitical and realist agendas.

3.6 The Dual Duties of the State

For those focused on achieving emancipatory idealism, exploring the nature of the State and identifying its primary duty through the work of Schmitt and Foucault's biopolitics suggest that the primacy of the State has become a problematic disposition of international law. The structure of international law is brought into question for it becomes apparent that the State is battling to calm the tensions of the two duties that it possesses. The first duty is one that has been covered extensively throughout this chapter, which is the one the State has to its territory as described by Schmitt and Foucault. This duty sees the State utilise 'international law norms to help construct national identities and interests through a process

[142] A. Buchanan, *Justice, Legitimacy, and Self-Determination: Moral Foundations for International Law*, (2003), 211.

[143] Z. Nevo & T. Megiddo, 'Lessons from Kosovo: The Law of Statehood and Palestinian Unilateral Independence', (2009) 5.2 *Journal of International Law and International Relations* 89, at 114.

[144] J. Crawford, *The Creation of States in International Law*, (2007), 194.

of justificatory discourse.'[145] The second is the duty the State has to the international community and obligations it has to ensure international peace and security, either through the UN Charter or various international legal agreements or documents. This second duty encompasses emancipatory idealism and to ensure that all individuals or communities of individuals are protected from modes of oppression. Thus, there is the expectation—for those focused on achieving emancipatory idealism—that when crises arise or international injustices occur, States—as the primary subject and object of international law—should seek to achieve utopian focal goals regardless of how this may affect its own realist or biopolitical goals. States are expected to contribute to UN efforts to deal with humanitarian crisis effectively and to work within the Security Council framework to effectively respond to individuals or communities of individuals regardless of their primary duty. Indeed, Article 2.5 of the Charter stresses this expectation, establishing Member-States' responsibility to assist 'in any action [the United Nations] takes in accordance with the present Charter.'[146]

Yet this highlights the competing tensions States are dealing with when interacting with international law. These two duties do not always align, and States tend to compromise utopian focal goals for their realist goals if faced with the decision to choose between the two. Modern international law has vastly developed since its birth at the Peace Treaty of Westphalia, where the focus was placed upon maintaining healthy relations amongst the European powers. Both the League of Nations and the United Nations had come about in order to achieve international peace and security, following the horrors of the wars that had paved the way for their creation. International law had expanded the Westphalian model, becoming much more than just about maintaining State relations. As Foucault details, the role of the sovereign had shifted from being centrally concerned with a disciplinary society that utilised individuals for its own maintenance and furtherance,[147] to a sovereign power sovereign power that 'invests [in] life through and through, and its primary task is to administer life.'[148] This can even be seen in the evolution of international

[145] Koh, *supra* note 12, at 2602.

[146] *UN Charter* (1945), Article 2(5).

[147] Foucault, *supra* note 122, at 135–145.

[148] Hardt & Negri, *supra* note 111, at 24.

law when analysing the development from the Westphalian model of international law to the liberal international institutions we have regulating the international community today. Thus, the League of Nations and the United Nations—along with the development of various international legal instruments—became a forum to potentially achieve emancipatory idealism. The aim was to create an international legal system that would establish peace and that would protect individuals or communities of individuals from modes of oppression. The fallout of such large-scale crisis was far-reaching, and it was civilisational development that was at risk. Considering that 'the state system is a political and legal order that attributes rights and obligations to states,'[149] it seems appropriate to expect States to attempt to achieve such utopian focal goals.

However, it is the duty placed upon States to simultaneously work towards achieving emancipatory idealism within the international community and exercise its domestic duties that can be deemed utopian in the negative sense. The position States have been placed into—and it is their own doing that they are in such a position—is untenable. This in itself is one of the central reasons that international law, as a project attempting to ensure international peace and security, has continued to fail in achieving utopian goals of international law on a consistent basis. It is highly optimistic to expect States to sacrifice their own domestic situation for the sake of the international community if the two focal goals (realism and utopianism) of international law do not align.

Thus, Henkin's argument holds considerable weight in the current discussion:

> Since there is no body to enforce the law, nations will comply with international law only if it is in their interest to do so; they will disregard law or obligation if the advantages of violation outweigh the advantages of observance.[150]

His point of analysis highlights that the structure of international law allows for States to behave in this manner, cementing what seems,

[149] L. Murphy, 'International Responsibility', in S. Besson & J. Tasioulas (ed.), *The Philosophy of International Law*, (2010), at 303.

[150] L. Henkin, *How Nations Behave*, (1979), 49.

'the sovereign's absolute power'[151] within the international community nurtures the State's freedom to dismiss duties to achieving utopian focal goals in order to focus on their individual realist goals through the use of international law. Franck outlines that a central reason that States feel compelled to comply or 'obey powerless rules' is because of considerations of legitimacy.[152] This argument hovers over why States interact with international law and their perception of the legal system. It first indicates that States tend to interact with international law in order to legitimise the achievement of their realist agendas, and furthermore the State's perception of the international legal system is one that is malleable to its objectives. More so, it identifies that States' interaction with international law revolves around its obligations to its own populace.

In the light of such assertions regarding States' interaction with international law, Phillip Allott's claim that 'the State turned inside out'[153] and that this is problematic for a conception of international law focused on humanity. Allot stipulates that 'the State having developed as a way of internally organising a certain sort of society, such State-systems came to be conceived also as the external manifestation of the given societies.'[154] He rejected the State as the primary unit of authority and the current 'reconstruction of world affairs,' for it 'encapsulates a fundamental misconception about what matters: it authorises the pursuit of specifically State interests to the detriment of those of humanity.'[155] Allott pushes this claim further by stating that the interests pursued by States in the world of States is 'related to the survival and prospering of each of those State-societies rather than the survival and prospering of an international society of the human race.'[156] It is Allott's focus on humanity that corresponds with the central aims of emancipatory idealism, justifying the rethinking of the State as the primary unit of the international legal system. For in the current system of international law, according

[151] T. Endicot, 'The Logic of Freedom and Power', in S. Besson & J. Tasioulas (eds.), *The Philosophy of International Law*, (2010), at 245.

[152] T. Franck, *supra* note 28, at 477. See also Koh, *supra* note 12, at 2601–2602.

[153] P. Allott, *Eunomia: A New Order for a New World*, (1990), 243.

[154] Ibid.

[155] I. Scobbie, 'Thinking About International Law', in M.D. Evans (ed.), *International Law*, (2018), at 75.

[156] Allott, *supra* note 153, at 247.

to Allott, 'morality becomes discontinuous between the domestic and international spheres'[157] which allows States to 'murder human beings by the million in wars, tolerate oppression and starvation and disease and poverty, human cruelty and suffering, human misery and human indignity.'[158] Such a prospect is permissible for the focus for States in their interaction with international law is the protection of their own domestic territory, and not humanity, which in the famous words of Philip Allott 'cannot be how the world was meant to be.'[159]

Amidst States fulfilling their duty to their own populaces, the importance of attempting to achieve emancipatory idealism can easily be forgotten. Yet one should not be quick to criticise the State for doing so. Even for those focused on emancipatory idealism as a utopian focal goal of international law, it is important to remember that the State was specifically constructed to achieve the protection of its own territory. Foucault's biopolitics outlines that the State has been shaped in a way as to act as a shield for the citizens of its own territory, especially post-nineteenth century. If the State fails to protect its people from modes of oppression then who is responsible for ensuring order, peace and security of the territory? Its own territory could potentially be endangered if the State prioritises its international duties over its domestic ones. Inevitably, the duty the State has to its own territory supersedes any other duty the State may have. Both the modern and classical theories of sovereignty are primarily focused on ensuring a stable domestic situation, and it is clear to see that the manner in which the State has been developed—even after the nineteenth century—has been constructed to serve such a specific purpose.[160] The traditional conception of the State before the introduction of its international duties was not to ensure the achievement of emancipatory idealism within the international community.

It is also important to note that the duties the State has within the international community only emerged in the last century.[161] The duty

[157] Ibid., at 244.

[158] Ibid., at 248.

[159] P. Allott et al., 'Thinking Another World: "This Cannot be How the World was Meant to Be,"' (2005) 16 *EJIL* 255.

[160] Foucault, *supra* note 122, at 140.

[161] P. Allott, 'State Responsibility and the Unmaking of International Law', (1988) 29 *Harv. Int'l. L. J.* 1, at 9.

it has to its people, on the other hand, is a long-standing one harking back centuries.[162] The utopian goals of international law are attempts to further develop the role of the State beyond its own boundaries. Considering the fundamental purpose of the State to its own territory, it is clear to see that such progressions—that at times rally against its fundamental purpose—will not occur swiftly. In fact, such duties the State now has within the international legal system are somewhat of a relatively alien concept for the State to grapple with. Allott's critique on the ILC's work on State Responsibility is indicative of this. He emphasised that, 'the International Law Commission symbolizes this world. It is a physical manifestation of the underdevelopment of the public life of international society.'[163] It is important to go back to the Peace Treaty of Westphalia and highlight the first discussions about the concept *ius gentium* were not focused upon establishing international peace and security. The discussions amongst nations were rather to ensure healthy relations amongst nations.[164] Certainly, such a goal can work towards achieving peace and security on an international level, yet this is not what nations set out to achieve. It is a far cry from the international legal system currently in place, and its predecessor. Such utopian duties were only established in the international community with the emergence of the League of Nations. Thus, the first initial discussions about the emergence of *ius gentium* in the seventeenth century were advanced by the nations in order to protect the stability of their own territories, and not necessarily to ensure international peace and security.[165] The argument can be put forward that the interest in *ius gentium* professed by States at the time would consequently ensure international peace and security, yet it only ensures peace and security to a certain point. This, in contrast with the contemporary system of international law, where the advancement of the R2P doctrine for example or for general humanitarian intervention, becomes less so about States protecting their own territory and fully realising peace and security and more so about the achievement of emancipatory idealism in the international community. States continue to adjust to their new duties within international law, attempting to find a balance between exercising

[162] Koskenniemi, *supra* note 58, at 495.

[163] Allot, *supra* note 103 at 9–10.

[164] Koskenniemi, *supra* note 100, at 11.

[165] P. Malanczuk, *Akehurst's Modern Introduction to International Law*, (1997), 11.

their dual duties. Currently, it seems that the State is struggling to strike a balance between its domestic and (relatively) newfound international duties.

3.7 Conclusion

The State as an entity within the international legal system will continue to offer an important contribution to the international community. It has been vital in ensuring the more important advancements in international law to ensure the achievement of emancipatory idealism. If it were not for the contribution of the State, international law would not be where it is now, making the influence it has to ensure international peace and security. To do away with the State has never been the intention of those who would seek to achieve emancipatory idealism. Moreover, it has not been the intention to undermine the value the State plays in helping achieve utopian goals of international law. However, there is a need to re-evaluate the primacy States enjoy.

Too many occasions have slipped by where States have misappropriated their position, leading to individuals and groups of individuals falling prey to modes of oppression without any recourse to justice. For the State to juggle such shared utopian aspirations of the international community alongside the sole responsibility, it has to its citizens has proven at times to be untenable. States enter international law to advance their self-interests. Schmitt and Foucault exemplify this notion adequately. By establishing the importance the State places upon protecting its own populace, its interactions with the international legal system become clearer. The *ad-hoc* nature of international legal development, the lack of rigour in the international legal system, and the difficulty of ensuring State compliance all are somewhat weakly justified by its primary duty to protect its populace. However, for those seeking the achievement of emancipatory idealism as a focal goal of international law, the characteristics that the international legal system exhibits are not entirely conducive. Those seeking to achieve emancipatory idealism emphasise the value of every individual. Their contribution to civilisation could be a pivotal step, and it is for this reason international law should strive to establish mechanisms to protect such individuals. For those seeking the achievement of emancipatory idealism, large concepts such as civilisational development are at stake. If the international community's central aim is to prevent a stunt in civilisational development and the decline that would precede such a stunt in growth, reassessing the influence the State plays in the international legal system is of prime importance.

CHAPTER 4

The Life and Death of the League of Nations

4.1 Introduction

Chapters 2 and 3 have laid out the theoretical framework of the project, helping to establish the key themes to be explored. In regard to the theoretical framework, Chapter 2 established that emancipatory idealism as a utopian focal goal of international law aims to develop and utilise the international legal system for the sake of protecting individuals and communities of individuals. This is so that human civilisation can continue to advance on a technological and sociological level. Chapter 3 then established that a State has dual duties; one is to its domestic territory and the other is to the international community. The fact that these duties can come into tension is problematic for the international community, as the State tends to prioritise its domestic duty over its international duty. This is outlined by the exploration of the nature of the State, and the fact that it is inherently designed to serve its domestic populace. From the theoretical framework, two hypotheses can be established. First, the central aim of emancipatory idealism—which is the protection of individuals and groups of individuals from modes of oppression—plays a significant role in the development of international law. Second, the primary position States enjoy in the international legal system has at times been a barrier to achieving utopian focal goals of international law.

D. Mawar, *States Undermining International Law*, Philosophy, Public Policy, and Transnational Law, https://doi.org/10.1007/978-3-030-64789-6_4

The next two chapters seek to prove these hypotheses. This shall be done by examining the creation of both the League of Nations and the United Nations. Such examination will highlight how the central aim of emancipatory idealism has helped shape international law. Whether it is the creation of various treaties, or the construction of the Covenant of the League or the UN Charter in order to maintain international peace and security, the attempt to protect individuals and groups of individuals is apparent when analysing State interactions with international law. Analysis will predominantly focus on State interactions with the executive organs of the League of Nations and the United Nations. This approach has been adopted as it best illustrates the second hypothesis, which is the fact that States can be an obstacle to the achievement of emancipatory idealism. Analysing both the League and the UN leads to the suggestion that States undermine the utopian goals of international law when seeking out their realist interests. By analysing the workings of these international institutions, such a suggestion becomes apparent when assessing the manner in which States have interacted with the legal system and how States have enjoyed their position as the primary subject and object of international law. It is this particular facet of international law that makes the system so dependent upon the will of States. For those seeking to ensure utopian goals of international law through the use of the international legal system, an important factor to achieving such goals is whether the more influential States of the international community are similarly focused on utopian focal goals.

This chapter shall analyse the League of Nations and State interactions with the Council. The initial successes of the League in dealing with threats to international peace and security and the various developments that emanated out of the international institution have been considered. This will help to prove the first hypothesis, showing the significant role utopian goals of international law play to the development of the international legal system. The first half of this chapter shall analyse the creation of the League of Nations and its first ten years of development. After such exploration of the League's early days, its failures shall then be analysed in order to highlight how the commitment of States is such an integral factor for achieving the central aims of emancipatory idealism and the overall functioning and efficiency of the international legal system and its primary international institution. Furthermore, analysing the League's failure will demonstrate how the State's primary position in international law is problematic, as it prevents the achievement of emancipatory idealism as a utopian focal goal of international law. The second half of this chapter shall focus on the League's inability to cope with the effects of the Great Depression, the disarmament movements and various threats to international peace and security in the 1930s that eventually led to its collapse.

4.2 Aspirations for a Long-Lasting Peace: Creating and Preserving the League of Nations

4.2.1 Starting the World All Over: The Paris Peace Conference and Woodrow Wilson's Fourteen Points

The period between the end of World War I and the start of the second was an interesting period in history as it was an era when idealism significantly influenced the movement of the international community. Many States, particularly the victorious Allied forces, pushed for the establishment of an international institution 'in order to promote international cooperation and to achieve international peace and security.'[1] One could surmise that post-World War I, international law had its most prime opportunity for success. The international community entered this venture with a clean slate. It was not strained by the heavy burden of failure for the League was the very first of its ilk in human history. Many believed that the League would be a resounding success and there would be little difficulty in ensuring peace and security. The international community was in consensus on the fact that after the atrocities of World War I, nations would be reluctant to take actions that would potentially lead to large or small-scale violence. Thus, States were more willing to cooperate with the League before the Great Depression in 1929. This was one of the attributing reasons to the League's success during its first decade of activity. Although the League did suffer a blow when the United States did not become a member, the remaining States that participated were enthusiastic and willing for the international institution to work. What this movement demonstrated was the international community's desire to protect individuals and groups of individuals from modes of oppression. The focus in this period was especially on preventing war or another comparable large-scale crisis.

[1] Covenant of the League of Nations, (1920), Preamble.

Even during the war period, calls for the League were being brought to the fore in many debates regarding the state of international relations. The assertion was that the League would be a prime advocate for ensuring peace for the international community. The President of United States at the time, Woodrow Wilson, shared such an assertion. In his 'Peace without Victory' speech on January 22, 1917, Wilson committed himself for the first time not only to the League but also to the international spirit. He stated that the United States would join the League only if the peace it guaranteed was one with no resentful loser.[2] The peace needed to be founded upon pillars of 'democratic liberties for all peoples, territorial transfers only with the inhabitants' consent, freedom of the seas, and limitation of armaments.'[3] Wilson also revealed his fourteen points programme for peace, which played a relative influence on the establishment of the League. The fourteen points asserted liberal and idealist ideologies and was an exhaustive list of the kinds of transformative effects the international community required for the assurance of international peace. Points I–IV and XIV, for example, reasserted principles of open diplomacy, freedom of navigation on the seas in peace and war, the removal of economic barriers, the reduction of armaments 'to the lowest point consistent with domestic safety,' and the creation of a League of Nations. The fourteen points did not want to render the Central Powers crippled nations and merely requested that they 'return' territories to nations that they had invaded. For Wilson this was not a matter of retribution but a move towards actual peace that was intended for the international community as a whole. Wilson was consistently in talks with Lloyd George and Clemenceau and when it was time to negotiate an armistice, Wilson did so with the fourteen points being the structural composition of the negotiated end to the war.

However, before the League came into fruition in 1919, the creation of an international organisation had been a topic that had been widely discussed by several circles in several parts of the world. Most of the work that had been conducted in establishing some form of an international legal order was done in vagueness and inconclusiveness 'couched in the language of aspiration rather than political science, nevertheless some solid work had been done, both officially and reached in these studies on

[2] D. Stevenson, *Cataclysm: The First World War as a Political Tragedy,* (2004), at 256.

[3] Ibid at 256.

the Atlantic.'[4] However, with all the variations of the League, the central idea was to establish peace. The outbreak of war and its repercussions gave many of the figures who drafted models of the League the impetus to do so as they were all deeply affected by the terror that unfolded during the war and its foreseeable long-lasting implications. In June 1915, a group from the United States came before the public with a set of proposals and an organisation, named 'The League to Enforce Peace,' to address the objectives of achieving international peace.[5] Lord Bryce led the British group who discussed the issue and this group formed the conception that was later known as the League of Nations. A study group was also formed in the Netherlands and entered into relations with the British and American groups. The members of all these groups were inspired and determined to work on drafting an international organisation under one simple ethic—*never again*. These groups were not necessarily focused on stopping the war that was raging on in their time, but rather they looked forward to the future and the goal of ensuring that history did not repeat itself in allowing such a devastating scale of conflict to reoccur. The American draft was to see the League as the peace-enforcers of the world: 'The Signatory Powers shall jointly use forthwith both their economic and military forces against one of their number that goes to war, or commits acts of hostility, against another of the signatories before any question arising shall be submitted as provided in the foregoing.'[6] The British plan drafted twenty articles in comparison with the American draft, which only consisted of four, however the foundations were very much similar as the aims were to settle disputes peacefully and provide substantial safeguards against war. However, it must be stated that none of the parties prohibited the recourse to war. Though they encouraged the use of peaceful settlements to state disputes, none of the parties prohibited the use of war if all other means of settlement were ineffective.

In 1918, acting on a suggestion put forward by Lord Cecil soon after he became Minister in December 1916, the Foreign Secretary, Mr Balfour had been appointed a Committee regarding the League of Nations. Following similar precedent to the previous groups who had drafted plans for the League, it was their primary concern to create an international

[4] A. Zimmern, *The League of Nations and the Rule of Law*, (1998), at 161.

[5] Ibid., at 161.

[6] Ibid., at 164.

legal structure that would prevent another large-scale war. The committee reported on March 20, 1918, and a copy of its report was given to Wilson. However, the 'Philmore Plan' was an unsatisfactory hybrid of the American and British plans. Their model for an international institution seemed to establish an Alliance rather than a League. The French scheme, on the other hand, sought to establish a 'Society of Nations' where both law and order were perfectly provided for.

However, the most substantive developments regarding the formation of the League of Nations occurred during the Paris Conference 1919. Twenty-nine countries were represented in Paris, all keen to take part in shaping a post-war international community.[7] The significance of the five months of the Paris Conference was so momentous, the likes of Wilson and Clemenceau considered it a virtual world government.[8] There were several issues that required attention during the Paris Conference, including the drafting of peace treaties, the awarding of German and Ottoman overseas possessions as mandates (primarily to Britain and France), reparations imposed on Germany, the drawing of new national borders to better reflect ethnic boundaries across Europe, Asia and Africa and of course the creation of the League of Nations.[9] In regard to creating the League, 'when the Peace Conference created the Commission on the League of Nations, the room resounded with noble sentiments,'[10] during which, a British and American collaboration on a common draft of the Covenant was revealed.[11] This common draft detailed the plan for the League with an executive council of Five. This was however altered as the smaller powers pushed for the right to vote in four additional members.[12] Whilst the American and British continued to collaborate on the first draft Covenant, French representatives wished to

[7] Foreign Relations of the United States, (1919), vol. 3, at 492, at 537. See also M. MacMillan, *Paris 1919: Six Months That Changed the World*, (2001), 89.

[8] Clemenceau stated a day before the Paris Conference ceremony, 'We are the league of people,' whilst Wilson replied, 'We are the State.' See L.A. Marescotti, *Nuovi ricordi*, (1938), at 102; Foreign Relations of the United Nations, (1919), vol. 3, 614, at 620–622.

[9] O.A. Hathaway & S.J. Shapiro, *The Internationals: How a Radical Plan to Outlaw War Remade the World*, (2017), at 113.

[10] Macmillan, *supra* note 7, at 132.

[11] Cecil, *A Great Experiment*, (1941), at 63; P. Raffo, *The League of Nations*, (1974), 166; Papers of Woodrow Wilson, (1919) vol. 54, at 152.

[12] Foreign Relations of the United States, (1919) vol. 3, at 176–201.

'give the League teeth.' This meant 'if there were disputes among League members, these would automatically be submitted to compulsory arbitration. If a state refused to accept the League's decision, then the next step would be sanctions, economic, even military.'[13] They also 'advocated strict disarmament under a League body with sweeping powers of inspection and an international force drawn from League members.'[14]

By February 13, 1919, the first draft of the League's Covenant was ready. It was comprised of twenty-six articles with the 'main outlines of the League in place: a general assembly for all members, a secretariat and an executive council where the big five would have a bare majority.'[15] No League army was put into place, nor was there compulsory arbitration or disarmament. However, 'all League members pledged themselves to respect one another's independence and territorial boundaries.'[16] Moreover the Covenant also contained provisions that would satisfy the demands of those seeking to utilise international law for the protection of individuals and groups of individuals. 'It contained an undertaking that the League would look into setting up a permanent international court of justice, provisions against arms trafficking and slavery and support for the spread of the international Red Cross. It also established the International Labour Organization to work for international standards on working conditions.'[17]

Much of the drive to create the League can be explained by utopian aspirations. It is perhaps poignant to highlight that creating the League was an attempt to shed the pre-war conations imbued with a sense of imperialist inspired chaos and tyranny that was such a prevalent feature of the non-organised operation of international law that led to the breakout of the Great War.[18] The League was thus established to set aside concepts such as 'chaos' and 'tyranny' that was so harmful to the international community. 'To do so, the literature often characterises those dimensions

[13] Macmillan, *supra* note 7, at 134–135.

[14] G.W. Egerton, *Great Britain and the Creation of the League of Nations*, (1978), 134–135; H. Miller, *Drafting of the Covenant*, (1928), vol. 1, 209, at 216–217.

[15] Macmillan, *supra* note 7, at 137.

[16] Ibid. See also Papers of Woodrow Wilson, (1919), vol. 55, at 120 & Cecil, *supra* note 11, at 72.

[17] Ibid.

[18] This is reference to the pre-World War Westphalian model of international law. See D. Kennedy, 'The Move to Institutions', (1987), 8 *Cardozo Law Review* 841, at 868.

of "war" and "peace" which the League will set aside or continue in somewhat less charged terms.'[19] It made 'socialists' of lawyers and non-lawyers alike tasked with discussing international affairs, although not in the 'conventional' interpretation of socialist, but in the sense that 'social questions had assumed a prominent place in our politics and that they had come to stay.'[20] The war maintained its influence upon the construction of the League and the drafting of the Covenant, for 'it must never be forgotten that the Covenant was drawn up by men filled with the recent experience of the war. It affected different minds in different ways, but it deeply affected them all.'[21] Thus, the war signalled a significant rupture in the international stage and this particular model of international law. It was in fact a breakaway from the pre-World War I environment and thus an opportunity to remedy and prevent the reasons that were the catalysts for such a large-scale crisis. Kennedy suggests that in this vein 'the War was "a catalyst", "a crucible", "a sudden storm" sweeping away the old order.'[22] It is on this basis that the creation of the League of Nations was considered such a revolutionary advancement in international law. Oppenheim suggested that the 'League would be founded upon a solemn treaty, whereas the old model hitherto was only based upon custom.'[23] It was a suggestion that was duly followed for the belief was that in order to 'make war or abolish it altogether,' the international stage needed to operate on an organised basis.[24] Not only was the international legal system significantly reformed, but by moving to an institutionalist model, with a central institution and a Covenant given central responsibility to regulate international affairs, the objectives of the legal system had drastically changed. International law was not solely focused on ensuring healthy relations between States but was now also engineered to maintain international peace and security.

[19] Ibid., at 868.

[20] A. Zimmern, 'International Law and Social Consciousness', (1934) 20 *Transactions of the Grotius Society* 25, at 25.

[21] Ibid., at 137–138.

[22] Kennedy, *supra* note 18 at 852. See also B. Schmitt & H. Vedeler, *The World in the Crucible 1914–1919*, (1984), at 27.

[23] L. Oppenheim, *The League of Nations and its Problems-Three Lectures*, (1919), at 6.

[24] Ibid., at 6. See also Kennedy, *supra* note 18, at 904.

Therefore, using international law to protect individuals and groups of individuals from modes of oppression had had a drastic change on the international legal system following World War I. The legal system had moved away from the classical positivist model of international law espoused by the likes of Oppenheim, Verdross and Weil. As mentioned above, international law was no longer strictly and solely about the State. In fact, the argument could be made to suggest that international law was focused also on humanity and its prosperity and survival. Indeed, the creation of the League of Nations was a dramatic shift for international law showing the significant influence of utopian focal goals of international law in the development of the international legal system.

Nonetheless, it is important to note that the first steps of the League were not easily taken. There were several issues that the League and its members needed to overcome before establishing the *modus operandi* of the institution. As mentioned above the United States' decision not to become a member of the League was a crucial blow. First of all, the presence of Woodrow Wilson throughout the post-war negotiations was intrinsic to establishing the League. Wilson was an influential figure whose enthusiasm and determination to maintain peace and security was one of the central reasons as to why the League became a reality. His famous fourteen points were a cornerstone concept that helped establish the League. He was dedicated to the cause of establishing the organisation as soon as possible.[25] Wilson felt that if the Covenant was not adopted in the early stages of the conferences held between the Allied nations, instead of leaving such discussions to the end, it might never be adopted at all.[26] The fact that he would not be able to participate further as a representative of the United States in the work of the League was evidently a detriment. Secondly, the United States was at the time a rising power that had not been affected by the war as significantly as Britain or France for example. The United States was therefore in a better situation to support the work of the League and make it a more effective regulator of the international community. In fact, for Britain, US participation was a precondition for the success on any League.[27]

[25] P.J. Yearwood, *The Guarantee of Peace: The League of Nations in British Policy 1914–1925*, (2009), at 88.

[26] F.P. Walters, *The History of the League of Nations*, (1969), at 31.

[27] Yearwood, *supra* note 25, at 138.

When it became apparent that the United States were hesitant on becoming a member of the League, Britain had sent an ambassador, Viscount Grey, to attempt to help support Wilson in order to push through ratification of the treaty. However, when Wilson had suffered an incapacitating stroke, Grey's task became ever more difficult. Furthermore, Republican opposition to the treaty had hardened, with Senator Henry Cabot Lodge introducing fourteen reservations.[28] The issue with Lodge's reservations were that they were fundamentally incompatible with the Covenant. For example, the most striking reservation was that:

> The United States assumes no obligation to preserve the territorial integrity or political independence of any other country or to interfere in the controversies between nations—whether members of the League or not—under the provisions of article 10, or to employ the military or naval forces of the United States under any article of the Treaty for any purpose, unless in any particular case the Congress, which, under the Constitution, has the sole power to declare war or authorise the employment of the military or naval forces of the United States, shall by act or joint resolution so provide.[29]

Concerned with the damage such reservations would cause to the League and the fact that China had already been told that no reservations were allowed,[30] Britain strongly opposed them. With this outcome, the United States had rejected the treaty on November 19, 1919.

This predicament drastically changed the international situation, the claim that the League would be an established and effective world authority required reassessment. With US refusal, onus was placed upon France and Britain to take up the mantelpiece of the League and lead their work. In the light of US refusal to become a member, Britain, for example, shrank in its responsibilities to the League. Britain had joined the League in 1919, accepting the obligations of the Covenant in the belief that the United States would also be accepting such obligations. Britain believed that US defection made the League of Nations an unworkable project. Lord Balfour supported such an argument, stating that:

[28] Foreign Office 371/4251.

[29] Walters, *supra* note 26.

[30] Council of Four, 25 June 1919, Link (ed.), *Deliberations*, ii. 551–552.

> The League of Nations in its present shape, is not the League designed by the framers of the Covenant. They no doubt contemplated and, so far as they could, provided against, the difficulties that might arise from the non-inclusion of a certain number of States within the circle of League membership. But they could never suppose that among these states would be found so any of the most powerful nations of the world, least of all did they foresee that one of them would be the United States of America.[31]

For Balfour, the League could no longer adopt a Concert of Powers model. Britain became a reluctant party to the League, and subsequently they worked hard to weaken the interpretation of both Article 10 and 16. These two articles in particular allowed the League to become more involved in dealing with disputes that posed a threat to international peace and security.[32] By using the loophole provided through the second clause of Article 10 in order to weaken the powers of the League,[33] Britain used the League for its own political advantage and to evade its responsibility. The United States' refusal to join the League also is an indication of States undermining utopian goals of international law in order to safeguard their own interest. It hindered the operation of the League when influential States were not fully supportive of it, so much so that from the outset it had limited some of the intended functions envisaged. What remained was the Hague system for dealing with disputes, but it could not impose sanctions, 'and the system of World-services, to which additions had been made in the treaties.'[34]

[31] See Lord Balfour's remarks at the eight meeting of the Council, August 2, 1920. This quote can also be found in A. Zimmern, *The League of Nations and the Rule of Law*, (1998), at 311.

[32] Article 10 of the Covenant of the League of Nations covers the obligation Member-States have to respect and preserve the territory of other States and refrain from the use of external aggression on the territorial integrity and existing political independence of all Members of the League. Article 16 stipulates the consequences of Member-States resorting to acts of war, and subsequently the steps the Council may take to deal with such situations.

[33] Article 10 stipulates that 'In case of any such aggression or in case of any threat or danger of such aggression the Council shall advise upon the means by which this obligation shall be fulfilled.' In such a circumstance Britain sought to avoid the obligation to 'police' the international community and instead would use the Council to advise or make recommendations on how to deal with acts of aggression not permitted by the Covenant.

[34] A. Zimmern, *supra* note 4, at 312.

Alongside this issue of State hesitancy, there was also the problematic nature of organising an international institution that would appease the needs and wishes of all States. In a theoretical sense, all participants agreed to the aims of creating the League, however, the path to such goals tended to differ from State to State. Most notable is the discord of Soviet Russia. The first attempt to establish a relationship of tolerance between the League and Soviet Russia ended in failure. 'The Bolshevist government replied with a stream of violent criticism of everything that was being done in Paris, and in the universal condemnation the Covenant was, of course, included. The League was a sham, intended only to preserve the capitalist system, and to muster all the imperialist powers, including Germany, in an unholy alliance against the Soviet regime. All Socialists were advised to have nothing to do with the League.'[35]

However, even in such an environment the League was able to negotiate some successes. Such achievements were down to a sense of practicality that Member-States administered when dealing with the predicament of the League at the time. It was not the institution that Wilson and the other Allied forces had imagined, and therefore the League needed to be malleable to the situation it was in. Although there were differing goals between members, the sentiment at the time was still heavily anti-war. Conditions were favourable as many States were willing to participate in reasonable efforts to make the League operate successfully in order to establish international peace and security. Thus, the League worked tirelessly with expert preparations before meetings, attempting to make sure such meetings were conducted in a calm and regular manner, rules of procedure known to and respected by all and a Secretariat was in place which assured confidence due to its knowledge, efficiency and impartiality.[36] The commitment displayed by the League and its members was the reason as to why the first decade of the League's existence was met with relative success. It was the Member-States' 'will to cooperate' that was influential in the League's success and its ability to establish international peace and security.[37] It seemed that the initial

[35] Walters, *supra* note 26, at 94.

[36] S. Pederson, *The Guardians: The League of Nations and Crisis of Empire*, (2015), at 46–50.

[37] Typifying such sentiments is Dean Inge, who led the official League of Nations sermon in Geneva Cathedral: '... during the war we all sinned together in vilifying our opponents. We now feel that the nations all went stark mad together and brought upon

fear of tension and cohesion had dissipated, replaced by a strong desire to collaborate together towards a certain focal goal as Walters stipulated:

> Indeed from the early days of the League, there had been observed an unexpected, yet constantly recurring, phenomenon- the successful issue of conferences, or of sessions of the Council or the Assembly, which had been preceded by many signs of discord and seemed destined to lead to complete deadlock. Delegates who arrived with the expectation of meeting irreconcilable opposition, and with the intention of showing equal obstinacy on their own side, would soon be using all their energy and intelligence in seeking grounds of arrangement, and would find their opponents doing the same. New suggestions for compromise would be put forward, new safeguards would be discovered, new concessions would be exchanged, and the session would close with results, which all concerned could regard as satisfactory. Such experiences were often ascribed to a sentimental or even a mystical state of mind induced by what was known "as the atmosphere of Geneva."[38]

So out of practicality and an initial inability to find a common policy between Member-States, the League became something quite different to the initially envisaged supervisor of the international community. It was not necessarily the organisation that actively prevented any threats to international peace and security, but it became, as Alfred Zimmern remarked—'a centre of influence.'[39] However, it was a mode of operation limited to tasks such as promoting ideas, organising discussion, initiating projects and setting up standards for example.[40] It appeared that the power to make decisions rested firmly with the government and peoples of the Member-States. Yet, the League's limitations did not render the institution ineffective. It was quite the contrary, especially during its first ten years as it utilised the technical experts from within

themselves and each other a calamity as unnecessary as it was disastrous. Our plain duty now is to restore the solidarity of European civilization, to help the crippled nations to recover and to create whatever safeguards that are possible against another outbreak, from which there could be no recovery. Our justice must be touched with generosity and we must help to bear one another's burden, moral as well as material.' Quote taken from C. Howard-Ellis, *The Origin, Structure and Working of The League of Nations*, (1928), at 36.

[38] Walters, *supra* note 26, at 296.

[39] Zimmern, *supra* note 4 at 305.

[40] Pederson, *supra* note 36, at 55–57.

itself to tackle the issues arising in international affairs. Thus doctors, bankers, child welfare experts and the 'intellectual co-operator' were all able to contribute and discover the best solutions for particular problems that followed along their lines of expertise. Zimmern believed that this approach to international affairs would usher in a new era of international relations:

> Thus there emerged, in League circles, what may be described as a new form of the old Fabian or gradualist doctrine, based upon the assimilative power of the Geneva spirit and of the institutions, which it was creating. Little by little, so it began to be believed, the morass of 'high politics' would dry up along its edges, as one issue after another was drained off to Geneva. Thus eventually there would be a world-wide co-operative system held together by a network of contacts between government departments (other than Foreign Offices), professional organisations and individual experts.[41]

Although the League suffered setbacks, the fact that the general consensus within the international community was to focus upon achieving utopian goals of international law, Member-States' flexible approach proved to be decisive. The initial phase of establishing the League quickly displayed how important a factor the will of States was to the successful achievement of emancipatory idealism's central aims within the international law framework. The emergence of the League of Nations through the various phases of diplomacy following the end of World War I demonstrates the international community's focus on creating the stable environment for the prosperity and survival of humanity and the furtherance of civilisational development. The construction of an institutionalist model of international law, bearing a central organisation focused on maintaining international peace and security, represents the influence of utopian goals of international law. Such an evolutionary turn in the international legal system proves the validity of the first hypothesis, for creating a framework to prevent the emergence of international conflict highlights the international community's effort to protect individuals or groups from modes of oppression.

[41] Zimmern, *supra* note 4, at 329.

4.3 A Successful Decade: The League in Action

4.3.1 Upper Silesia

It appeared that the League had successfully navigated around the initial pitfalls that had emerged when creating the first large-level international organisation. It may not have been the organisation that the international community envisaged, but it maintained enough influence that the potential was there for the League to prevent wide-scale violent conflict. The ability for the League to focus on achieving the aims of emancipatory idealism, through maintaining international peace and security, remained very much possible in the manner in which the League was designed to operate. In fact, for emancipatory idealists, the first ten years of the League's tenure was a relatively effective period for the protection of individuals and groups, as their efforts to deal with the breakout of conflict were largely successful. This signified a carry through of the utopian influences that were prevalent when the League had been drafted, with a commitment towards maintaining international peace and security. Although the League and its model of international law did not fully realise Allott's aspirations of an international legal system that prioritised the individual over the State, the legal framework put into place did create the desired safeguards for individuals and groups. The League's success in dealing with threats to international peace and security during the 1920s represents how the central aims of emancipatory idealism played a significant role in the development of international law.

Alongside significant change the international stage underwent with the emergence of the League of Nations, the creation of the Permanent of Court of International Justice (PCIJ) in 1921 further demonstrated a period of accelerated development for the international legal system. W.J. Curtis believed that 'the organization of this Court is doubtless the greatest advance that has occurred during the last century in the domain of international law.'[42] He argued that the establishment of the PCIJ was an avenue for international dispute settlement without resorting to the ordeal of war.[43] Indeed, when taking a more placid approach towards the PCIJ, it can still be considered a relative success. 'The Court

[42] W.J. Curtis, 'Permanent Court of International Justice', (1992) 8 *American Bar Association Journal* 158, at 158.

[43] Ibid.

handed down thirty-two judgments in contentious cases, mostly between European states, and twenty-seven advisory opinions which assisted in clarifying rules and principles of international law. Operating within a still limited and relatively homogeneous society of nations, it enjoyed considerable authority, more than was to be accorded later to the International Court of Justice.'[44] The significance of the emergence of the PCIJ is similar to the League of Nations, in that there was a formal legal process to maintain international peace and security and to maintain healthy relations amongst States. It must be noted that the Permanent of Court of Arbitration (PCA) had been established earlier than the PCIJ; however, the former had been overshadowed by both the latter and its predecessor, the International Court of Justice. In fact, the name of this 'Court' is misleading. Each state party to the Hague Convention 1899 (which established the PCA) can nominate four persons to serve on a panel of arbitrators, and disputing states may select arbitrators from this panel in the traditional way. Therefore, in reality the Hague Convention did not create a court; it merely created the machinery for setting up arbitral tribunals.[45] Thus, the PCIJ was the first of its ilk; an international court with judges possessing expert knowledge of international law to settle State disputes.

With the League and the PCIJ established, tests of the League's effectiveness came relatively swiftly with the Upper Silesia territorial dispute between Germany and Poland. This was a dispute that was a result of the plebiscite of March 1921 on the area of Upper Silesia, with the Allied governments policing the area. The area was of particular interest for both parties because of the 'Industrial Triangle,' which held an industrial complex. Although the result was favourable to Germany, it was suggested that the plebiscite area should be divided between the two nations for the sake of fairness. Yet there was confusion as to where the frontier line should be drawn. 'The German nation had convinced themselves that every legal, moral, and economic principle was favourable to their claim and that the cessation of any part of the area would be a tyrannical violation of the laws of both God and man.'[46] Britain and Italy proposed to

[44] P. Malanczuk, *Akehurst's Modern Introduction to International Law*, (1997), at 24.

[45] H.J. Schlochauer, 'Permanent Court of Arbitration', (1981) 1, *EPIL* 157, at 157–163.

[46] Walters, *supra* note 26, at 153.

give the 'Industrial Triangle' to Germany, and to Poland 'certain country districts which could be cut off from the rest without making the frontier completely unworkable.'[47] The reason that Britain and Italy took this stance was based on the potential inability of Germany to pay the war reparations if they had lost the Silesian industries. France on the other hand believed that the complete Triangle and a majority of the remaining territory should go to Poland. They favoured such an outcome as they sought to weaken Germany. However, Poland demanded an even more extensive share and in May 1921 they attempted to occupy the territory by force, resulting in hostilities and the loss of lives.

In light of the hostilities, the Council was forced to settle the dispute and draw up the frontiers. The Council used expert advisors to lay down a number of conditions. This approach was adopted in order to bring such a dispute to the most practically possible solution. Rather than talking to the representatives of the contesting States, they called in for consultation from industrial and trade union leaders of both nationalities. With the help of these groups, the advisors were able to draw up a plan that if accepted and carried out by both Germany and Poland, would enable the Triangle to carry on as an industrial and trading unit even after it had been politically cut in two. The finer details of this regime were negotiated with Poland and Germany, with the help of the League, which was formally encompassed in a treaty between the two parties. Although the regime lasted a relatively successful fourteen years, there were grievances on both sides. The German people had felt that they had been unfairly treated with the promise of the whole area, a false hope, which was especially exacerbated by the British press. They felt that the same hands that had developed the area should control the vast resources. For Germany, Upper Silesia should not be transferred to an 'inexperienced and unbusinesslike nation.'[48] However, it would have been unfair for such an outcome to come into fruition considering that 'the original intention of the Peace Treaty had been to transfer Upper Silesia to Poland without further discussion.'[49]

[47] Ibid., at 153.

[48] Ibid., at 155.

[49] Ibid., at 156.

4.3.2 Albania

Shortly after dealing with the Upper Silesian dispute, the Council was called upon to deal with another threat to peace on Albanian frontiers. The Assembly and Council intervened on the basis of the powers and duties established under the Covenant, and they were met with a large measure of success. Albania was a relatively new independent State but during and after the war the country's stability and survival was endangered. Italy wished to annex Albania's coast, whilst Greece desired the whole southern section of the country and Yugoslavia also sought-after Albanian territory. Though discussions between these nations and the Allied Powers took place, negotiations nonetheless proved unsuccessful, 'partly through mutual jealousy, partly through American hesitations, chiefly through the courageous attitude of the Albanians.'[50]

It was clear from these discussions that Albania's frontiers needed to be decided anew. Consequently, the Supreme Council undertook such a task with the agreement of Yugoslavia and Greece, however, Albania was not consulted.[51] They subsequently refused to recognise the right of the Supreme Council to change their frontiers without their consent.

Such a situation all but exacerbated the hostility between the Albanians and the Yugoslav, Greek and Italian troops. Hostilities were rising to the point that by 1921 Albania, now a member of the League, appealed to the Council to settle its frontiers dispute and to free its territory from foreign occupation. However, Greece and Yugoslavia contended that only the Conference of Ambassadors could decide the territorial question; something the Great Powers of the Council agreed to. In an attempt to bring the dispute to a resolution Albania brought the issue before the Assembly. British, French and Italian delegates guaranteed Albania that a decision regarding the frontier would be announced imminently. However, developments were in fact still working at a pedestrian pace as the debate was repeatedly postponed. The Great Powers of the Council still hoped to leave the matter with the Ambassadors. The possibility of a definitive conclusion to matters continued to be absent, with Lord Cecil considering the behaviour of the Ambassadors as unacceptable. Such delays allowed for further violence to unfold as men and women were being

[50] Ibid., at 158.

[51] By this stage of the dispute Italy had withdrawn their troops and detached themselves from the dispute.

killed, jeopardising peace and security within the region. Nevertheless, even with such a situation facing the Assembly, Yugoslavia were tentative to be in direct conflict with the Allied Powers. It was only when Britain aroused their fears of a threat to peace did the situation undergo a remarkable change. The British government took seriously Albania's warnings, convinced that there was an imminent danger of war. British Prime Minister Lloyd George demanded that the Council should be summoned immediately 'and should decide that, if Yugoslavia did not carry out forthwith her obligations under the Covenant, she should be forced to do so by economic sanctions.'[52]

Even after such an aggressive call, the Council was still slow in conducting itself, taking ten days to get the process up and running. Yet this delay proved to be advantageous for once as Yugoslavia eventually decided that in order to avoid economic sanctions it would have to accept the Ambassadors decision and withdraw its troops from the frontiers. As a result, when the Council did meet to discuss Albania's frontiers the task was much simpler. 'The danger of war was over, and the Council could contend itself with giving good advice to all concerned' and consequently, 'Albanian re-occupation were carried out peaceably and in order.'[53]

It was apparent that until Britain's direct effort to prevent such a dispute from disturbing European peace and security, the League was cumbersome in dealing with the issue at hand. Nonetheless, the League had eventually been successful in dealing with the dispute and further highlighted that if the Covenant was used effectively, threats to international peace and security could be overcome with the full commitment of the Great Allied Powers.

4.3.3 *Locarno Treaties*

The League was garnering a respectable name within the international community following the successful resolution of both the Upper Silesia and the Albanian dispute. It had seemingly overcome its early failures and developed into an effective mechanism for ensuring international peace and security. Opportunities to highlight the progress of the League were emerging constantly and the negotiation of the Locarno Treaties was

[52] Ibid., at 160.

[53] Ibid., at 161.

another example of the League strengthening relations between powerful European nations.

In 1925, German Foreign Minister, Gustav Stresemann, proposed a Rhineland pact, which would entail Germany, France, Britain and Italy agreeing the inviolable character of the Franco-German Frontier. Britain's Foreign Minister, Austen Chamberlain, saw the advantage of such a suggestion. Germany would reaffirm its acceptance of not only the loss of the Alsace-Lorraine region but also the demilitarisation of the Rhineland. Furthermore, Britain and Italy could jointly guarantee a reciprocal promise of non-aggression between France and Germany. It was the perfect opportunity to ensure the peace of Western Europe be held together far stronger than any ordinary alliance could potentially do so. Chamberlain believed that such an agreement could help achieve security and disarmament, and the best method to achieve such goals would be through 'promoting special arrangements between those powers whose relations with one another were most important for the preservation of peace.'[54] With such a proposal brought before the Council, Germany, France, Britain, Italy and Belgium gradually discussed the Locarno pacts. Discussions continued to ensue throughout the year, yet by October, with the close of the Sixth Assembly meeting, the seven nations concerned gathered in Locarno to draw up the final texts.[55] For much of the international community the initiation of the Locarno Pacts opened the possibility of a lasting peace. This was partly due to the specific guarantees against war but also because of reconciling the hostility between Germany and France.[56] The pacts were a symbol of optimism for it seemed 'that the world was about to return to those normal international relations which the drafters of the Covenant had contemplated as the natural condition of its working.'[57]

[54] Ibid., at 286. Speaking to the British Press, Chamberlain claimed that the Locarno Treaties were the 'real dividing line between years of war and years of peace.' Quote taken from C.A. Macartney, 'Survey of International Affairs 1925, Vol. 2', (1928) 33 *Royal Institute of International Affairs* 1895, at 1956.

[55] J. Wright, 'Stresemann and Locarno', (2008) 4 *Contemporary European History* 109, at 111.

[56] J. Jacobson, 'The Conduct of Locarno Diplomacy', (1972) 34 *The Review of Politics* 67, at 69.

[57] Ibid. at 291.

The legal significance of such agreements was also substantial. Prior to 1925, the three most fundamental articles of the League—Articles 10, 11 and 16—remained practically a dead letter.[58] But the signing of the five agreements at Locarno rekindled the importance of these articles. This was due to the agreement of the five powers to 'put into effect the principle of collective responsibility for mutual protection.'[59] However, such obligations to each other did not mean that the wider circle of States supported such a motion. The parties of the Locarno Pacts had committed themselves to some more general obligations:

> First in order comes the general pledge to keep the peace by mutual respect on the part of each state for the independence and territorial integrity of the others; next comes the pledge of mutual aid in an event of an attack by any one of their group upon another; lastly, a comprehensive and unqualified obligation, to which two additional Powers were parties, to submit to arbitration.[60]

There were also more specific guarantees established between the parties involved. For example, the Treaty of Mutual Guarantee bound Germany, Belgium and France to regard their existing frontiers, and the demilitarised zone of the Rhineland, as inviolable. Furthermore, these parties also agreed that in no case could either party attack, invade or resort to war against one another. Another factor was that Germany needed to become a member of the League, which was an obligation that Germany did agree to, albeit with some reservations.

Much of the international community saw the outcome of the Locarno Treaties as a positive one. Even in Germany, the treaties were welcomed as a whole.[61] The belief was that the League had made significant strides forward by enacting the Locarno Treaties. It paved the way for a new era of security, prosperity, and it brought about the potential of disarmament.[62] The fact that nations that only a decade ago were in conflict

[58] C.J. Fenwick, 'The Legal Significance of the Locarno Agreements', (January 1926) 20(1) *AJIL* 108, at 110.

[59] Ibid., at 110.

[60] Ibid., at 111.

[61] Wright, *supra* note 55, at 112.

[62] E.M. Borchard, 'The Multilateral Treaty for the Renunciation of War', (1929) 23 *AJIL* 116, at 117.

had now established a treaty that ensured peace between them all was a monumental advancement for those focused on achieving utopian focal goals of international law. It was clear that national interests of many nations aligned with utopian focal goals of international law at this point in this time. Moreover, the Locarno Treaties was an indication to the fact that the League was proving to be an effective organisation to maintain international peace and security.

4.3.4 Mosul Dispute

Another dispute that was comparable to Upper Silesia in regard to the threat to peace and security occurred in the Mosul territory. The parties involved were Turkey, Britain and Iraq. Turkey claimed that the province of Mosul belonged to them on the basis of a historical right as the area had been under their rule for centuries. However, Britain had conquered Mesopotamia during the war, and was guiding the newly created State, Iraq, to self-government. Although under the Treaty of Sèvres, Turkey had agreed to award Iraq with the Mosul province, Turkey had back-tracked on its promises. During the drafting of a new treaty, the Turks insisted on retaining it. In fear of an escalation of the dispute, the matter was taken up to the Council.

Although proceedings in Council meetings at Geneva were progressing easily and quietly between the representatives of each party, on ground disputes were becoming heated. Each side claimed that they upheld their obligations to not disturb the status quo, but it had appeared that both Britain and Turkey were making attempts to strengthen their grip. Reports of minor clashes with some loss of lives were being sent to the Council. By October 9, the situation had heated up to a level at which the British government had delivered an ultimatum. They threatened military action unless all Turkish troops were withdrawn within forty-eight hours, beyond the line, which, according to the British view Turkey was bound to respect. Following such an ultimatum, a special meeting was held in Brussels. Acting as the rapporteur of the Mosul dispute from within the Council, Hjalmar Branting proposed that the Council should settle the current circumstances by a temporary demarcation. This settled British hostilities as each side gave a solemn promise to prevent any civilian or soldier from crossing the line drawn established in the meeting in Brussels. This allowed the Commission of Inquiry to begin working on an effective settlement of the dispute.

The resulting report of the Commission was not all together favourable for any party. They established that the Brussels line should be the fixed frontier between Turkey and Iraq, which meant that Iraq had most of the Mosul territory. This conclusion was difficult for Turkey to take, due to the historical claim over the region but Britain and Iraq were equally not content with the outcome. The Iraqis believed they were capable of self-government. However, the terms of the mandate established by the Council asserted that the British government should undertake the same responsibilities it had undertaken when guiding Palestine, and similarly French guidance over the Syrian State building movement. British opinion was not enthusiastic regarding the terms of the mandate. A large contingent of the British opinion considered the mandate as 'useless, expensive, and dangerous, and, in the hope of forcing its abandonment, had actually sustained the Turkish demand for Mosul.'[63] Britain attempted to push their luck by suggesting that Iraq be awarded more territory whilst Turkey challenged the power of the Council. These claims were rejected by the Council and it proved another occasion on which the League was successful in preventing a large-scale conflict from breaking out.

Incidentally, the Turkish claim of the Council operating beyond its powers brought about some degree of consternation within the Council. It did not want to be seen as acting outside of its remit. Turkey claimed that the Council could not make a decision on the matter without the consent of the two parties, or to adopt any resolution on the subject except by unanimous vote. As a result of such a claim, the Council requested that the PCIJ deliver a ruling as to the nature of the powers, which it was to exercise under the Treaty of Lausanne. The PCIJ stated that the Council's decision required unanimity, but the votes of the two parties were not to be counted. The court asserted that:

> It follows from the foregoing that, according to the Covenant itself, in certain cases and more particularly in the case of the settlement of a dispute, the rule of unanimity is applicable, subject to the limitation that the votes cast by representatives of the interested Parties do not affect the required unanimity.[64]

[63] Walters, *supra* note 26, at 308.

[64] *Article 3, Paragraph 2 of the Treaty of Lausanne (Frontier Between Turkey and Iraq)*, Collection of Advisory Opinions, 21 November 1925, PCIJ at 31–32.

The jurisprudence of the decision was subject to a great deal of debate amongst international lawyers. This position was more so scrutinised when looking at the manner in which the PCIJ tackled such issues in the future such as in the *Lotus* case, for example. Regardless of the disparities and whether such an advisory opinion was legally sound, the judgement was clear and practical. Irrespective of the criticism drawn towards the PCIJ for their advisory opinion, this contributed in paving the way to the end of the conflict over Mosul. It highlighted the fact that many parts of the League were working effectively in collaboration with each other in order to ensure international peace and security.

4.3.5 The Greco-Bulgar Crisis

Although the League did grow in stature and confidence, the criticism still remained that it was a 'weakened League.' Indeed, the League had proven itself to be an effective international organisation, but for many the question remained whether there were adequate safeguards for maintaining peace. It had managed to manoeuvre itself over the initial disappointments and changed its ability to deal with disputes between nations, but if a large-scale crisis emerged, many were uncertain what the League could do to counteract such an event.

Scholars such as Zimmern suggested that in the great flexibility of Article 11, there was the ability to prevent large-scale crisis from emerging.[65] He suggested the article did not bind the League to one particular procedure, but it allowed it to 'take any action that may be deemed.'[66] Therefore, it was up to the Great Powers to configure effective safeguards to the peace of nations when deemed necessary. The British government stipulated that 'the strength of the Covenant lies in the measure of discretion which it allows to the Council and the Assembly in dealing with future contingencies which many have no parallel in history and which therefore cannot, all of them be foreseen in advance.'[67]

An opportunity to display Article 11s potential to deal with a threat to international peace and security came in 1925, with the Greco-Bulgar

[65] Zimmern, *supra* note 6, at 379.

[66] Covenant of the League of Nations, (1920), Article 11.

[67] 'Reduction of Armaments', (May 1928) 9(5) *The League of Nations Official Journal* 608, at 703.

crisis. On October 23, 1925, the Bulgarian government announced numerous Greek forces had entered Bulgarian territory, with artillery and air bombing support. This Greek advancement was a result of small-scale hostilities on the frontier three days earlier. Bulgaria requested an immediate meeting of the Council to deal with the imminent threat to peace and security. The chances of alphabetical rotation had brought round the Presidency of the Council to France during this particular period. This fortunately meant that Aristide Briand was President of the Council during the time of Bulgaria's request. He sent telegraphs to both parties immediately urging them to stop all military action and withdraw their troops back to their own respective sides of the frontier. These telegraphs were met with surprising success. 'At 6am, on October 24th- exactly twenty-four hours after' the Bulgarian government sent their telegram alerting the Secretariat of the encroaching conflict, 'a Greek commander was about to launch an attack on the Bulgarian town of Petrić with one thousand men and three batteries.'[68] Both sides were full of anger and there was a very real prospect of an 'obstinate and bloody engagement on a scale which would have made it difficult to prevent another Greco-Bulgar war.'[69] Fortunately, however, the Greek forces had received orders from Athens to suspend all offensive operation, which was a result of Briand's telegram.

Although the conflict had passed its peak, the situation remained hostile, as small skirmishes continued to occur. In order to bring a complete end to hostilities, the Council declined to listen to the legal and moral justification of each side until both sides ceased all fighting and troops were withdrawn behind their respective frontiers. Bulgarian representatives tried their utmost to comply with the Council's demands, as no Bulgarian troops stood on Greek soil. The Greek representative had a more difficult time convincing military dictator, General Pangalos, of compliance as he deemed it national dignity and security to continue their advancement in Bulgarian territory. Briand and Chamberlain were in no mood to be defied by 'a small and shaky dictator.'[70] Although no threats were made in public, there was discussion of a naval demonstration and even the use of sanctions through an application of Article 16

[68] Walters, *supra* note 26, at 312.

[69] Ibid.

[70] Ibid., at 313.

of the Covenant. Whilst such threats were made, the British, French and Italian military envoys were only sent to report to the Council that the demands that they had set out were met. When the military envoys were in a position to investigate the area, they had found that withdrawal had already commenced. With successful compliance and no further danger of a renewal of hostilities, the Council was willing to listen to the arguments and complaints of both parties.

As had become usual custom, a Commission of Inquiry was sent to the region to 'not only report on the rights and wrongs of the case, but also to study the general situation on each side of the frontier with a view to preventing the recurrence of any similar crisis.'[71] By the time the Council had reconvened for its regular session on December 7, 1925, the Commission had already completed its work and was in a position to report back to the Council with a full account of hostilities. The Commission had found that the responsibility for the outbreak of conflict was divided, as both parties were to blame. In the original skirmish 'a Greek officer, advancing under the white flag to stop firing, had been shot dead, and it was natural that this aroused great indignation. But the Greek government, instead of laying its grievance before the League in accordance with the Covenant, had taken the law into its own hands and invaded Bulgarian territory.'[72] For the compensation of the moral and material loss inflicted on Bulgaria, the Commission decided that an indemnity of 30 million leva should be paid to Bulgarian by Greece. Furthermore, an indemnity was due to Greece for the death of its officer killed under the white flag. Though some small protests were made to such arrangements by both sides, it was met largely with agreement and the League had managed to prevent another large-scale conflict from occurring.

4.3.6 The Kellogg-Briand Pact

Following the Greco-Bulgar crisis, the Council re-evaluated its ability to intervene in the instance where a threat to international peace and security emerged. Consequently, the Council set up a Committee to research two matters. Firstly, the Council wanted to plan all the material arrangements

[71] Ibid., at 313.

[72] Ibid.

necessary for the effective functioning of the League in times of crises. Secondly, the Committee was set up to research Article 11, with particular interest to its application in cases of emergency. In respect of Article 10, the Commission's report considered that Article 16 should be kept in the background as Article 11 became recognised in Geneva as the emergency *par excellence*.[73] For this reason, resorting to Article 15, which was the gateway to 16, was discouraged.

The feeling amongst many of the central figures of the League was that greater efforts were required to ensure that international peace and security would be sustained for a longer period of time. This feeling correlated with the Council's intention to understand how the League could be more effective in times of crisis. The German government submitted a proposal that asserted that 'Members of the League should bind themselves in advance, to accept and carry out any recommendations which the Council might make in order to reduce the danger of war- such as the cancellation or mobilisation orders, the withdrawal of troops, or even the cessation of hostilities if these have already begun.'[74] Though the German proposal did not come to fruition, the Arbitration and Security Committee did propose a model treaty that renounced all recourse to force and promising mutual assistance if one of the parties should violate its pledge. This work was effectively the foundation for the Kellogg-Briand Pact, which was signed by fifteen countries in Paris on August 27, 1928, and opened to the signature of all. The treaty was also known as the 'General Treaty for the Renunciation of War as an Instrument of Nations Policy.' It was a perfect time for the emergence of such a treaty. The Council was at its peak of power and influence. The Assembly was firmly established as the annual meeting-place of Ministers, for the 'economic and social agencies of the League were growing swiftly in authority, efficiency, and reputation, and were extending their activities in every continent.'[75] The response to such a treaty was generally positive,[76] as the

[73] Zimmern, *supra* note 4, at 383.

[74] Walters, *supra* note 26, at 381.

[75] Ibid., at 384.

[76] When addressing the public, when the Kellogg-Briand pact was being signed, Aristide Briand declared that this day 'marks a new date in the history of mankind, and the end of selfish and wilful warfare,' for this treaty attacked 'the evil at its very root' by depriving war of its 'legitimacy.' U.S. Department of State, *Treaty for the Renunciation of War: Text of the Treaty, Notes Exchanged, Instruments of Ratification and of Adherence, and Other*

Kellogg-Briand Pact was regarded as a step forward for the international community.

In fact, the magnitude of such a moment should not be overlooked. The Kellogg-Briand Pact was the most ratified treaty in history at the time, having been joined by sixty-three nations. Oona Hathaway and Scott Shapiro contend that the Kellogg-Briand Pact was 'the most transformative events of human history,' as it 'marked the beginning of the end- and, with it, the replacement of one international order with another.'[77] Although this could be considered a strong claim (something that Hathaway and Shapiro agree that it could be), there is some justification in such a proposition. Their argument is that it changed the culture of the international community dramatically. Though the Pact itself failed, but:

> By prohibiting states from using war to resolve disputes, it began a cascade of events that would give birth to the modern global order. As its effects reverberated across the globe, it reshaped the world map, catalysed the human rights revolution, enabled the use of economic sanctions as a tool of law enforcement, and ignited the explosion in the number of international organizations that regulate so many aspects of our daily lives.[78]

Before the end of World War I, States often used war as a legitimate method to rights wrongs. Resorting to war was considered an instrument of justice, relied upon and rewarded.[79] Moreover, 'the Old World Order also granted immunities to those who waged war—in effect, authorizing mass homicide. If an ordinary person killed another outside of war, it was a murderous crime. If an army killed thousands during a war, it was not only lawful but glorious. To wage war was to be necessarily immune from criminal prosecution.'[80] Though Hathaway and Shapiro have perhaps underappreciated the transformative effects World War I had to the international community and its relationship with war, the Kellogg-Briand Pact made a significant contribution to move international law into a new

Papers (Washington, DC: U.S. Government Printing Office, 1933), 308–309 (French original text) and 313–14 (English translation).

[77] Hathaway & Shapiro, *supra* note 9, at 10.

[78] Ibid., at 12.

[79] Ibid.

[80] Ibid., at 13.

order. It signified the move away from the old format based heavily upon the act of war into an era of denouncing war and where new approaches to international relations began to prosper. It further highlights the claim that the aims of emancipatory idealism have played a significant role in the development of international law. The international realm was less and less a chessboard for States to advance their various strategies for superiority. The international community was now becoming conscientious of the effects of war, seeking to utilise international law to protect individuals and groups of individuals. No longer was the legal system's focus only on maintaining healthy relations between States. The transformative effects the international legal system underwent demonstrated that it would also be used to maintain peace and security, for 'every country wanted to achieve its policy without war, and therefore stood for peace.'[81]

The Kellogg-Briand Pact was a symbolic and literal representation of the fact that the first nine years of the League had been successful. By 1929 it seemed as if a new international system had replaced the discarded Concert Powers system of the pre-war days. Though it was not completely the organisation Member-States had envisioned the League it to be, the international organisation had managed to disprove naysayers that such a project would be a failure. It comes back to the willingness of States to make the League work. The Great Allied Powers were cooperative in ensuring that this new international system would be more effective. This rooted from the idealism and optimism of such a predicament. Charles Howard-Ellis reiterated similar sentiments at the time, suggesting:

> that in the League the nations themselves our nation and most of the other nations of the world have pledged themselves to conduct their foreign policies through certain machinery, in certain conferences, and on the basis of certain obligations providing for international co-operation and peaceful settlement of disputes. Whether this effort succeeds or not depends in the last resort on the will of every citizen, but that such pledges should have been implemented, and that such an association of states as the League should actually exist and be working, is something new in the history of

[81] E.H. Carr, *The Twenty Years' Crisis 1919–1939: An Introduction to The Study of International Relations*, (1946), at 140.

> the world, something that fifteen years ago every statesman would have declared wildly Utopian.[82]

Member-States had thrown themselves into making the League an effective machinery for preventing threats to peace and security. The successful settlements of the disputes outlined discussed thus far and the creation of international treaties such as Locarno and the Kellogg-Briand Pact that advanced international peace and security are all but an indication of this. The central reasons for the League's success were rooted in the commitment of Member-States to prevent another catastrophe that would rival the Great War. Occasions when Member-States have acted for their own self-seeking interests have tended to result unfavourably in settling disputes as in the Upper Silesia crisis. Britain, France and Italy attempted to manipulate the situation for their own individual benefit, and it was only the Council's use of the expert advisors, who were neutral to the dispute that a successful resolution was found.

4.3.7 The Rise and Fall of the League

It is necessary to stress the importance of Member-States' compliance to the League. Even in examples such as Great Britain, who were reluctant to continue on with the League following the withdrawal of the United States, compliance was not an issue. This falls back to the fact that much of the international community wished to see the League be a success. Regardless of whether States were members to the League or not, the international community was committed to putting the horrors of the Great War permanently behind them.[83] The League was an opportune pathway to ensuring that such large-scale violence would be prevented in the future. In order for the League to work, compliance was a necessity. Occasions where compliance was doubtful were quickly snuffed out when the likes of Briand and Chamberlain threatened with declarations of naval intervention.

Therefore, the first decade of the League was a successful period in terms of achieving the central aims of emancipatory idealism. The ethic that was espoused during the drafting of the League, *never again*, had

[82] C. Howard-Ellis, *The Origin, Structure and Working of The League of Nations*, (1928), at 58.

[83] Walters, *supra* note 26, at 227.

seemingly maintained a strong influence upon the workings of the institution. With States' realist agendas aligned with those aspirations focused on protecting individuals and groups of individuals, it was the ideal environment for such a focal goal to prosper and successfully be achieved. In fact, Allott's claim that international society and its legal system should be utilised for humanity's prosperity and survival[84] is typified by the successful nine years the League initially enjoyed. The manner in which any threat of hostility was dealt with is indicative of this argument. The accelerated development of the international organisation coupled with the States' 'will to contribute' displayed the idea that the protection of individuals and groups of individuals, continued to bear influence upon international law and international relations well into the 1920s. This strong desire for peace motivated the leading nations of the League to effectively deal with disputes such as Upper Silesia or Mosul, establish the need for disarmament, or even negotiate treaties such as Locarno or the Kellogg-Briand Pact. The international community sought to protect itself from the sort of stunt in civilisational development that it had suffered due to the destabilising repercussions of the Great War. It is in highlighting the accelerated phase of development international law underwent during this period that the first hypothesis of the paper can be proven. As international law transitioned from the traditional Westphalian non-institutionalist model to the institutionalist model of the League of Nations focused on maintaining international peace and security, it becomes apparent how the aims of emancipatory idealism play a significant role in the development of international law. Furthermore, such analysis of the first nine years of the League indicates that it is precisely when following a large-scale crisis, that such utopian goals influence the international legal most significantly.

Additionally, it is interesting to note that the successful influence of utopian foals of international law coincides with a period where State compliance was never fervently disputed. What is indicative of this phenomenon is how international relations and international law is heavily reliant upon the nature of the States, more specifically, the States that are most influential in the international community. For this reason, the first decade of the League could be considered as one of the longest periods of sustained success any international organisation has ever maintained in

[84] P. Allott, *The Health of Nations: The Society and Law Beyond the State*, (2002), at 387, para 18.30.

terms of achieving the utopian goals of international law. Such a period shows how influential the position of the State is, as the primary subject and object of the international legal system. States play a major role in determining the development of international law. Thus, it seems that the achievement of emancipatory idealism's aims relies upon a vested interest for States to seek to realise such focal goals. E.H. Carr supports this position, stating that 'after the collapse of the Disarmament Conference, it became apparent to all that the League of Nations could be effective only in so far as it was an instrument of the national policy of its most powerful members.'[85] Between 1920 and 1929, for the more influential States seeking the achievement of utopian focal goals of international law is reasoned by the need for such States requiring a period of stability. Most States involved in World War I were economically, socially and politically weakened. In order to create a certain level of stability, the protection of individuals and communities of individuals was the most suitable means through which to prevent a further stunt in civilisational development.

4.4 A Slow Death: The Rise of Protectionism During the *Interbellum* Period

Although the League of Nations had achieved so much in its first nine years some still saw the organisation as 'a weakened League.' US withdrawal was still considered to be a big detriment to the effectiveness of the League and the question remained whether or not it would continue to sustain its success. Up until now, the utopian goals of international law and the realist objectives of the more influential States in the international community were aligned, establishing a perfect climate for the League to successfully operate within. The true test for the League would come when such interests bifurcate and come into conflict. Moreover, even though the disputes the League had settled thus far were vital to maintaining international peace and security, they were not large-scale conflicts that could dramatically destabilise international relations.

This predicament further cemented the powerful position States, and the more influential States, in particular, enjoyed in the international legal system. International law was structured in such a way that for the system to work effectively, it heavily relied upon the commitment of

[85] Carr, *supra* note 81, at 140.

States as the primary subject and object of the international legal system. Through such analysis, an important question arises; could the League and its utopian goals to maintain international peace and security survive if States displayed less commitment to comply with the legal system? It is by answering such a question the second hypothesis shall be proven. Showing how States undermined international law during the *interbellum* period demonstrates the League's failure to achieve utopian focal goals of international law, which led to World War II.

The Great Depression in 1929 sparked a significant change in the international community. With the emergence of such a shift, it became apparent that such a phenomenon would have deep repercussions not only for the international community but also for those focused on achieving utopian aspirations. The international legal system derailed emphatically as States lost interest in achieving the utopian goals of international law or even ensuring the effectiveness of the international legal system itself. The events that emerged after the first nine years of the League outlined such fears. Given the option to undermine the utopian goals of international law in order to focus on their realist agendas or to maintain international peace and security and commit to achieving the utopian goals of international law, it was the former option that proved more popular for States. The following ten years saw the League crumble under the pressure of maintaining international peace and security, as States abandoned the League and the utopian goals of international law to eventually ready themselves for another World War.

4.4.1 Effects of the Great Depression Upon the International Community

Before delving into the coming failures of the League, it is important to ponder over the Great Depression momentarily. The negative effect of this event was monumental and played a significant role in the changing landscape of international relations. A series of events caused the global economy to decline in catastrophic fashion. The stock market crash of October 1929 was the result of a 'knee-jerk reaction on the Federal Reserve Board of the United States,'[86] that followed with investors selling

[86] D. Rothermond, *The Global Impact of the Great Depression*, (1996), at 2.

stocks at a rapid pace. Such a reaction exacerbated the economic situation leading to the matter becoming more than just a domestic issue.

The global standard of gold also played a role in causing the Great Depression. 'This standard had guaranteed monetary stability and economic growth for several decades.'[87] Considering the fact that the post-World War I period was considered a golden age, many figures such as David Hume for example advocated such an approach. The advantages of such a standard had been because 'it provided an equilibrium by means of a simple mechanism which seemed to work as if governed by a law of nature.'[88] However, this misconception became apparent when it was clear that such a standard depended on a powerful lender of last resort.[89] When the Bank of England was unable to play such a role, it spurred on a detrimental effect upon the global economy, as 'the ensuing deflation' that followed the response to the failed global standard of gold, 'depressed the price level, discouraged investment, increased unemployment, etc.'[90]

On top of these economic pitfalls, the matter of war debt and reparations also played a role in the emergence of the Great Depression. The problems—which plagued post-war monetary policy in several European countries—were due to the dilemma of war debts owed by the British, the French and several smaller European countries to the United States, on the one hand. On the other hand, however, Germany was obliged to pay France, Great Britain and Belgium. 'The debt service of the war debts was an essential part of the American budget: if they were struck off or reduced, the government would have to raise taxes to that extent.' Altogether, the United States was owed twelve billion dollars by Great Britain, France and other smaller states. However, in order for Britain and France to be in the position to repay the United States the debt they owed; they needed the reparations from Germany. Whereas the war debts were fixed in rather precise terms, the reparations, which Germany obliged to pay to the Allies according to the Treaty of Versailles, were not fixed until a committee appointed for this purpose specified an amount of 132 billion

[87] Ibid., at 19.

[88] Ibid., at 19.

[89] B. Eichengreen & D.A. Irwin, 'The Slide to Protectionism in the Great Depression: Who Succumbed and Why?', (2010) 70 *The Journal of Economic History* 871, at 873.

[90] Rothermond, *supra* note 86, at 31.

gold marks in 1921. This amount was never fully paid but the continued pressure of reparations remained. The French were particularly stubborn as they were eager to claim their pound of flesh, invading the Ruhr region as compensation.[91] The big issue of the situation was that although reparations were demanded their means to fulfil their obligations were also restricted. The French invasion of the Ruhr for example did not help, as their ability to generate funds was hard to establish.[92] Although the United States put in place the Dawes Plan, and combined it with Locarno, it came some way to assist tensions on both an economic and political level, yet it did little in the way of establishing a more stable future. As a result, the Great Depression hit Germany especially hard and this was one of the contributing factors as to the rise of Fascism in Germany.

What is noteworthy of the effect the Great Depression had, is the protectionist standpoint adopted by States not only on an economic level, but also how this filtered into their political activity in the international arena. 'In the face of an unprecedented economic collapse,'[93] many States adopted a protectionist policy to ensure their own economic survival. Thus, the 'will to cooperate' was seemingly strained by the economic and political climate and the commitment shown earlier with great exuberance seemed to falter. During this period also, several States had become extreme in their political ideology, an obvious example being Germany, which was a cause for concern in relation to international peace and security. In regard to the League, there were two direct consequences of the Great Depression. Firstly, the structure of economic cooperation had broken down. With Britain abandoning the gold standard, allowing the pound to depreciate, the effects 'sent shockwaves through the world economy.'[94] Other countries responded to Britain's actions by imposing restrictions on international trade and payments which dealt a severe blow to world commerce. World trade volume fell sixteen per cent from the third quarter of 1931 to the third quarter of 1932. Between 1929 and

[91] C. Fischer, *The Ruhr Crisis 1923–1924*, (2003), 223–224.

[92] C. Fischer, 'The Failure of the Détente? German-French Relations Between Stresemann and Hitler', in Frank McDonough (ed.), *The Origins of the Second World War: An International Perspective*, (2011), 87–91.

[93] Eichengreen and Irwin, *supra* note 89, at 894.

[94] Ibid., at 876.

1932 it fell twenty-five per cent, and nearly half of this reduction was due to higher tariff and non-tariff barriers.[95]

This consequently led to the second direct impact which has already been touched upon lightly and that was the growing tensions between some Member-States such as France's relationship with both Germany and Italy.[96] Both were apparent when the Convention on the Treatment of Foreigners and the Convention for the Abolition of Import and Export Prohibitions and Restriction were being drafted. Additionally, the Tariff Truce was indicative of the fact that 'the whole movement towards a freer flow of international trade had now actually been reversed.'[97] The League's economic organs warned Member-States of the pitfalls of their protectionist position; however, such warnings were largely ignored. Now that central guidance was more necessary than ever, States had instead looked into their own defences and were less willing to listen to international institutions.

The Great Depression was more than simply financial distress and unemployment for a large part of the world; it also affected the political stability of the international community. As States began to grow more protectionist, their interest for the 'slow process of rebuilding the political stability' of the international community had been undermined. It was a signal to the League of what to expect when threats to international peace and security had emerged and the response of the States that had initially committed themselves wholly to the cause would now treat the matter differently. Furthermore, the attitude towards the League was also now to change, as the disregard of its economic organs was just a taste of what would occur in the next decade of the League.

4.4.2 *Disarmament*

The League's endeavour on the disarmament front accurately encapsulates the history of the international organisation. It is an indication of the transition from a League that was so successful in their first decade, into an organisation failing to ensure international peace and security in the

[95] League of Nations, *Review of World Trade*, (1938), at 62.

[96] C. Fischer, 'The Failed European Union: Franco-German Relations during the Great Depression of 1929–1932', (2012) 34 *The International History Review* 1, at 3.

[97] Walters, *supra* note 26, at 429.

second half of its lifespan. The whole disarmament story between 1920 and 1938 precisely represented the attitude of Member-States throughout the existence of the League, not only on this subject matter in particular, but the whole operation of the international organisation. The first decade of success was due to Member-States' enthusiasm, whilst the second decade was a failure because such enthusiasm was lacking from Member-States. It became apparent that the most important component for a successful international organisation regulating the international community was State commitment.

Very early on with the development of the League there were discussions regarding disarmament. This movement derived from the desire of many States wishing to prevent another large-scale conflict that could match the devastation of the Great War. A suggested solution to this was decreasing the amount of munitions each State possessed. Between 1920 and 1933, the disarmament agenda was continuously brought to the forefront in regard to the aims and activities of the Assembly and the Council's sessions. 'Committees and Commissions, some composed of men of high political rank, other specialists and technicians, held innumerable meetings on the subject.'[98] All in all, a strong desire was exhibited by most of the powerful States, including the United States in this instance, towards such an initiative. It was on this basis that such a prerogative was adopted when the Covenant was drafted. Article 8 of the Covenant stated that 'the maintenance of peace requires the reduction of armaments to the lowest point consistent with national safety.'[99] In retrospect, such an article within the primary legal source of international law at the time is illustrative of how influential the utopian goals were during this period. Moreover, there were discussions to bring national armaments to the lowest point consistent with national safety,[100] whilst the preamble to the arms reductions clauses of all the peace treaties signed with the defeated powers insisted that their enforced disarmament was taking place in order 'to render possible the initiation of a general limitation of armaments of

[98] Ibid., at 217.

[99] The Covenant of the League of Nations, (1920).

[100] 'The Question of Armament Notes', (1921) 2 *League of Nations Official Journal* 256, at 256–259.

all nations.'[101] Several bodies were designated the task of dealing with the matter of disarmament during the League's reign, such as the Permanent Armaments Commission, the Temporary Mixed Commission on Armaments, the Preparatory Commission for the Disarmament Conference and the Disarmament Conference itself.[102] There was a genuine belief within the League and its members that States would adhere to such a disarmament movement and follow such a protocol. It was a bold step outlining the dedication towards international peace and security.

Therefore, the initial consensus was a positive one. Most countries were already engaged in reducing their forces from the high figures confirmed just before the Armistice. Although the Permanent Armament—which was mostly composed of the Great Powers—advised that drafting a scheme of armaments reduction would not be possible at the time, the Assembly pushed onwards and continued to exert pressure in regard to disarmament. Their persistence paid off as the Temporary Mixed Commission was established, in order to prepare a plan for the consideration of the Council. The Commission was slow in productivity, but its first report in 1921 did address the technical and political hurdles in the way of ensuring disarmament.[103] The momentum of this report carried on in the Washington Conference made 'further delay impossible.'[104] There was more support from the Great Powers; however, there remained a level of hesitancy in regard to the push towards disarmament following the Washington Conference. Many nations were still concerned about the safety of their domestic situation and the potential threats that could emerge from external forces. Certainly, for nations such as France, the possibility of Germany once again rising as a potential threat created a level of French reluctance. Even with Britain's Lord Esher's plan, where 'forces should be restricted according to a fixed ration, following the naval precedent of Washington' was quashed swiftly, France, Belgium, Poland and other

[101] For the peace treaties with Germany, Austria, Hungary, Bulgaria and Turkey, each of which incorporated the Covenant of League of Nations, see *The Treaties of Peace, 1919–1923*, (1924), at 2.

[102] A. Webster, 'The Transnational Dream: Politicians, Diplomats, and Soldiers in the League of Nations' Pursuit of International Disarmament 1920–1938', (2005) 14(4) *Contemporary European History* 493, at 495.

[103] See 'Temporary Mixed Commission for the Reduction of Armaments', (1921) 2 *League of Nations Official Journal* 743, at 743–745.

[104] Walters, *supra* note 26, at 220.

European countries contended that although they wished nothing more than to reduce armaments, the fact that the presence of munitions quelled any insecurities and fears of attacks, made them reluctant to commit fully.

With this setback, Lord Robert Cecil, who was also contributing to the Temporary Mixed Commission, therefore, began to look for an alternative, as he sought out a more feasible option that would still achieve disarmament. Cecil admitted that 'certain States believed that they could not undertake any obligation to disarm without receiving additional guarantees of security.'[105] The Commission concluded that a new Treaty of Guarantee would be the most successful means towards achieving disarmament. The Treaty would be designed in such a way that once each signatory had reduced its armaments according to an agreed plan, if another attacked a signatory, they would be assured immediate support from all other signatories in the same continent. With this in mind, a new plan was laid before the Third Assembly in Geneva. The Temporary Commission affirmed that: firstly, disarmament could not be successful unless the safety of their country was guaranteed; secondly, that a lot of governments would be reluctant to reduce armaments unless the safety of their nation was guaranteed; thirdly, that such a guarantee could be provided.[106] Such a declaration of policy was the fourteenth resolution adopted by the Assembly regarding the issue of armaments. Resolution 14 proved to be a pivotal and influential advancement by the League for it proved to be the starting point of all subsequent efforts to establish disarmament by constructing a system of security. 'Resolution 14 of 1922 led on to the Treaty of Mutual Assistance drawn up in the Assembly of 1923, to the Geneva Protocol of 1924, and to the Geneva Protocol of 1924, and to the Locarno Treaties of 1925.'[107]

With Resolution 14 playing a significant role towards achieving disarmament, Cecil and the Temporary Mixed Commission set to work on a draft treaty with an Assembly mandate. The core proposals of the treaty were that in addition to the League, the Council should take it upon itself to draw up certain special guarantee treaties for the benefit of particularly exposed States. In the event of an outbreak of war the Council

[105] Ibid., at 223.

[106] 'Temporary Mixed Commission for the Reduction of Arms Note', (1922) 3 *League of Nations Official Journal* 316, at 316–317.

[107] Ibid., at 224.

had to determine which State was the aggressor within a four day time period, whereupon the defence organisation was to be set in motion, the command of the common force being assumed either by the attacked party or be a State designated by the Council. Cecil and the Commission accepted that such a system of military guarantees was not possible for the world as a whole, and therefore, they proposed that the obligations be only applied in the continent in which the aggression occurred. When the draft treaty was submitted to the Permanent Advisory Commission, it was rejected on the grounds that 'the idea that the Council should draw up the special treaties of guarantee' was not favourable. Colonel Réquin of France drafted a substitute. Eventually, the two drafts were amalgamated to produce the Treaty of Mutual Assistance.[108] The treaty was brought before the Fourth Assembly in 1923. Unfortunately, many governments, such as Russia and the United States, rejected the treaty. Britain responded to the proposition of such a treaty with little enthusiasm, as they insisted that they had the 'intention to call a world-wide disarmament conference as soon as the moment seemed favourable.'[109] There were some States that did approve the treaty such as France,[110] and Italy who expressed a general approval, except the provisions for special agreements.[111] Lesser States such as 'Poland, Czechoslovakia, Belgium, the Baltic States, Finland and others who feared aggression'[112] supported the treaty.[113] However, in July 1924, when Britain rejected the treaty, it signalled the fact that the Treaty of Mutual Assistance was fated for failure. Even though Cecil, a member of the Conservative party, was an influential presence in drafting the Treaty of Mutual Assistance, a central reason for British rejection was that before the Fourth Assembly ended, a new Labour government had come into power. The new Labour

[108] Webster, *supra* note 102, at 506.

[109] Walters, *supra* note 26, at 226.

[110] France's stated that: 'The Government of the Republic is extremely desirous of affording co-operation, in as wide a measure as possible, with all efforts which aim at maintaining peace and at enabling a reduction of armaments to be effected by means of a definite and effectual scheme for mutual assistance between States Members of the League.' 'Reduction of Armaments Note', (1923) 3 *League of Nations Official Journal* 1073, at 1080.

[111] Ibid., at 1081–1082.

[112] Walters, *supra* note 26, at 226.

[113] 'Reduction of Arms Note', *supra* note 111, 1073–1095.

government—led by Prime Minister Ramsay MacDonald—held particular reservations in regard to the military commitments stipulated in the treaty.[114]

What came after the failed Treaty of Mutual Assistance was a result of public opinion, as it reflected a frustration in the standing of international relations. Britain's reluctance was not met with much favourability:

> It was said with truth that the very government which had proclaimed that its whole foreign policy would consist of strengthening the League, had now not only destroyed by a single gesture the result of all the efforts of three Assemblies and the Temporary Mixed Commission, but had done so in a tone which reflected the dislike for the older generation of officials and for the institutions of Geneva and by arguments which seemed intended to undermine the foundations of the Covenant itself.[115]

Britain's inability to support all the work that had been accomplished by the League on the issue of disarmament highlights an instance of States undermining utopian goals of international law. One of the key sources of inspiration for the workings of the League was the protection of individuals or a community of individuals from modes of oppression. The disarmament movement was in the mould of such utopian focal goals as an essential reason to limit the amount of munitions each nation holds is to ensure international peace and security and protect individuals or communities of individuals. However, when States become self-seeking in carrying out their duties as Members of the League, advancing utopian goals of international law becomes a secondary notion. States' influence on the League's proceedings bore a detrimental effect in ensuring such focal goals. Britain's lack of support of the Treaty of Mutual Assistance was indicative of this. Given the chance States have tended to prioritise their own interest over the interests of the international community.

As a result of the backlash Ramsay MacDonald met after such a move, the British Prime Minister was anxious to bring forward new proposals. Some believed that there was no need to add external additions to the obligations already substantiated in the Covenant. Instead, a practical guarantee that Britain and the other chief power intended to carry out

[114] 'Reduction of Armaments Note', (1924) 5 *League of Nations Official Journal* 1035, at 1036–1039.

[115] Walters, *supra* note 26, at 227.

their obligations as Members of the League was called for. Though there were strong arguments for this—as the Covenant should be an adequate enough legal obligation to ensure disarmament—this fell short of a full commitment that a secondary legal source would be established. The existence of another treaty or scheme alongside Article 8 of the Covenant would have exerted more pressure upon States to take the matter of disarmament seriously and to go ahead with such a scheme.

However, with the success of the Locarno Conference in 1925, the Council once again turned their attention to planning a general Disarmament Conference. A new organ was established which focused on the planning of such a conference. In December 1925, the Preparatory Commission for the Disarmament Conference, also known as the Preparatory Commission, was created. The Preparatory Commission was composed of politicians or diplomats, along with two bodies of technical experts—at the disposal of the Council—that were present as support to the initiative. Germany, the United States and Soviet Russia also had representatives in the Preparatory Commission.

When the Preparatory Commission met for the first time in May 1926, it was considered a monumental moment in history, for it was the first ever occasion that such a task had been seriously undertaken. The Preparatory Commission sought to tackle many issues such as: 'how should armaments be defined? How could they be compared? Could offensive weapons be distinguished from those intended only for defence? What were the various forms which limitation or reduction might take? Could the total war strength of a country be limited, or only its peace establishments? Was it possible to exclude civil aviation from the calculation of armaments? How could such factors as populations, industrial resources, communications, geographical position, be reckoned in preparing an equitable scheme? Could there be regional schemes of reduction, or must reduction necessarily be planned on a world scale?'[116] This endeavour was evidently taken with a significant deal of determination for the Commission were fully investigating how to make disarmament a practical reality. Though there was a great deal of disagreement and reservations in the discussions, by March 1927, when the Commission met for a second time, the French and British delegations each submitted a draft

[116] Ibid., at 365.

Convention to serve as a basis for the preparatory work for the conference.[117] Even when the two drafts were wildly different on core ideas, and debates and disagreements continued on amongst various members within the Commission it could not be denied that progress had been made on the front of disarmament, still no agreement was foreseeable as of yet.

By September 1928, proceedings did not seem to follow a positive direction as the attempt to make progress through diplomatic conversations had merely led to mutual ill temper between Britain and the United States, and between France and Italy. Germany also began to grow more suspicious on the basis that 'any compromise arrived at by such means were sure to be based on the consent of each party not to press for reductions to which the other might object.'[118] The issue of disarmament was becoming increasingly futile with attitudes simply unfavourable for disarmament to become a reality. However, it was around the time of the Kellogg-Briand Pact, that the disarmament movement generated momentum once again. Several central powers, including the likes of the United States and Soviet Russia, expressed a growing sense of urgency to deal with the matter of disarmament, stressing that no further delays could be afforded. The Preparatory Commission began to work on a second draft Convention put forward by Russia. This particular draft Convention did not call for total disarmament, but instead proposed a large reduction in 'offensive weapons, such as bombing aeroplanes, long-range guns, heavy aircrafts, tanks [and] aircraft-carriers.'[119] Nonetheless, a majority of the participants of the Commission did not favour Russia's draft, and the members decided to start discussions all over again on a new basis. Consequently, the Preparatory Commission opted to proceed with a second reading of its own draft Convention of 1927.[120] A similar tradition of a slow process of development followed with neither a clear result

[117] League of Nations, Special Commission for the Preparation of a Draft Convention on the Private Manufacture of Arms and Ammunition and of Implements of War, *Report of the Special Commission to the Council on the work of its first session*, C.219.M.142.1927.IX, (April 27, 1927).

[118] Ibid., at 372.

[119] Ibid., at 373.

[120] League of Nations, Assembly, *Arbitration, Security, Disarmament and the Work of the Preparatory Commission for the Disarmament Conference*, A.124.1927.IX (September 26, 1927).

nor a consensus between members of the Preparatory Commission established. The likes of Britain and the United States could not agree with the limitation of the trained reserves or of materials, whilst France and Italy agreed to compromise on the methods of naval limitation. Japan, on the other hand, 'with unfailing amiability declined practically every form of reduction.'[121]

Nonetheless, by 1931 there was adequate support for holding a disarmament conference. Pressure was building although there remained a belief that the time was too soon to hold a conference, the pressure of German claim to equality, for example, and the general claim for disarmament was now far too urgent for such a discussion to be prolonged. The conference that did take place was a historical achievement, for never had so many nations participated[122] in a serious discussion on achieving disarmament before. A whole host of discussions ensued with Britain, France, Italy and the United States taking a central stage in proceedings but the various proposals that were brought forward by the conference participants did not become a reality. The atmosphere in which the conference was being held made the idea of reducing each State's level of munitions became more and more unlikely. The change of government in Germany, with Hitler's rise to prominence, was for France a more threatening prospect than ever before. Furthermore, the inability to protect China from Japanese hostilities hinted to the failure of the League and the fact that an alternative safeguard to the Covenant was required. The United States had little to offer, and similar to Great Britain, was not seeking to accept any new obligations. The German delegation stated that they could no longer collaborate in the work of the conference until the principle of equality of rights had been recognised.[123] Nations were evidently becoming more protectionists, growing more concerned about

[121] Walters, *supra* note 26, at 374.

[122] 'All sixty-four recognised countries of the world, except four of the smallest Latin American Republics were present. By the eminence of the principled delegates; by the numbers and qualification of expert advisors; by the importance for the whole world of the work they had assembled to perform; by the public interest, as shown by the crowds of journalists who reported its proceedings; it was at least the greatest since the Paris Conference of Peace.' See: Walters, *supra* note 26, at 501.

[123] League of Nations, Preparatory Commission for the Disarmament Conference, *Documents of the Preparatory Commission for the Disarmament Conference entrusted with the preparation for the Conference for the Reduction and Limitation of Armaments*, C.4.M.4.1931.IX (January 15, 1931), at 366.

ensuring their individual safety rather than achieving international peace and security. The utopian spirit that was so prevalent when the League was being created was seemingly fading away as a whole host of hostilities now seemed foreseeable. Even though the conference was wrought with difficulties by December 11, 1932, the four European powers, with US assistance, had agreed upon a formula. The formula had two primary objects: firstly, that the culmination of the conference would lead to the conclusion of a Convention in which Germany would possess 'equality of rights in a system which provide security for all nations'; secondly, all European States should reaffirm that they would never under any circumstances, attempt to settle their differences by resorting to hostile behaviour.[124] Although there was still a great deal to be debated in regard to the substance of such a formula, it was a good starting point from which the discussion of disarmament could expand upon. Furthermore, the guarantee for equality of rights ensured German participation.

When the Disarmament Conference had reconvened in 1933, the political environment had substantially altered, and it was not for the better. By this point, Japan and Germany had turned against the League and were already obstructing and threatening all the forms of cooperation the League was intending to salvage. France had grown increasingly more defensive against the 'Italo-German' campaign for treaty revision. During this period Mussolini became attracted to the 'warlike capacities of Italy' and for this reason was inclined to side with Germany. He had already supported Germany's equality of rights claim made in the conference's first year. Certainly, the unequal treatment of Germany was a cause for them to have such a bitter feeling towards the League and its leading members. Although the French and the British insisted on the validity of the Treaty of Versailles, the limitation and discrimination of Germany on several levels be it economic, militarily and territorially was one of the root causes to the threat that Germany had become, inevitably leading to the collapse of the League and World War II. Germany by 1933 began to remilitarise and France, however, could not accept such a flagrant treaty violation. France was eager to push forward with drafting a Convention with the imminent threat of Germany looming larger. The British delegation, led by Eden and Alexander Cadogan, were entrusted with such a responsibility. The result was a Convention that included specific levels

[124] Walters, *supra* note 26, at 374.

and amounts of munitions permitted and used much of the past work conducted in the area. It was a clear and practical plan, which might well have won general acceptance if it had been proposed only but a year earlier. In order to allow each delegation to consider the necessity for amendment, the conference had been adjourned for a month.[125]

Unsurprisingly, Germany did not respond favourably to the draft Convention. The thirst for war that was such a prominent feature in the Nazi movement had seen the claim for equality of rights now manifest into a more aggressive mission for German expansion. Though some attempts were made to appease initial German unfavourability—Mussolini's proposal of a Four-Power Pact being an example—it proved to be a failure and by October 1933 Germany had withdrawn from the League and continued to expand irrespective of the prohibition of rearmament established in the Treaty of Versailles.[126] With this the United States grew even more isolated, seemingly abandoning the conference. Italy believed that the conference was meaningless now that Germany had withdrawn entirely, and Italian delegates were consequently instructed to participate only as observers. The British and French were now bearing the weight of the conference in the aim of ensuring that it would not collapse. However, it was to no avail for Germany's withdrawal, combined with its rearmament, created a cloud of uncertainty as to the future of the international community. States needed to defend themselves if the time came when Germany began to act out towards other States aggressively. It was apparent that the conference could not continue. The prospect of disarmament now seemed a fantasy and although other attempts were made to reignite the debate during the remainder of the League's tenure, they proved unsuccessful.

With the League's endeavours to establish the disarmament movement, there were several moments, scattered throughout 1920–1933, when it seemed that such a goal would be reached. But there was always 'matters of higher importance' that stunted the momentum gathered towards achieving such a goal. Yet even in moments when enthusiasm had died down, a key event such as Locarno or the Kellogg-Briand Pact would reinvigorate the debate and desire of many of the leading States

[125] League of Nations, Conference for the Reduction and Limitation of Armaments, *Draft Proposals by the United Kingdom Delegation*, 1933.IX.1 (January 30, 1933).

[126] 'Notification by the German Government of its Intention to Withdraw from the League of Nations', (1934) 15 *League of Nations Official Journal* 16, at 16.

to continue the struggle towards limiting instruments of war. Nonetheless, the failure to achieve disarmament was rooted in the unwillingness of States to commit fully and to cooperate with each other and the League. States' internal feuds and constant search to find gaps in which to advance their own realist gains was a central feature to the inability in achieving disarmament. Whether it was Britain's reluctance, or French fears of Germany, or even Germany's mission to expand militarily, as much as they voiced their desire for limitation on munitions, when forced to act the central powers' protectionist policy was in contradiction to ensuring utopian goals. Focusing on Germany specifically, once Hitler did come into power, his speech in the Disarmament Conference in 1933 was a rousing declaration of the importance for peace and disarmament. It was all but a sign of the supposed dedication of Germany to cooperate with the League and the other States. However, several months later, Germany's withdrawal virtually dismantled the Disarmament Conference and any future work made towards such a goal. It was a clear example of how dependent the effectiveness of international law and the achievement of emancipatory idealism's central aims were reliant upon the commitment and cooperation of States. The disarmament movement also highlighted another problem, which was establishing laws that States would follow without an entity that could enforce the compliance to established legality. An issue that came up when drafting the various treaties or conventions during this period was creating practically possible laws that States would foreseeably comply with, such as limiting each States level of munitions, agreeing to what is defensive and offensive weaponry and so forth. Many of the figures that had got involved realised that if States displayed an unwillingness to comply with international law, it would undermine the legal system and consequently the drafting of legislation was a precarious endeavour filled with much deliberation.

Thus, to advance the central aims of emancipatory idealism, the role of the State—or more specifically the role of hegemonic States—was a pivotal one. The Italian ambassador, Dino Grandi's, was accurate when depicting the pivotal role the Great Powers play in the operation of the League and international law:

> We are faced at Geneva with the following reality: that the Powers- large and small- carry their difficulties and their conflicts of interest to the League of Nations. These conflicts do not shrink at Geneva; they expand… All the disputes brought to Geneva finish sooner or later, either directly

> or indirectly, are conflicts between the Great Powers. During my stay in Geneva I never saw a dispute of any importance settled otherwise than by an agreement between the Great Powers. They alone are responsible for the situations that arise. A few States that remain outside of fixed diplomatic combinations, and are therefore able to maintain an independent attitude, have from time to time exercised a conciliatory influence at Geneva. But this only happens in the case of secondary disputes, and moreover these lesser Powers, not having at their disposal the forces that might become necessary to back their action, are themselves compelled to have recourse to the Great Powers. The whole of the Geneva procedure is, in fact, a system of detours, all of which lead to one or other of these two issues: agreement or disagreement between Great Britain, Italy, France and Germany.[127]

International law operated with great difficulty without the willingness of States. The following events covered support this argument as the collapse of the League of Nations occurred slowly over the second half of the League's existence.

The disarmament movement perhaps best displays the validity of the two hypotheses emanating from the theoretical framework established in Chapters 2 and 3. Firstly, the influence of the central aims of emancipatory idealism is demonstrated by the international community's ability to gather key players of international relations to discuss the possibility of disarmament alongside the League's success to hold the various conferences and commissions on the topic. It represents a commitment to protecting individuals and groups by pushing towards the possibility of weakening States' abilities to resort to hostilities. However, the claim that the primacy of States in the international legal system is problematic for emancipatory idealist is also strengthened when the failure to achieve disarmament during the *interbellum* period is a direct result of a lack of State commitment for the achievement of such a goal. The disarmament movement represents a significant step towards creating a stable economic, social and political environment for individuals and groups to contribute to the development of civilisation on a technological and societal level. However, it is the realist approach States have taken to the disarmament movement that has jeopardised international peace and security and the achievement of emancipatory idealism. The failure to achieve

[127] H.F. Armstrong, *The Foreign Policy of the Powers, France, Germany, Great Britain, Italy, Japan, Soviet Russia, the United States*, (1935), at 86–87.

disarmament during the *interbellum* period ultimately demonstrates the dangers of State primacy in international law.

4.4.3 *Japanese Disruptions and the Manchurian Crisis*

The failure of the disarmament movement suggested that the feuds that erupted amongst Member-States weakened the League. This subsequently left the League ripe for States such as Japan, Italy and Germany to undermine the international organisation and see it crumble. As a result of the Great Depression and the ill feeling generated amongst Member-States when dealing with the matter of disarmament, States abandoned the international spirit to 'concentrate their attention on their own most immediate interests regardless of the effects of such a policy upon their relations.'[128] It became apparent that by 1929 the 'Geneva spirit' was unrecognisable to the one present in 1920.

By the 1930s France had allied itself with States such as Belgium, Poland and later Russia for example in order to prepare for any Franco-German disputes. Germany did the same by allying itself with Italy. The period from 1930 onwards was characterised by a play of power in the course of which Europe rapidly descended back to the 'new order' that existed in the eighteenth century. 'Geneva became an immense chess-board on which not only the Great Powers but knights and bishops and multitudinous pawns practiced the art of manoeuvre.'[129] Alongside the power play in Geneva, the Locarno system had disintegrated following French withdrawal from the Rhineland and Germany reclaiming the area in an unprecedented tactic, which confirmed the breakdown in Franco-German relations. The League was proving itself increasingly unable to ensure international peace and security. The rising tensions indicated a possible turn to hostilities and another possible stunt in the development of civilisation on both a sociological and technological level. The recourse to war was seemingly becoming a foreseeable option for States, even if the League continued to dedicate itself to the cause of international peace and security. The ethic *'never again'* that had inspired the creation of the League and the need for an international legal system was swept aside for sake of States' protectionism.

[128] Zimmern, *supra* note 4, at 410.

[129] Ibid., at 417.

As much as Germany was causing consternation within the international community, no one had foreseen the change in Japan that shook the foundations of the League in a profound manner. So horrific was the Japanese invasion of Chinese territory that F.P Walters declared the event as the 'rape of Manchuria.'[130] At first, there was relatively little interest and understanding of the severity of such an incident in the League. The Assembly was not aware of the implications it would have upon the international community, the League and international law. Japan had long desired the Manchurian territory from Chinese rule, for they feared that 'sooner or later it would be completely merged in that Chinese commonwealth, weak, formless, unorganised, torn by faction.'[131] Some attempts were made to find a peaceful settlement to matters, however the circumstances under which such attempts towards peaceful settlement were made were not feasible nor a realistic solution. Japan was looking to bully their way into gaining the territory of Manchuria and China were helpless to resist the merciless methods of Japanese diplomacy and its military might. Japanese endeavours to settle the dispute through diplomacy was a direct violation of Article 12 of the Covenant, as they sought to settle the dispute by force rather than submitting it to arbitration, judicial decision or examination by the Council. This was the first sign of Japanese conduct dismantling the legal structure and composition of the League.

Unsurprisingly, these attempts for a peaceful settlement paid little difference to the overall dispute as hostilities eventually broke out. It was whilst the Assembly was dealing with the details of Italy's motion for an armaments truce on September 19, 1931, when news came of a Japanese incident in Mukden. Japanese forces swiftly moved through the territory with the Chinese opposition, 'though overwhelmingly superior in numbers,' unable to match 'the Japanese in discipline, moral or equipment.'[132] China lacked confidence in their ability to defend their territory against a vastly superior military force, and subsequently both Chang Hsueh-liang and the Chinese government gave orders to not resist Japan's invasion of Manchuria. Over the following months, Manchuria was successfully under Japan's control, whilst China looked towards international authorities for support and justice. Chinese representatives called

[130] Walters, *supra* note 26, at 467.

[131] Ibid., at 468.

[132] Ibid., at 471.

upon the Council to act with haste on the matter and expressly agreed to whatever decisions the Council would make on the matter.[133] Although Japanese representatives were clearly stalling for time when the matter was brought forward by the League—by requesting a short adjournment—the Council called for both sides to do everything possible to prevent an escalation to hostilities.

The situation was set in a precarious place as the failure to settle the dispute and Japanese conduct would undermine the Kellogg-Briand Pact, the Washington Treaties and the Covenant. The Council set out to establish a Commission of Inquiry,[134] composed of men near to the spot. This was usual custom for the Council, and China had agreed that such a move to be taken immediately, however Japan opposed such a measure. Instead Yoshizawa, the Japanese representative in Geneva, informed the Council that he had received government instruction and was able to submit a formal statement. Yoshizawa stated that there was no military occupation; Japanese forces were reluctantly forced to take minimum precautions against Chinese attacks; Japan had no warlike intentions and no desire for territorial gains; they had already withdrawn most of their troops and intended to withdraw the remaining troops once the lives and property of Japanese subjects in Manchuria were no longer in danger, which it believed would be imminent.[135] Surprisingly, the Chinese representative stated that his government was ready to guarantee the safety of Japanese lives and property. Consequently, Japan had no excuse to not withdraw troops immediately, which would then allow for each party to prepare for negotiations, with the Council present.

Such declarations attempted to establish at least a momentary respite, however during on-going Council sessions, the situation in Manchuria worsened. Japanese forces failed to uphold Yoshizawa's promises, as military activity intensified. The Japanese government became increasingly more hostile as it argued that China's boycott of Japanese goods was a violation of the Kellogg-Briand Pact, and because China was not trying to establish a settlement through pacific means, Japan was entitled to

[133] 'Appeal of the Chinese Government under Article 11 of the Covenant', (1932) 13 *League of Nations Official Journal* 283, at 283–305.

[134] 'Appeal of the Chinese Government under the Covenant', (1932) 13 *League of Nations Official Journal* 956, at 956–957.

[135] 'Seventh Meeting (Public) Sixty-Fifth Session of the Council', (1931) 12 *League of Nations Official Journal* 2304, at 2307–2308.

take such counter-action through whichever means they deemed fitting. The choice of action they followed was a tragic one, as the bombing of Chinchow caused the Council to meet yet again on October 13.[136] The Council was anxious to find an agreement with Yoshizawa as to when Japanese troops would completely withdraw from the territory. However, these attempts to press for a time limit within which Japanese withdrawal was possible failed. Japan was willing to repeat the promises they had made but would not consent to a binding agreement. The Council seemed to be ineffective to settling the dispute and were reluctant to use Article 11 of the Covenant and adopt a more forceful measure to ensure peace and security. Not only was there a sense of reluctance to adopt such a measure, but there was also flaw within the construction of Article 11 which made it difficult to adopt. The League adopted the theory that an effective decision under Article 11 required the consent of all members of the Council, not excluding the Member-State whose aggressive conduct was under scrutiny. Therefore, any impartiality members of the Council would attempt to influence upon the decision-making process could potentially be vetoed by the Member-State whose conduct is attempting to regulate. This subsequently made Article 11 potentially redundant for it was far too easy for Member-States to bypass a crucial legal mechanism to ensure international peace and security. The ill-conceived drafting of Article 11 outlines the central issue of international law in the fact that States possessed too much power, making it permissible for the undermining of utopian focal goals. This phenomenon is most evident when analysing the Manchurian crisis. The Council seemed to be ineffective with curtailing Japanese aggression in Chinese territory, and it seemed that Japan was fully aware of the Member-State's capabilities to dismantle the international legal system.

Whilst the Council failed to negotiate a settlement between Yoshizawa and the Chinese representatives, the fighting intensified, as Japanese forces were ruthless and determined in fulfilling their objectives. More Japanese troops were arriving into the territory and the area of occupation was expanding. Chinese troops did their best to hold back the Japanese assault, however they continued to march on invading Tsitsihar, capital of the Northern Province of Heilungkiang, and also territories south of the Great Wall that had held 'valuable foreign interests.' The Council was

[136] 'Eight Meeting (Public) Sixty-Fifth Session of the Council', (1931) 12 *League of Nations Official Journal* 2309, at 2309–2312.

torn between making two decisions; either accept that it would be unable to deal with the situation or utilise Article 15 of the Covenant, which would allow a decision to be taken without the vote of the parties and would incur the threat of sanctions. The first choice was an option the Council would not take; however, the second option was deemed too dangerous to consider. Such a move would run the risk of a greater escalation in violence; a situation that the Council would find even harder to control.

It was at this point that Yoshizawa proposed that the League should send a Commission of Inquiry to investigate the situation both in Manchuria and China. The Lytton Commission set off for the Far East on February 3, 1932.[137] However, the establishment of this Commission of Inquiry was slow, and to the detriment of the League and the dispute. The crisis had lasted three months and the 'League had already suffered a severe loss of prestige and public confidence.'[138] Once the beacon of a brighter and peaceful future, the League was now facing claims of futility. It seemed unable to prevent hostilities and the frailties of the international legal system that it had established were becoming increasingly evident. Before the Lytton Commission had even set off for the Far East, the dispute had ascended to greater levels of violence, as heavy fighting broke out in Shanghai. The Chinese did their utmost to mount a defence against such an invasion, yet it was to no avail as Japanese forces were victorious. It was a brutal attack as the Japanese campaign began by bombing the densely populated Chinese district Chapei, resulting in the deaths of thousands of civilians.[139] The Chinese continued to fight on against the ever-ruthless Japanese forces. They used their naval and air might—combined with their heavy artillery—to continue their advancement upon Chinese territory until the early days of March when an armistice was finally arranged. As the Council session had opened January 25, the news of the conflict had seeped through and for the first time the Council had utterly lost confidence in its own ability to ensure international peace and security.[140] The Council and its members seemed resigned to the fact

[137] 'Nineteenth Meeting (Public) Sixty-Fifth Session of the Council', (1931) 12 *League of Nations Official Journal* 2371, at 2374–2376.

[138] Walters, *supra* note 26, at 483.

[139] Ibid., at 484.

[140] 'Second Meeting (Public) Sixty-Sixth Session of the Council', (1932) 13 *League of Nations Official Journal* 326, at 327. Chinese representative Yen Hui-Ch'ing: 'At the

that it was unable to alter the cause of the events and steer the Far East towards a peaceful settlement.

Having witnessed the inadequacies of the Council, the Assembly attempted to step up and take hold of the Sino-Japanese situation. It was China that had brought the issue before the Assembly, who had responded by calling for the withdrawal of Japanese forces in Chinese territory. The Assembly went further to stress that Japan's conduct was contrary to the spirit of the Covenant and a settlement of the dispute through peaceful means should be found immediately. They set about establishing a special Committee to help bring about a definitive armistice in Shanghai and took over from the Council as it displayed 'weakness and hesitation' regarding the whole matter. A stark criticism of the Council was the fact that it was leaderless, as both Britain and France had failed to take command of the matter. It was another indication as to the importance of the State for the workings of the international law. If States were unwilling to dedicate themselves to ensuring the successful operation of international law, it undermined the utopian goals that were an integral part of the legal system. The Council's failings to reconcile the conflict between China and Japan demonstrate this. The frailties of international law become apparent and gaping once States display a lack of commitment to the functioning of the legal system.

Nevertheless, before the Committee, set up by the Assembly, could begin working on resolving the conflict, it needed to wait until the

very outset China had the choice between preparing for her own defence and placing her faith in treaties and in the League. China today is not a military nation. She chose to come to the League, especially when it was in session. This Council has patiently and earnestly devoted six weeks of its time at twenty meetings to a conscientious effort to adjust the matter. Two resolutions have been unanimously passed. Each one of them was predicated upon a solemn promise by Japan to withdraw her troops as rapidly as possible. The promise has-been broken. In place of progressive withdrawal, there has been progressive advance. Since the Council adjourned six weeks ago the aggression has been relentlessly continued until, in the words of the American Secretary of State, "the last remaining administrative authority of the Government of the Chinese Republic in South Manchuria, as it existed prior to September 18th, 1931, has been destroyed" Chinchow and the territory to the south including Shanghaikwan have gone the way of Mukden, Changchun, Antung, Yinkow, Kirn, Tsitsihar and a score of other cities. Japan is now invading the province of Johol, hundreds of miles from the railway from Mukden to Peiping, and endangering cities in north, central, and even south China, as witness the latest threats to occupy Foochow, Tsmgtao and Shanghai points far away from the borders of what hitherto has been known as Manchuria.'

report of the Lytton Commission had been received. This was considered to be the basis upon which proposals could be made for settlement. The report took till September 4 to be signed by the Lytton Commission and brought to Geneva to be 'translated and printed with every precaution of secrecy.'[141] The report contained a detailed account of the situation before and after the invasion of Manchuria, stating not only the unsatisfactory administration of the Chinese government before invasion but also how the Japanese had regulated Manchuria once it had aggressively procured the territory. Furthermore, the report went on to describe the battle of Shanghai alongside covering the economic interests of both Japan and China in regard to Manchuria. It was to no surprise that the report had confirmed Chinese allegations of the unlawfulness of Japanese conduct under international law. The Commission stated that the operations of Japanese forces following the Mukden incident could not be regarded as legitimate measures of self-defence. The report also rejected the claim that formation of the Manchukuo resulted from an unprompted independence movement by inhabitants of the territory. The Commission recommended that a new administrative arrangement be found for Manchuria that would be consistent with the principle of Chinese sovereignty and continued to protect Japan's invested interests and rights within the territory.[142] The Assembly supported such findings and it became the basis upon which future policies would be set in regard to the dispute.

In the face of the Lytton Commissions report, Japan did its best to delay proceedings within the Assembly as they avoided having to reply to the suggested means of the resolution proposed by the Commission. However, it was when the Special Committee—established by the Assembly—submitted a statement to the Assembly on the basis of the Lytton report, that Japan could no longer stall proceedings. F.P Walters accurately assessed the statement and the impact it had to the League's ability to settle the dispute:

> [The statement] adopted the whole of the description therein contained of the events which had led up to the clash of September 18th, 1931, and of

[141] Walters, *supra* note 26, at 490–491.

[142] S. Wilson, 'The Manchurian Crisis and Moderate Japanese Intellectuals: The Japan Council of the Institute of Pacific Relations', (1992) 26(3) *Modern Asian Studies* 507, at 508.

> those which had followed it- the occupation of Manchuria, the battle of Shanghai, the founding of the new State of Manchukuo. It recapitulated the efforts, the hopes, and the disappointments of the Council. It did not omit the failures of Chinese policy before the conflict began, but vindicated her action since that date, and left no doubt as to Japan's violation of the Covenant. It set forth its recommendations for a just settlement in the terms of the Lytton Commission's proposals, maintaining above all that Manchuria was in China's sovereignty and that the new State was neither legally constituted nor representative of the will of its inhabitants. It called on the two parties to open negotiations for carrying out the settlement thus recommended, with the help of a Committee set up by the Assembly. (This Committee was practically speaking a continuation of the Special Committee itself). Finally it affirmed that the Members of the League would not recognise the new State either de jure or de facto, nor do anything else that might prejudice the execution of the Assembly's recommendations.[143]

The Assembly subsequently adopted the statement on February 24, 1933. Japan responded in the most dramatic of fashions as it walked out of the Assembly meeting, and a month later on March 27, 1933, they had formally announced its decision to withdraw from the League of Nations.[144] With this declaration of withdrawal the League were no longer able to actively intervene in the Manchurian conflict.

It was the first time that the League had failed in such emphatic fashion to ensure international peace and security. The Covenant had been rendered useless in successfully dealing with the conflict. The Washington Treaties and Kellogg-Briand Pact also were unable to impose any possible prevention of hostilities. It became clear how fragile the system of international law truly was. The over-reliance upon the State to ensure the functioning of international law was the system's greatest undoing. The idealism that inspired the League of Nations model of international law believed in the idea that all States wanted to maintain international peace and security. Hence why the system was constructed around the State being the primary subject and object of international law. It was based in the belief that following the horrors of the Great

[143] Walters, *supra* note 26, at 494.

[144] 'Notification by the Japanese Government of Its Intention to Withdraw from the League of Nations', (1933) 14 *League of Nations Official Journal* 657, at 657–658.

War, States would commit themselves fully in ensuring that the international community does not fall into societal, political and economic instability once more and that objectives of emancipatory idealism would be achieved. However, the idealistic conception of international law that drew influence from achieving the central aims of emancipatory idealism was undermined when States realised that their lack of compliance bore no detrimental repercussions to themselves. Japan demonstrated how States undermined international law to the detriment of emancipatory idealism. Japanese conduct in the Far East region not only led to mass political, societal and economic instability, but there was no justice to be found for the victims who had suffered during the conflict. Moreover, the members of the Council had turned their back on the League and undermined international law by adopting a policy of protectionism. More concerned by their own internal situations, States playing a more influential role in the international community had allowed for the dismantling of the international legal system that had been dealt by the hand of Japan. This defeat of the League proved to be a pivotal moment not only for its own downfall, but for also highlighting the persistent weakness of international law, that being the position of the State in the legal system.

4.4.4 Abyssinian Crisis

The Manchurian crisis had begun to set a precedent regarding the League. Following its attempts to deal with the Sino-Japanese conflict, the League's reputation was tainted by the inability to regulate aggressive Japanese conduct, as all its legal instruments to ensure international peace and security were blunted by the primacy of the State. However, an opportunity had arisen for the League to reclaim some reputation lost. When Mussolini sought out to realise Italy's colonial ambitions, targeting Ethiopia as the country that would fall prey to such desires, the League faced another attack that threatened to disrupt international peace and security.

It was in the year 1933 that Mussolini began to strategise how to annex the whole of Ethiopia and prepare for war. With Fascism gripping the Italian nation fervently, the plans were set to create disaffection and disorder in Ethiopia. Military plans were established, with money being provided to bribe Ethiopia and for road making in Eritrea. By the end of 1934, Italy was ready to make its move. When the opportunity would arise, Mussolini was prepared to quickly react and deploy its well-planned annexation. The opportunity came on December 5, 1934, when there was a clash in Wal-Wal, which was a disputed area between Italian Somaliland and the Ogden province of Ethiopia. Over 100 Ethiopians and 30 Italian troops were killed and it was considered a serious enough incident with the possibility of more detrimental consequences. Italy deftly appropriated the circumstance to conceal their real purpose of annexation. The Ethiopian government proposed to the Italian government that Article 5 of the Italo-Ethiopian Treaty of Conciliation and Arbitration should be enacted. In response to such a proposition Italy declined the request for an arbitral decision. This subsequently and immediately led Ethiopia to address the Secretary-General in order to inform the League of the case of hostilities at the Wal-Wal.

By January 3, 1935, matters had become increasingly more hostile as Italy gathered troops before the Ethiopian post of Gerlogubi. With Ethiopian troops killed and Italian planes constantly flying over the territory, there was definitive reason for concern. Ethiopia requested an application of Article 11 of the Covenant, that every measure be taken to safeguard peace.[145] By January 19, however, both Italian and Ethiopian representatives in the League formally stated their desire to the Secretary-General for the application of the procedure stated under Article 5 of the Italo-Ethiopian Treaty instead of mediation under Article 11 of the Covenant.[146] It was clear that Ethiopia were open to any method to settle the dispute, however, it was initially unclear as to why Italy had backtracked in regard to the use of the Italo-Ethiopian Treaty. It was a strange manoeuvre from the Italians considering the fact that Mussolini believed it beneath his dignity to submit the dispute before arbitration. Italian representatives had indicated 'that discussion of the dispute before the Council might prejudice the outcome of the direct negotiations being pursued by the parties to the dispute.'[147] However, all matters and intentions became clear two months later when Ethiopia argued that the Italian government was deliberately preventing a successful

[145] 'Annexes', (1935) 16 *League of Nations Official Journal* 193, at 252.

[146] 'Eight Meeting (Public) Eighty-Fourth Session of the Council', (1935) 16 *League of Nations Official Journal* 161, at 162–163.

[147] J.H. Spencer, 'The Italian-Ethiopian Dispute and the League of Nations', (1937) 31.4 *AJIL* 614, at 616.

outcome when they were demanding reparations.[148] Furthermore, the Italian government declined the offer of mediation by a third Power and they were in direct violation of the Italo-Ethiopia Treaty and the agreement made before the Council on January 19 when Italian troops had been mobilised on to Ethiopian frontiers. It was apparent that Italy's conduct deliberately created obstacles to achieving a dispute settlement. Consequently, the Ethiopian government requested that the dispute be brought before the Council in its whole entirety on the basis of Article 15 of the Covenant.[149] The Italian government responded by rejecting the use of Article 15 for the dispute in question and for the Council to influence matters. The Italian government contended that the stage of ordinary diplomatic negotiations specified in Article 5 of the Italo-Ethiopian Treaty had not yet been exhausted, 'and even if that were the case, there remained still the further procedure (conciliation and arbitration) provided for by the article.'[150]

The dispute was playing out over an elongated period of time in the Council with both parties making several claims about the other. With Italy's latest response, Ethiopia affirmed that direct negotiations were failing and for this reason, processes of conciliation and arbitration should be evoked. However, with conciliation being a profitless endeavour, it seemed more suitable for parties to seek a process of arbitration to resolve matters. Such a process appeared not only as an effective method for resolution, but it was also in the spirit of the Italo-Ethiopia Treaty. By March, the Ethiopian government had communicated with the Secretary-General, outlining Italy's failure to agree to calls for a resolution through arbitration. They implored the Council to react to Italy's violation of the Covenant and obligations under the Italo-Ethiopia Treaty. It was then when the Council responded with the adoption of two resolutions on May 25, 1935. The first resolution confirmed that direct negotiations under the Italo-Ethiopia Treaty had been exhausted and both parties should conclude processes of conciliation and arbitration by August 25, 1935.[151]

[148] 'First Meeting (Private) Eighty-Fifth (Extraordinary) Session of the Council', (1935) 16 *League of Nations Official Journal* 546, at 546.

[149] 'Annexes-Notes of the Ethiopian Government of March 16th and 17th 1935', (1935) 16 *League of Nations Official Journal* 569, at 571–572.

[150] Spencer, *supra* note 148, at 618.

[151] 'Fifth Meeting (Public) Eighty-Sixth Session of the Council', (1935) 16 *League of Nations Official Journal* 639, at 640.

The second resolution specified that if the four arbitrators for the settlement of the dispute had not reached an agreement on the dispute or selected a fifth arbitrator by July 25, the Council would meet again to discuss matters in regard to the dispute.[152] Furthermore, the second resolution also held that if the dispute were not resolved through conciliation and arbitration by the August 25, the Council would meet in order to examine the situation.

With the resolutions in mind the Ethiopian representatives specifically asked Italy to confirm their agreement to the proposals set forth by the Council and to not send additional troops, munitions or specialists to East Africa. The Italian response was not the one that Ethiopia or the Council were hoping for. During the months of June, July and August various negotiations took place that were unsuccessful as it was apparent that Italy was doing all that was in its power to stall proceedings and avoid a peaceful resolution. The League was struggling to contain the ambitions of a Fascist Italy. With this predicament, the League was also hesitant on dealing with the issue. They allowed a constant postponement of negotiations, killing any momentum gained towards a resolution. Integral members, such as France and Britain, showed a reluctance to face Italy's aggressive conduct and the Council's generally slow deliberation on matters.

By July 25, it was clear that the Council would be required to examine the situation. When the Council held a special meeting, no mention was made of the increasing concern of war—apart from the Ethiopian delegate who did voice his concerns on such a possibility—as discussions were strictly focused on the Wal-Wal arbitration. Despite such an exclusion of matters external to the Wal-Wal dispute, the Council did adopt a resolution to meet on September 4, to discuss the whole question of Italo-Ethiopian relations. By September 3, the Commission of Arbitration adjudicated its final award. The decision was that neither Italy nor Ethiopia was held responsible for the Wal-Wal incident on December 5, 1934. Consequently, there was no international liability to be incurred for the events discussed. The following day the Council met to discuss the whole question of the Italo-Ethiopian conflict, which was in conformity with the resolution adopted in August. Before the meeting took place, Mussolini had spent many speeches ridiculing the League and declaring

[152] Spencer, *supra* note 148, at 618.

Italian defiance to its work openly. Thus, when he sent Italian representatives to Geneva, Mussolini had sent him instructions to justify its aggressive conduct on Ethiopian frontiers before the League. Now that the Wal-Wal incident had been resolved according to the Council, Italy claimed that there was nothing further for them to discuss. As soon as the Council had opened the meeting, Italian representatives presented a memorandum with wide array of maps, photograph and annexes to justify their claim against Ethiopia. The Italian representative went further as he declared that 'Italy was reluctantly forced to consider Ethiopia beyond all question her enemy; as a barbarous State whose signature could not be trusted; and as no longer entitled to claim the rights of the League membership or the benefits of the Treaty of Friendship. It had been a mistake ever to admit her to the League.'[153]

Moreover, the contents of the memorandum were also concerning for those who sought to maintain international peace and security. The memorandum asserted that Ethiopia had failed to carry out its treaty obligations towards Italy. According to Italy, Ethiopia had prevented the delimitation of its frontiers with Eritrea and Somalia. Although both parties had signed the Treaty of Friendship, Italy claimed that Ethiopia had blocked all Italian attempts to acquire land, to carry on mining or other commercial activities, or to even collaborate in the administrative or technical development of the country. Furthermore, the memorandum outlined a number of 'outrages against Italian diplomats and consuls, injustices to Italian subjects, [and] raids across the frontiers of the Italian colonies.'[154] The outrages were trivial as petty thefts or discourtesies to the more serious incidents of murder and large-scale robbery. Thirdly, Italian representatives argued that Ethiopia was in fact incapable of being a member of the League for it was not an organised State. Initially, there was the ancient State of Abyssinia, however, this State had 'subdued and annexed vast countries outside its borders, inhabited by peoples of other races, languages and religions.'[155] The Ethiopia in question was a ruling minority that was contained and controlled by cruel techniques. 'Flourishing lands had been laid waste, peaceful tribes had been enslaved and

[153] Walters, *supra* note 26, at 642.

[154] Ibid., at 642.

[155] Ibid., at 643.

almost exterminated.'[156] According to Italy it was a 'duty of civilisation' to liberate these oppressed people. Fourthly, Ethiopia had been permitted to become a member of the League on the condition that they would abolish slavery. Italian representatives stressed the fact that Ethiopia had failed to meet such a condition and they had done little to commit to such a demand.[157] Another section of the memorandum dealt with the traffic in arms. Ethiopia's admission to the League was also based on a secondary condition that they would conform to the principles of the Convention of St. Germain, which stipulated that arms should not be sold to any unauthorised persons. Yet such a condition had not been carried through by Ethiopia for the Emperor Haile Selassie, had sold large quantities of arms and ammunition to his personal followers.[158] Italy's memorandum gave a detailed account as to why Ethiopia was not a suitable member of the League as it was unable to carry out its duties as a member of the organisation. In the light of this Italy contended that they were not violating the Covenant, in fact they were 'defending the prestige and the good name of the League of Nations.'[159]

Italy had played a clever game. Initially, the view had been that Ethiopia was the victim, yet the memorandum skilfully tipped such a perspective on its head to outline Ethiopia as a perpetrator of many violations of international law. Regardless of such a game, the ploy was unsuccessful as many of the claims made by the Italian representatives were not entirely accurate and in fact unfair. The memorandum had detailed Ethiopia's shortcomings without noting the Emperor's plans for

[156] Ibid.

[157] 'First Meeting (Private, Then Public) Eighty-Eighth Session of the Council', (1935) 16 *League of Nations Official Journal* 1132, at 1137. Italian representative Baron Aloisi: 'While the League Covenant states that the wellbeing and development of backward peoples form "a sacred trust of civilisation" while the treaties lay down the fundamental guarantees to be required of Governments Members of the League of Nations and the International Labour Office in order to ensure a minimum of rights, well-being and equitable treatment for all their nationals, the terrible scourge of slavery still exists in Ethiopia. Whole populations of vast areas conquered by her in the past fifty years are still decimated by raids and subjected to slavery in all its cruellest forms. Civilised nations must refuse friendship with a State which allows such customs to continue. To claim that Members of the League are bound to observe the rules of the Covenant in their relations with a Member who has always persistently failed to observe them is contrary to every principle of right and justice.'

[158] Walters, *supra* note 26, at 643.

[159] Ibid., at 644.

reform. Such plans for reform were not only genuine but also proving to be successful. Furthermore, it was known that much of the Italian grievances were its own doing, as they had secretly been encouraging local chieftains to defy the centralised government. Also, even if the entire contents of the memorandum had been completely accurate, it could not justify Italy's actions to engage Ethiopia in a war. Moreover, Italy had violated the Covenant already by persistently refusing to allow the Council to deal with the substance of the dispute.

With the Council dissatisfied with Italy's memorandum, they decided to set up a Committee of Five—Britain, France, Poland, Spain and Turkey—to seek out a peaceful settlement.[160] The Committee of Five was firmly focused on ensuring conciliation between the two parties and subsequently drafted a report on methods of resolving the dispute effectively. The proposals brought forward by the Committee of Five were for both parties to recognise the public services in Ethiopia. The proposals went further to suggest that there should be 'certain territorial exchanges between Ethiopia and Italy in the region of the Somaliland Coast.'[161] France and the UK also consented to recognise a special Italian interest in the economic development of Ethiopia. Many of these proposals were based on the one hand to resolve the dispute in a manner in which Ethiopia felt that that justice was guaranteed for the strife they had endured, but also on the other hand to not create any animosity between the League and its central members with Italy. The central members of the Council in particular did not want to lose Italy as an ally nor did they want to insult or infuriate Mussolini any further, who was increasingly becoming an unpredictable and somewhat dangerous figure within the international community. Nevertheless, Italy rejected such a process of conciliation under such terms even though Ethiopia had agreed.

Conciliation processes had clearly failed, and the first steps were taken towards the application of sanctions, under Article 15, paragraph 4. The Council set up a Committee of Thirteen—encompassing representatives from all members of the Council—to draft a report on the facts of the dispute and final recommendations for a settlement.

[160] 'Third Meeting (Private, then Public) Eighty Eighth Session of the Council', (1935) 16 *League of Nations Official Journal* 1143, at 1145.

[161] Spencer, *supra* note 148, at 622.

It was seemingly becoming a repetition of the League's dealings with Japan. States' expansionist and realist interests undermined the reason behind assembling the League. The likes of Japan and Italy became aware of their ability to undermine the international legal system and utopian focal goals. Moreover, such States were not afraid of violating international law to seek out their own interests. Italy at every turn defied the League and undermined international law by continuing their conflict with Ethiopia. However, in order to seek out their interest it was a risk Italy was willing to take as the frailties of the international legal system were becoming increasingly more apparent. This was proven on September 25; when in response to Ethiopian mobilisation beyond the thirty-kilometre zone, Italian troops had entered Ethiopian territory, as Mussolini had ordered for operations to commence. The Italian government had informed the Council that they had to take the necessary measures for defence. A few hours later, Ethiopian representatives had informed the Council that the Italian army had crossed the frontier and Italian planes had begun bombing Ethiopian territories.

In light of the escalation in hostilities the Council issued its report on October 5. The report ultimately rejected the Italian justification for the invasion of Ethiopian territory, in a manner that was purposefully polite. It asserted that the Covenant, the Kellogg-Briand Pact, the 1928 Treaty of Friendship and the Optional Clause of the Statute of the Permanent Court were for both parties, solemn undertakings, prohibited the resort to arms.[162] If Ethiopia had been seen as violating its obligations, then it was for the Council to decide the next course of action. Such a decision was not given to a sole State to decide how to deal with such violations. It was a successful moment for the Council as such a judgement had represented the collective decisions of thirteen Member-States 'who were anxious to view Italian policy in the most favourable [manner] possible'[163] but in fact had achieved a decision that was the complete antithesis of their desires. This decision was successful in ensuring that the utopian goals of international law were safeguarded. In this instance, States had placed that objective before its own alliances with Italy, irrespective of the fact that they wanted to ensure such a relationship would remain a

[162] 'Fifth Meeting (Private, then Public) Eighty-Eighth Session of the Council', (1935) 16 *League of Nations Official Journal* 1209, 1209–1213.

[163] Walters, *supra* note 26, at 653.

healthy one. Unsurprisingly, Ethiopia voted for such a report, whilst Italy voted against it. Nevertheless, their votes were not to be recognised, so that the report was unanimously adopted. On the day that the report was presented, the Council proceeded to set up a Committee of Six—UK, Chile, Denmark, France, Portugal and Romania—to evaluate the report of the Committee of Thirteen in light of the recent hostilities that had broken out. The report of the Committee of Six was quick to respond with the declaration that:

> The Members of the League are not entitled without having first complied with the provisions of Articles 12, 13, and 15, to seek remedy by war for grievances they consider they have against other Members of the League. The adoption by a State of measures of security on its own territory and within the limits of its international agreements does not authorise another State to consider itself free from obligations under the Covenant... After an examination of the facts stated above, the Committee had come to conclusion that the Italian Government has resorted to war in disregard of its covenants under Article 12 of the Covenant of the League of Nations.[164]

Such a conclusion bore great significance as the fact that the Committee deliberately reiterated the opening words of Article 16 implied that verdict was not just a verdict on Italy's claim to war. It went further to confirm that the acceptance of such a verdict meant that it was their legal duty to apply sanctions. Both members of the Council and the Assembly voted to apply sanctions. Of course, Italy voted against such measures, but so did Albania, Austria and Hungary. These countries did so on a basis of not wanting to violate their allegiance with Italy.

A new Committee of Sixteen (later to become a Committee of Eighteen) was established and by October 11, the new Committee had met and taken its first substantive decision to prohibit the export of arms to Italy. By October 14, proposals for such sanctions were expanded to the prohibition on the importation of Italian goods, and exports to Italy. On October 31, the Committee of Coordination decided to confirm that November 18 would be the date when such sanctions outlined in proposals III and IV made by the Committee of Eighteen would be

[164] 'Seventh Meeting (Public) Eighty-Ninth Session of the Council', (1935) 16 *League of Nations Official Journal* 1125, at 1226.

implemented.[165] The effects of these sanctions were being felt by Italy, as they endured economic strain coupled with the Italian public's disappointment with the lack of resounding success in regard to the annexation of Ethiopia. Public opinion strongly supported the League's measures to apply sanctions even though the likes of the United States, France, Switzerland and UK protesting against the loss of business.

It seemed to be that the current situation saw the League in the stronger position, so much so that although the Committee of Eighteen had decided to go forward with the application of sanctions, conversations were on going between France, UK and Italy with the objective of reaching a settlement of dispute. Mussolini reached out to French Prime Minister Pierre Laval as he threatened to leave the League and move troops to the French frontier. Such a brash statement however caused little concern on Laval's part, as he was still committed to help Mussolini and Italy. Whilst discussions were being conducted between the three nations, the Sanctions Committee was to meet before the end of November to consider the possibility of applying further sanctions. UK and France at this time were also expected to announce 'their individual willingness to stop all their own exports of coal, steel, and oil to Italy, and thereafter to take a joint decision on behalf of the Members of the League as a whole.'[166] There was especially greater pressure for the embargo on the exports of oil to Italy as the fighting that was taking place in Ethiopia saw the Italians fighting in planes, tanks and other such mechanical means of transport. If Italy's supply of oil had been cut, they would have been forced to eventually retreat.

Although the Committee of Eighteen were to be summoned on November 28, Laval had requested a postponement of such a meeting, and it was subsequently rescheduled for December 12. During this time Laval, with the British Secretary of State for Foreign Affairs, Samuel Hoare, secretly developed a plan that consisted of two proposals. Firstly, the Hoare-Laval plan proposed the exchange of territories, which 'consisted of the cessation by Ethiopia to Italy of three areas, two in the north contiguous to Eritrea, one in the south-east contiguous to Somalia.'[167]

[165] Proposal III prohibited the imports of Italian goods, whilst proposal IV provided an embargo on exports to Italy.

[166] Walters, *supra* note 26, at 667.

[167] Ibid., at 669.

All together this would be 60,000 square miles of land transferred over to Italy. In return, Ethiopia would be given an outlet to the sea through the cessation by Italy of some 3,000 square miles in the South-east corner of Eritrea. If Mussolini had refused such a proposition, then an equivalent area would be taken from French or British Somaliland and given to Ethiopia. The second proposal was that the whole southern half of Ethiopia should be 'a zone of economic expansion and settlement reserved to Italy.' This specified zone was to remain under Ethiopian sovereignty and administration; however, Italy would oversee such an administration whilst it exclusively enjoyed the rights of economic exploitation, the right of ownership of unoccupied territories and the unlimited rights of immigration and settlement within the region.

When this plan was made public on December 10, it was met with widespread shock and anger. Firstly, the fact that such a plan had so heavily favoured Italy and robbed Ethiopia of so much land was a major outcry of injustice. Leading up to the unveiling of the Hoare-Laval plan, the League had seen Italy as the perpetrator that violated the Covenant and the applications for sanction under Article 16 of the Covenant were being promoted to ensure international peace and security. For the Hoare-Laval plan to completely reverse that cause of action and instead applaud Italy for such a violation of international law was a major setback to achieving the utopian goals of international law. Moreover, the League's initial position to apply sanctions was symbolic of the international organisation tackling the growing concern that Fascism had become to the international community. It was clear that both the UK and France had gone on to pursue their own personal agenda to ensure healthy relations with Italy. By December 11, the plans were delivered to Italian representatives, whilst the Ethiopian representatives received the plans on December 12. The Ethiopian government without much surprise disapproved the Hoare-Laval plans. On the same day, the Ethiopian government requested that the Assembly be convened for a debate on such proposals. However, much to the Ethiopian government's disappointment, the Secretary-General had stated that the Assembly would await the outcome of the debate in the Council, as the dispute had been submitted before it.

Both France and the UK had undermined the goal of achieving utopian focal goals. Their actions were inconsistent with the Covenant and furthermore had inadvertently further persecuted the victim of such a conflict. Such a manoeuvre had had longer lasting implications as it demonstrated how easily States could manipulate the international legal order for their own interest. The proposal of the Hoare-Laval plan outlined that the States' position as the primary object and subject of international law can be an obstacle to achieving the utopian goals of international law. If utopian goals are contrary to the objectives of the more influential States, undermining utopian focal goals can occur with relative ease.

With Ethiopia's disapproval of the Hoare-Laval plan, Mussolini and the Italian press severely criticised Ethiopian behaviour. Mussolini claimed that had Ethiopia not objected to the plan so strongly, Italy may have accepted it. Although the plan had been rejected by both parties to the conflict—as it had proven unfavourable with the Members of the League and was also dropped by the UK and French government—it had managed to postpone any extension of sanctions. This was precisely what the UK, France and especially Italy had hoped for. The Hoare-Laval plan had also shaken the confidence and unity of the League and now the Members had become unsure on the direction they would take. By December 18, it was clear that the Hoare-Laval plans would not be utilised and the following day the Committee of Eighteen had postponed any consideration of an embargo on oil. The next regular session of the Council was on January 20, and Ethiopia took this opportunity to demand, without any more delays, further sanctions. Ethiopia also referred back to the request submitted on January 3, that a committee of inquiry should be established to investigate the alleged *ius in bello* violations as well as the request for financial assistance made on November 1, 1935. On the basis of financial assistance, the Council were quick to reject such a request. Furthermore, the Committee of Thirteen declined to respond to Ethiopian demands for further sanctions and that such measures would be supervised and considered by the Coordination Committee and the Committee of Eighteen.[168] The Committee of Eighteen decided to establish a Sanctions Committee to investigate the technical aspects of a possible embargo on oil. On February 12, the Sanctions Committee reported that such an embargo would likely take approximately three to four months to be effective. The report of the

[168] Spencer, *supra* note 108, at 629.

Sanctions Committee was taken into account as the Committee of Eighteen decided to meet on March 2, in order to decide upon the adoption of such an embargo.

Whilst in Geneva discussions continued on, with the situation in Ethiopia heavily tilted in Italy's favour. Italian forces were ruthless as they advanced deeper into Ethiopian territory with the 'use of dum-dum bullets; [the] bombing of open towns; and deliberately attacking field hospitals from the air.'[169] Italian forces used gas bombs and shells, however worst of all was the use of mustard gas, which not only affected both armies but also the Ethiopian women and children. With the situation in Ethiopia growing more harmful for the international community, the Council decided to reassert the focus on bringing a peaceful end to the war through conciliation—a strategy proposed by French representatives. However, the Committee of Thirteen had previously stated that conditions were not ideal for a successful process of conciliation. Nevertheless, on March 3 a meeting of the Committee of Thirteen took place, which led to the message being relayed to both parties for 'an urgent appeal for the immediate opening of negotiations in the framework of the League and in the spirit of the Covenant with a view to the prompt cessation of hostilities and the definite restoration of peace.'[170] On March 5, the Ethiopian government replied to such a call for negotiations by agreeing 'to the opening of negotiations, subject to the provisions of the Covenant being respected.' Italy agreed to the same on March 8, however, their agreement to open negotiations seemed to possess a tentative outlook on the potential of such proceedings.

Yet at this time, reports came into Geneva confirming that Germany had denounced the Locarno Treaties, which unfortunately diverted the League's attention towards this matter. This meant that the proposed date set to examine the conflict was pushed back from March 10 to March 23. During this period, where the League's attention was elsewhere, reports came in indicating that Italy and Ethiopia had conducted direct negotiations to settle their dispute. On June 29, Italy had submitted a memorandum to the Assembly that they had 'attempted to establish confidential contacts, which took place at Athens and Jibuti between

[169] Walters, *supra* note 26, at 767–677.

[170] 'Annexes', (1936), 17 *League of Nations Official Journal* 395, at 395.

delegations of the two parties.'[171] To this Ethiopia responded by stating that they were not interested in any form of dispute settlement unless the League was present and that such proceedings would be negotiated within the framework of the League. When discussion did commence on March 23, and the initial objective of the Committee of Thirteen Chairman, Madariaga, was to turn Italy's attention towards their use of gas on the Ethiopian northern front. This had been an issue that Ethiopia had been protesting against for some time and Madariaga felt that this was a matter that needed to be dealt with swiftly before any procedures of dispute settlement could take place. The Chairman was thereupon ready to commence negotiations between the two belligerent parties. The Ethiopian representatives replied swiftly with an assured intention to comply. Italian representatives, on the other hand, requested for more time in order to make a request to their government to designate a delegate for such a process of negotiations. This was another example of States postponing and slowing down the processes adopted by the League to deal with matters of peace and security in order to stall their work and achieve success through such a detrimental circumstance for international peace and security. Nevertheless, time was permitted for the Italian government to elect a delegate for such a matter. By April 2, Italy had stated that they were prepared to send a delegate to Geneva immediately after Easter in order to open negotiations with Ethiopia. Moreover, Madariaga was invited to Rome for discussion with the Italian government, to which he agreed. This meeting was unfortunately a consolidation of the fact that the League would fail to ensure peace and security.

With Germany's aggressive behaviour becoming more concerning, especially in the light of their denouncement of the Locarno Treaties, France and Britain wished to keep relations with Italy healthy. This was a key objective for both nations in order to protect themselves from the imminent danger that faced them. France and Britain's approach to the Abyssinian crisis was indicative of States' realist interest undermining the utopian goals of international law in such an emphatic manner that they were willing to carry through such processes regardless of the repercussions. Walters accurately summates how little States would care for international law and the ideals that it attempted to preserve when their own self-preservation was at risk:

[171] 'Annexes' (1936), 17 *League of Nations Official Journal* 15, at 20.

> And if Italy were to be a guarantor of the Franco-German frontier, was it not the height of folly not merely to alienate her good will, but to undermine her resources? Why continue to widen the gulf, sacrificing Italy's old friendship with Britain and new friendship with France, and forcing Mussolini to maintain in Africa the armies and airplanes which might be deployed in defence of the Rhine? All this to satisfy an ignorant and sentimental public opinion, to preserve the independence of a barbarous Empire, to uphold a Covenant whose true purpose was to restrain aggression in Europe. The French government had at least made up its mind: if it had to choose between Mussolini and the League, the League must give way.[172]

The landscape of international relations had changed so much from the times when nations were calling desperately for the establishment of an international organisation. The days when idealism had inspired the need for an international system and the aims of emancipatory idealism influenced the need for safeguards for the international community were long gone. Now came a period when the most influential Members of the League were willing to sacrifice the League for its own security. Mussolini was well aware of the fact that Britain and France were willing to give into his demands and when he met with Madariaga he played a diplomatic game that gave him equal amounts of profit and pleasure. Although he felt a great deal of resentment towards the League, he did not want to officially break away from it, as not only would it deprive Italy of their position to bargain a deal for their best interest, but it would also openly indicate their alliance with Germany. Moreover, Mussolini had no intention to negotiate a peace settlement with Ethiopia. The game Mussolini played with the League, and Britain and France especially, was to delay discussions and processes of dispute settlement so that the Italian armies would be able to successfully annex Ethiopia with little resistance from the international community.

Whilst Madariaga held meetings with Mussolini in Rome, on April 1, the Ethiopian representative submitted to the League—as well as the Committee of Thirteen and Eighteen—a declaration for financial assistance, the removals of obstacles and hindrances placed by several States for Ethiopia's transport of munitions, the reinforcement of sanctions under Article 16 as well as the application of additional sanctions, and finally,

[172] Walters, *supra* note 26, at 678.

urgent representation in Rome to immediately stop the use of the gas on the Ethiopian northern front.

With more delays caused by the Italian representatives, the Committee of Thirteen finally met on April 18 to review the status of the negotiation processes. Following the meeting Madariaga had with Mussolini, he reported to the Committee and later to the Council, that the Council's attempt to negotiate peace between the two parties had failed and any further efforts should be abandoned. Following the Committee of Thirteen's report, the Council met on April 20. Italian diplomat, Pompeo Aloisi, was present for this meeting alongside the Italian representative in the League. The Council were forced to listen to Aloisi proclamations that Italy had suffered injustices at the hands of the League; and that Italy had acted in the spirit of the Covenant.[173] They had brought freedom and civilisation to an Ethiopia, ravaged by a barbarous rule. Aloisi stated that they were ready to negotiate with the presence of the League, however not in Geneva. Furthermore, Ethiopia needed to accept an armistice, which contained the condition that they would agree to a complete occupation. It was even clearer that Italy never intended to negotiate within the framework of the League.[174] Instead of seeking a peaceful resolution, Italy had violated the Covenant, the Kellogg-Briand Pact, the Treaty of Friendship with Ethiopia and the anti-gas protocol.

Yet in light of Aloisi's speech and Italy's disregard for international law, the Council made no attempt to intensify the use of the Covenant to counteract such a violation. Instead, the members of the Council accepted defeat and subsequent calls for reforming the Covenant were made. Such calls for reform proposed that the Covenant should move away from being a system that acts as a defence mechanism against war to simply a system of discussion and consultation. Regardless of such claims, the Council voted to continue applying the sanctions already in place. The Council also pressed Italy on the matter of using gas on the northern front of Ethiopia, to which Italy responded by saying that as Ethiopia had breached *ius cogens*, as they had dishonoured their signature of the 1925 Gas Protocol. The Council rejected such a claim and as much as they continued to press the matter, Aloisi moved the attention away from their

[173] 'Tenth Meeting (Private, Then Public) Ninety-First (Extraordinary) Session of the Council', (1936) 17 *League of Nations Official Journal* 376, at 377.

[174] Walters, *supra* note 26, at 618.

own violations and demanded that the atrocities Ethiopia had committed were not given sufficient attention by the Council.

By this point in time, Italy's annexation plan was in full swing and successful at every turn. By May 2, 1936, Italian forces had invaded the Ethiopian capital and their last organised army was defeated. The loss of Ethiopian lives was monumental. Emperor Haile Selassie was forced to flee the country, whilst some of the Ethiopian people continued to resist unnecessarily. It was evident that the war had been won by Italy. By May 11, the Council received a document from the Italian government, declaring the official annexation of Ethiopia. A further document from Aloisi stressing the fact that there was no longer an Ethiopian State, and any Ethiopian representative should not be permitted to take part in Council sessions. The very same day there was a Council session, yet when Ethiopia took its seat in the Council, Aloisi withdrew himself from the session in protest to such an illegitimate acceptance of the Ethiopian representative.[175] The following day, the Council decided that more time was required to consider the effects of the annexation and agreed to reconvene on June 15. The Council also agreed that the sanctions already in place should continue to be applied. However, it was evident that the League had been defeated and that the sanctions had failed to impact the conflict in the desired way. The Council had also swiftly agreed to leave the matter with the Assembly. The Council agreed that the Assembly should meet on June 30 to discuss the matters at hand.

When the Assembly did meet the Members needed to address two matters in particular. The first was whether there was any justification to continuing the application of sanctions given the circumstances of the conflict. The second issue was on whether the Assembly should recognise Italy's annexation of Ethiopia.

Many members of the Assembly agreed that the sanctions should be lifted, and that the League should accept that the Covenant and the various other legal instruments to ensure international peace and security had failed. Yet there were members in the League who believed that the

[175] 'First Meeting (Private, Then Public) Ninety-Second Session of the Council', (1936) 17 *League of Nations Official Journal* 534, at 535. Baron Aloisi: 'I beg to state that the Italian delegation cannot agree to the so-called Ethiopian representative being present at the Council table. Nothing resembling an organised Ethiopian exists. The only sovereignty in Ethiopia is Italian sovereignty. Any discussion on a dispute between Ethiopia and Italy would accordingly be pointless. I am bound, therefore, not to take part in it.'

sanctions should continue to be applied as it had created a strain on the Italian economy. Although there was much secrecy to the inner political and economic workings of Italy, some Members of the Assembly believed that their breaking point was approaching. Furthermore, 'the purpose of sanctions was to prevent an aggressor from imposing his will by war, and the fact that the victim was no longer able to keep up the fight did not affect the legal or moral obligations of the Members of the League.'[176] If the sanctions still had the possibility of ending threat to international peace and security, then some Members of the Assembly believed that it was their duty to impose such sanctions. For these Members the continuation of such sanctions was for the sake of the international community and the upholding of the utopian goals of international law.

However, it was the resolve of the UK that had failed the possibility of ensuring that sanctions would continue to be applied. The UK had abandoned hope that the League could reprimand Italy and further action would be futile. Consequently, the UK representative recommended to the Assembly that the application of sanctions should not continue. Whilst the UK had recommended the discontinuation of sanctions, France declared that they would agree with any decision that would take place at Geneva. This was the nail in the coffin for the Italo-Ethiopian conflict as the sanctions began to dissolve. Businesses in the UK and France openly made arrangements to resume commercial exchanges with Italy as soon as possible. Eventually the Assembly succumbed to the fact that sanctions should be dropped. By July 6, 1936, the Coordination Committee established that a resolution should be adopted abrogating the sanctions that had been adopted in line with the recommendations made by the Assembly.

In regard to the second matter, the Assembly were leaning towards not recognising the annexation of Italy; with strong voices from Argentina for example stating such a line should be adopted. It was a doctrine that the Assembly and Council had adopted in regard to Manchuria that if territorial change had occurred through force then the League would not recognise such alterations. However, the UK and France were still seeking to appease Mussolini. A resolution was thus drafted that excluded any words, which could potentially bind the Members of the League to the non-recognition of the annexation of Ethiopia. The remaining members,

[176] Walters, *supra* note 26, at 678.

not wanting to worsen the relationship with Italy, were persuaded to agree to such a resolution.

The Abyssinian crisis was one of the greatest defeats of the League of Nations on several levels. Italy's dismantling of the international legal system was so severe that it led to calls for reform. Although the Manchurian Crisis had proven the fragility of the League of Nations' model of international law, what Italy had proven was not only the inability of such a system to ensure international peace and security but the fact that such a system was unable to administer justice to those that suffered at the hands of aggressors. The League was hindered by a series of complicated procedures and postponements, as the number of sub-committees and commissions of experts was counterproductive to resolving the conflict. The Covenant could not muster a defence against such acts of aggression. The use of sanctions was seen as a resounding failure as even though they had been applied worldwide, such measures were not able to prevent the war and quell the aggressor's chances of victory. Even if blame could be placed on the deceit of the Great Powers, it was clear that reform was required. Opinions were that either all Members should be effectively protected against aggression by the safeguards put in place by the Covenant, or the duties of Members should be revised. If the Covenant was unable to protect its Members, the obligations of Member-States should then be more lenient.

This furthermore outlined that if States were unwilling to commit to utopian goals of international law the system would not work. International law was far too dependent upon the voluntary compliance of States for its effectiveness and that States would use international law for the good of the international community as a whole. Smaller States in particular felt that they had been let down by the Great Powers. Such States felt that they could no longer depend upon the League to protect them from aggression. The antics of the Great Powers—with the Hoare-Laval plan, the postponement of oil sanctions, the attempts to capture Italy's favourability after Germany had disregarded the Locarno Treaties and finally the decision to abandon sanctions—were an integral (if not the most intrinsic) reason as to the failure of the League to deal with such a conflict swiftly and effectively. UK and France had been negligent in their responsibilities as the leading States of the League and much criticism circulated around them in particular. Whilst they proceeded to embark on achieving personal gains by deliberately saving Mussolini from defeat, they had sparked the collapse of the League's model of international law.

Every time there were opportunities to establish international peace and security, French and UK activities undermined the work of the League and the powers of the Covenant to neutralise aggression. Perhaps, the most frustrating part of France and UK's behaviour during the Abyssinian crisis was that it was a wasted effort. Their desire to maintain friendly relations with Italy had failed as they had become increasingly more aligned with Germany, pulling away from the rest of Europe. Although Italy did not withdraw from the League, if its allegiance with Germany came into conflict with the work of League, they tended to refuse participation to such proceedings.

The League's failure to deal with the Abyssinian Crisis effectively had serious repercussions for its objective of ensuring the aims of emancipatory idealism as a utopian focal goal. The ambition to ensure the protection of individuals or a community of individuals from acts of hostility or oppression had been jeopardised through the League's failure to deal with the crisis effectively. It had become apparent that international law had been broken down by Italy's strategic games. This not only outlined the shortcomings of the international legal system, but it also marked the degeneration of the international community during this period, leading to World War II.

Emancipatory idealism is underlined by the work of critical theorists and Hegel who suggested that civilisation is constantly seeking to develop itself technologically and sociologically. Not only is the Abyssinian Crisis a direct violation of emancipatory idealism on the basis of the sheer loss of Ethiopian lives, but also it had an adverse effect upon civilisational development. The League's model of international law could not achieve such goals if States were able to undermine it so easily. The protection of individuals, communities and civilisation were unachievable if States were unwilling to comply with international law or ensure that it operated successfully if it did not align with their interests. Subsequently, it became apparent for smaller States that international law would be unable to safeguard their rights if a larger State decided to invade their territories. Similarly, larger States became aware that international law could do little to prevent them from invading territories if they had played a calculated strategy, which both Japan and Italy did respectively. Civilisation was on the verge of another large-scale breakdown and the international legal system in place could seemingly do little to prevent such a phenomenon from reoccurring.

4.4.5 *The League and Lebensraum*

The final failure of the League was one that led to its collapse. This was dealing with Nazi Germany. Not only did German conduct lead to the defeat of the League, but it also sparked off World War II. Already some events have been mentioned above, with Germany withdrawing from the League after the Disarmament Conference, and a brief mention of Hitler's denouncement of the Locarno Treaties. However, it is necessary to delve deeper into how German conduct in the second decade of the League's existence was so pivotal to the failing of international law and the League in achieving utopian focal goals of international.

By 1935, the central powers in Europe had officially declared that a new armaments race had begun following the failure of the disarmament movement and the rise of a State protectionist culture within the international community. For many States this was a direct response to the speed at which Germany's forces were expanding. By March 16, 1935, Germany had established a law that had re-administered conscription and declared that they could not be accused of violating obligations in the Peace Treaty, considering the negligence of the victorious powers, who had refused to carry out their pledge that German disarmament would be followed by their own. The likes of France and the UK were deeply concerned with the manner in which Germany's army grew in size in such a short amount of time. Furthermore, a greater concern was the manner in which Germany had absolutely no regard for the Peace Treaty, and there was no attempt even to comply with the obligations it continued to have under such a treaty. Once Hitler had withdrawn Germany from the League, they approached international law with much disdain, as the system was unable to exercise any effective influence over the actions of the German government.

With such a predicament laid before the League and its members, the Allied nations were left with two options. The first option was to use or threaten to use force in order to reinforce the obligations Germany had under the Peace Treaty. The second option was to accept Germany's recent stance and discuss the control and limitation of armaments with Germany on equal terms. However, the League and its leading members kept with their traditional custom of taking no action, consequently allowing circumstances to drift out of their control.

When eventually the Council met to discuss matters in the Stresa Conference on April 11, 1935, it was a cause for greater concern as to the direction in which the international community was heading. It was UK, France and Italy who had taken part in such a conference. The President was Mussolini, who had no general plan to propose but suggested that Germany should be able to keep their troops, in order to ensure peace and security in Europe. This was done in part in support of their ally Germany and also to give justification for Italy's own expansion and modernisation of forces. Many critics of the Stresa Conference stated that though the conference was largely exploratory in nature, participants failed to deal with issues of particular difficulty. Either the participants chose to overlook such issues completely, such as Austrian independence, for example, or such matters were transferred to a special committee to deal with.[177] The greatest blow to the Council and the League was the manner in which the central powers had undermined the international organisation. The specific Member-States believed that the strengthening of Germany militarily would mean the strengthening of the system of collective security based on the Covenant. The remaining members of the Council felt that the central powers did not believe that the League's proposals would effectively deal with the growing concern of destabilisation in the international society. The three participants of the conference did stress the sanctity of all treaties, however, Italy had already annexed Ethiopia, violating a whole host of treaties along the way and Britain had little interest to ensure treaty compliance if such measures went against its own self-interest. Germany in particular was not to be held back by its treaty obligations and regardless of the Council's condemnations, Germany continued to rearm itself at a rapid pace.

As proof of such disregard, Germany had negotiated an Anglo-German Naval agreement with Britain only a few months after the conference. Germany reconstructed its fleet up to thirty-five per cent of the strength of the British navy, as agreed. This was yet another major violation of the Treaty of Versailles, and it was at this point that France condemned Germany's naval expansion.[178] French dissidence to such an agreement was not for the sake of ensuring international peace and security on a broader scale but more because such expansion would have concerning repercussions to its borders. Such naval rearmament meant that the

[177] H.L. 'The Stresa Conference, (April 1935) 11(2) *Bulletin of International News* 3, at 3.

[178] 'Fifth Meeting (Private) Eighty-Fifth (Extraordinary) Session of the Council', (1935) 16 *League of Nations Official Journal* 546, at 550–551.

French themselves were forced to start a new programme of naval building, in another display of State protectionism. However, such dissidence did not affect the pace at which Germany continued to expand militarily. One of the central reasons as to Germany becoming such a great threat to international peace and security was due to the lack of willingness States showed to ensure that the obligations of the Treaty of Versailles were not violated. It allowed Germany to grow in confidence and to become more daring in testing out the limits to the League's leniency with the violation of international law.

One of the responses of the League to such flagrant violations of international law was the proposal to extend the scope of financial and economic sanctions. This spurred on the creation of the committee to study the practical ways in which sanctions could be applied effectively. Although such a study helped establish sanctions against Italy that had proven initially successful, the Council was brought into disrepute as such measures were deemed worthless. Furthermore, Germany found such a study a reason to intensify its anger towards the League. This created more distance between the League and what it stood for and Germany. The most concerning outcome was the abandoning of the Treaty of Versailles by many Member-States. They were no longer concerned with upholding treaty obligations.

Germany's bitter relationship with international law continued to unfold for the worse. By April 1935, Hitler had renounced the Locarno Treaties and ordered German troops to remilitarise the Rhineland. This was a bold move and although Hitler had made such a grand proclamation, he still remained tentative. He had ordered his troops to retreat if they met any French resistance. Whilst Hitler had accepted the possibility of war, he was not ready to engage in such hostilities just yet. However, German troops met no resistance and such a mission had been a resounding success. No more was it evident that the instruments of the League, the agreements between nations to ensure international peace and security through the use of international law, had been abandoned. Such undermining of international law and the League's powers to ensure healthy relations within the international community had proven decisive and was an integral reason as to why several years later World War II had broken out. The League's failure to deal with both the Manchuria and Abyssinia crises effectively displayed the fragility of the international legal system and such a system's dependence upon the State for it to function effectively. However, the acceptance of Germany's renouncement of the

Locarno Treaties by the major powers had outlined that the commitment towards upholding international law had dissipated. The leading States sought other means to protect its territories and had lost faith with the League's capacity to ensure not only the protection of international peace and security but also utopian focal goals.

These events had caused greater concern for Germany's eastern neighbour, Poland. Germany's attention now turned to the Free City of Danzig. This was a semi-autonomous territory that contained the city of Danzig and several other towns, villages and various settlements. Although this area was not to be owned by either Germany or Poland, the League did protect the region and Poland were given full rights to develop and maintain transportation, communications and port facilities. Whilst there was a Nazi government in the Danzig Volkstag since 1933, they did not have the two-thirds majority required to make constitutional amendments in order to suppress freedom of speech and other liberties as such. However, by 1935, the Nazi party decided to override such constitutional barriers, as they dissolved the Volkstag and pushed through a vote of confidence in Hitler. In order to achieve a successful outcome only the Nazi party were able to broadcast, with any opposition sources prohibited from speaking. Surprisingly such tactics failed to win them the desired two-thirds majority and German opposition was still held at bay for the time being.

Opposition parties were encouraged by the election results, prompting calls for the results to be annulled. They were confident they could win a majority if a new vote was held. However, no such request was granted, and the Nazi government proceeded to disregard as much of the constitution as they had dared, since amendment was no longer possible. Through this turbulent period the League—through the Council—continued to keep its presence within the political workings of Danzig and worked with the Nazi government to hold back their tyranny.[179] But by the summer of 1936, the Council's control began to wilt. Witnessing the League's inability to control Mussolini's conduct in Ethiopia, Hitler had the confidence to defy the will of the Council. He openly declared that it was now time for Danzig to take the first steps towards breaking away from the relationship it had formed with the League. Using Nazi propaganda, an attack was launched at the constitution, expressing that until Hitler had

[179] 'Free City of Danzig Note', (1936) 17 *League of Nations Official Journal* 511, at 511–516.

control of the territory there would be no peace in Eastern Europe. Such use of propaganda had proven successful considering the fact that opinion of the League's presence in Danzig was considered ineffective in regard to establishing a fruitful relationship between the Free City and Poland. However, Nazi presence had seemingly mended relations between the two parties, as Hitler did genuinely seek peace within the region.

When the Council discussed the matter of Danzig on July 4, Nazi representatives chose such a moment to openly attack the League's presence in the region. The spokesman stated that he was not in fact the representative of the Danzig government but the German Reich.[180] He then withdrew himself from such a meeting abruptly. The members of the Council were furious with the humiliation they were forced to endure, however, there were no means through which they could enforce the Danzig government to comply with its obligations. With the Council no longer able to regulate Nazi tyranny, the German government was free to begin violating citizen rights of those within the territory.

With another victory for Nazi Germany against the League, they now pressed to form an alliance with both Italy and Japan, who were both in agreement in regard to the contempt they felt for the League. By November 25, 1936, the Anti-Comintern Pact had been signed by all three parties, which established agreements to combat any Communist ideology that had proven dangerous to their nation. Yet, the real uniting factor for such a pact was the desire to overthrow and defeat the League once and for all. All three States had pulled apart the League with relative ease and looked onwards to bring down the international legal system completely as it remained an obstacle to each States' goals for expansion and territorial dominance. Alliances were being formed as the road to war was becoming ever more apparent. These powers were determined in undermining the League as rearmament intensified at a greater level than ever. With other powers responding to such rearmament in similar fashion, the dream of disarmament had been long lost. Moreover, Italy and Germany both used a propaganda campaign to undermine the League and to bring closer attention to the futility of such an international organisation.

This all the more brought the defeat of the League to be the clear final outcome. All the sides that the League had taken in such conflicts

[180] 'Fifth Meeting (Private) Ninety-Second Session of the Council', (1936) 17 *League of Nations Official Journal* 757, at 762–769.

saw them on the side of the defeated. Be it their support for China against Japanese aggressors, or Ethiopia against Italy, the sides they had backed had been overrun by hostile and ruthless States besieged by their own self-interest. Moreover, by 1937 the principal Members of the League—Britain and France—had shown no sign to reassemble the League from its defeat and press on with ensuring international peace and security. Instead, such members stood in the background as the Axis powers became more confident, arrogant and united. By April 1938, the Axis programme was being carried out with full effect as Italian and German forces were acting in collaboration in issues such as support for General Franco in the Spanish Civil War.

Whilst the Axis powers helped Franco to victory, Hitler had also marched his forces into Austria. They met with no resistance as the Austrian government collapsed. Austria did not even call for support even though the League had asserted that its independence was a vital proponent to ensuring peace in Europe. Nor did the government suggest any appeal should be made to the League, indicating how much faith had been lost in its ability to regulate the international community. Austrian annexation was a clear violation of the Treaties of Peace, yet there was no objection or any calls to establish international peace and security.[181] International Law had been abandoned and Austria was forced to endure Nazi oppression with no access to justice. The League's reputation was severely damaged by this point, as the Council was forced to accept the state of affairs and give only sympathy to the likes of Ethiopia, China and Austria. It had accepted that it could do nothing to prevent these atrocities from occurring and embraced its position as a bystander to such widespread violations of the Covenant and international law in general.

[181] 'Situation of Austria: Declaration by the Mexican Government Note', (1938) 19 *League of Nations Official Journal* 239, at 239. 'In view of the suppression of Austria as an independent State as the result of armed foreign intervention, and since the Council of the League of Nations has not as yet been convened with a view to the application of Article 10 of the Covenant, which requires the Members of the League to respect and preserve as against external aggression the territorial integrity and political independence of all Members, I have the honour, acting on the instructions of the Mexican Government, to transmit to you the following declarations, and to request you to be good enough to bring them to the knowledge of the States Members of the League. The political extinction of Austria, in the form and circumstances in which it has taken place, constitutes a serious infringement of the League Covenant and the established principles of international law.'

Hitler did not stop at the annexation of Austria, as his ambition to press on was swift. His attention now turned immediately to Czechoslovakia. Germany began its advance towards Czechoslovakia in usual fashion, assuring them initially that they would see no hostility in their lands; before a propaganda campaign rallied support for a German assault; until finally such an assault became a reality. Hitler had accused Czechoslovakia of mistreating its German minority. However, Czechoslovakia was bound by the Minorities Treaty, which guaranteed safeguards for the rights Czechoslovakia's German citizens. The League had even possessed the role of overseeing such guarantees, indicating that Hitler's claims were questionable on a factual basis. Czechoslovakia turned to the Council, as had China and Ethiopia for help to settle the matter. However, many of the Member-States were taking precautions of their own for the expected war as the likes of Britain were seeking to free themselves completely of the obligations it had under the Covenant, for example. Many States declared that collective security should be abandoned, as under the current circumstances such a process seemed difficult to maintain. Many Council members believed that it would be a greater disaster to abandon the League completely than simply abandoning Article 16. Regardless, this was still a major defeat for the League, international law and its utopian focal goals. The few safeguards that the League had maintained were slowly dissipating. The Council consequently renounced their duty to save its members from attack, as they sought to expand the Council's capacity to deal with disputes from an early stage instead. The League no longer had the capacity to prevent any threats to international peace and security. This was for Czechoslovakia a major blow for there were no safeguards to its sovereignty if Germany decided to invade it.

Instead Czechoslovakia was forced to abide to the Munich Agreement signed on September 29, 1938, by Germany, France, Britain and Italy. This agreement permitted German annexation of the Sudetenland territory. The principal instigator of such an agreement was British Prime Minister Neville Chamberlain. He sought to appease Hitler in an attempt to prevent the possible breakout of war. Czechoslovakia was not even present for the agreement, however, with no other option apparent to them they were forced to honour such an agreement. Such an event led Russia to believe that Geneva was no longer capable of ensuring peace. Russian assessment was an accurate depiction of the events that had unfolded for the League was broken to the point that such damage was irreversible. It had sealed the end of the League of Nations as Germany invaded Poland on September 1, 1939, with Britain and France declaring war on Germany. This event brought an end to the Council's activity as the war times had brought its operation to a close.

4.5 Conclusion: Death and Rebirth

Although the League of Nations continued to overlook the war period its work had come to a close at the start of World War II. Through its twenty years of existence, it had endured a series of high and lows. It had been championed as the protector of the international community and ridiculed as a useless organisation unable to prevent the unfolding of another war that was far more catastrophic than its predecessor. Certainly the League was a failure, but it is important to remember that it did indeed have some successes. For a period of time, it had ensured international peace and security, quelled several conflicts and brought many nations all over the globe closer than they had ever been before. The utopian focal goals that it sought out to realise had been achieved at times as the aims of emancipatory idealism bore great influence in establishing international peace and security. The League garnered societal progress with the establishment of international laws that would influence its successor to go beyond what had already been achieved and further develop the system.

In fact, the first nine years of the League prove the first hypothesis of this project. Philip Allott's claim in *The Health of Nations: Society and Law Beyond the State* has clear resonance in the utopianism's potential to transform society:

> The health of a society, its degree of well-being, is determined by the ideas which take actual effect in the process of its day-to-day self-constituting as a society. To reform or redeem a society is to change those determining ideas. Our quality of life is a function of the quality of our ideas.[182]

It is in the aspirations of utopianists to protect individuals and groups of individuals from modes of oppression that allowed the international community to 'take power over the human future, to choose the human future, to make the human future conform to our ideals, to our best ideas of what we are and what we might be.'[183] Allott's claims are

[182] P. Allott, *The Health of Nations: Society and Law Beyond the State,* (2005), x.

[183] Ibid.

demonstrated by the development international law underwent during the first decade of the League's existence. The aims of emancipatory idealism manifested in the development of international law from a non-institutionalist Westphalian model to an institutionalist model of international law, the creation of the PCIJ, the Locarno Treaties and the Kellogg-Briand Pact. Such developments demonstrate the significant influence the aims of emancipatory idealism had had during international law's most accelerated phases of development.

Yet, the frailties of international law are most apparent when analysing the destruction of the League at the hands of its very subjects. Outlining the League's failures to achieve utopian focal goals and ensure the protection of all individuals and groups of individuals is a result of States undermining international law. The first nine years the League achieved remarkable feats that were only possible because the most influential States in the international community still felt the pain of World War I and never wanted such an event to repeat itself. The commitment of Member-States saw the international community establish and expand in its operation to ensure international peace and security. When upholding the utopian focal goals of international law was for these States coinciding with their self-interest, no problems arose. It was when a conflict of interest became apparent that the downfall of the first model of international law emerged. It is not just Germany, Italy and Japan to blame for the undermining of the utopian goals of international law. So too are the likes of Britain, France and the United States responsible for the outbreak of war and the failure to achieve utopian focal goals of international law. The societal, economic and political degeneration that ensued is a result of States unable to reconcile their role of ensuring peace in the international society with the responsibility of protecting its own populous.

Certainly, Harold Laski's claim that 'our civilisation is held together by fear rather than good will'[184] has clear resonance when detailing the fragility of State commitment to the League. This fear for States is first and foremost the breakdown of peace and security within its own territory. This is indicative of the protectionist stance States took following the Great Depression. E.H. Carr rightfully affirmed that self-assertion

[184] H. Laski, *A Grammar of Politics*, (1925), 20.

cannot be removed from political life.[185] The pursuit of domestic security has tended to drive much of State interaction with international law, which has been to the detriment of achieving utopian focal goals. Carr pauses upon Germany's violation of the Locarno Treaties by militarising the Rhineland to illustrate the importance of domestic security for States. Once the treaty had no meaning for Germany, and moreover, curtailed its ability to protect its domestic security, Germany did not hesitate to overthrow the demilitarisation clauses of the Versailles Treaty.[186] State prioritisation of their domestic duty over their international duty explains why the likes of Germany, Italy and Japan adopted revanchist policies. It justifies the argument that the State is inherently designed to tend to the needs of its own populace and ensure the prosperity and survival of its domestic population. Thus, it is in this chapter's attempt to show how States undermined the League and international law in order to pursue their primary duty to their populace the second hypothesis has been proven. Exploring how State conduct in the international community led to the breakdown of the League and its capacity to ensure international peace and security demonstrates such a claim, for it becomes apparent that the State 'seeks to bring into conformity with his own will the wills of others, so that he may the better attain his own ends.'[187] It is the result of self-assertion from the primary subject and objects of the international legal system that saw the League fail to achieve utopian focal goals of international law.

Thus, for those focused on achieving the aims of emancipatory idealism as a utopian focal goal of international law, the position of the State in the international legal system is of great concern. The lack of consistent and foreseeable commitment States exhibit to ensure the achievement of utopian goals of international law is not conducive to guaranteeing that individuals and communities of individuals are protected from modes of oppression in order to contribute to civilisational development. Consequently, the dangerous repercussions of States undermining utopian goals of international law bring into question—at least for those focused on achieving emancipatory idealism—the position of States as the primary object and subject of the international legal system. The *interbellum*

[185] Carr, *supra* note 81, at 97.

[186] Ibid., at 106.

[187] G. Catlin, *The Science and Method of Politics*, (1964), 309.

period and the death of the League of Nations suggest that States are incapable of setting aside their realist interest for the sake of the international community as a whole, regardless of how detrimental the repercussions are of undermining emancipatory idealism as a utopian focal goal of international law.

CHAPTER 5

The United Nations Security Council and Power Politics

5.1 Introduction

As with Chapter 4, this chapter examines the two hypotheses of the project; analysing the importance of utopian focal goals to the development of international law and demonstrating how and why State primacy in international law has led to an international body, here, the United Nations, to fail to achieve such focal goals. On April 26th 1945, the United Nations Conference was held in San Francisco to discuss the creation of a new international organisation that would replace the League of Nations. Forty-six world leaders gathered to deliberate how the international community would move forward and by June 26th, which resulted in the signing of the United Nations Charter. The League's Assembly had adjourned on April 18th 1946, in light of the fact that all the necessary steps were taken to terminate the existence of the League. Without much fanfare, the United Nations had replaced the League on August 1st, 1946 in Geneva.

The transition from the League of Nations to the United Nations entailed some pivotal differences, but in many ways the UN was a progression of what the League had been, rather than a drastically contrasting descendant.[1] The UN was founded upon the pillars of the past. Whilst

[1] M. Mazower, *No Enchanted Palace*, (2008), 14.

D. Mawar, *States Undermining International Law*, Philosophy, Public Policy, and Transnational Law, https://doi.org/10.1007/978-3-030-64789-6_5

the circumstances under which it was established differed from that of the League, it bore many of its characteristics. What is revealing is that the UN was considered more of an evolutionary progression rather than a revolutionary one.[2] This is reflected by the UN's composition, which was born out of the League's tradition.[3] This is demonstrated by the specific provisions within the Charter, such as: Article 4 that outlines the process of membership for States; and Article 14 of the Charter, being a descendent of Article 19 of the Covenant on the subject of the General Assembly's capacity to 'recommend measures for the peaceful adjustment of any situation, regardless of origin, which is likely to impair friendly relations among nations.'[4] The adoption of the Concert of Powers model with the Security Council is a feature synonymous with the League, and both organisations adopted the principle of Member-States' voluntary cooperation. Even on a base level there are indications of similarities in regard to the four central organs of both international organisations. The names of these organs may have been altered yet the function they carried out within the UN structure was more or less similar. Rather than a process of upheaval the four central organs were maintained in the UN, and instead underwent reform to ensure that they would be more effective in carrying out their respective functions.

Yet the stench of failure that followed the League, when assessing its ability to ensure international peace and security, forced the UN to move away from the idea that it was simply an evolutionary development. Public opinion at the time sought for a new international organisation that would be fresh and a marked upgrade from its predecessor. Hence, there was a push to enact superficial changes. Even during the UN's Conference, no mention was made of the League to substantiate the idea that the UN was an international organisation, which was the first of its kind and definitively distinct from the League's model.

Moreover, even though the composition of both the League and the UN are similar on several levels, the philosophical influences and traditions that it had adopted were contrasting. The League was influenced

[2] L. Goodrich, 'From the League of Nations to the United Nations', (Feb. 1947) 1.1 *International Organisations* 3, at 4.

[3] J.S Rofe, 'Prewar and Wartime Postwar Planning: Anecdotes to the UN moment in San Francisco' in D. Plesch & T.G. Weiss(eds.), *Wartime Origins and the Future United Nations*, 17 at 20.

[4] Goodrich, *supra* note 2 at 7.

by idealism, as the work of the French Idealists, such as Georges Scelle and Wilson's adherence to Kantian concepts of perpetual peace through his fourteen points, inspired much of the work that led to the creation of the League.[5] Such positions all encouraged a legal system that was driven by a synthesis of morality and law. On the other hand, the UN adopted a more scientific approach to international law, steeping itself in a positivist method, as the likes of Hans Kelsen advocated the idea that the League was far too politicised. Kelsen argued that a political approach to international law led lawyers to become 'amateur sociologists or dilettante moralists.'[6] Instead of adhering to the metaphysical notions of morality, Kelsen sought out a model of international law based on logic and reason that was grounded upon the basis of objectivity.

The discussion on similarities and contrasts of both the League and the UN has been the subject of broad and continued debate, yet the concern at this particular moment is whether the UN's model of international law has progressed enough to prevent the failings of its predecessor. In light of the UN being an evolutionary progression of what the League was, had the UN managed to remedy some of the problems that had hampered the work of the League in not achieving the central aims of emancipatory idealism? The previous chapter outlined that the League's failure to achieve of utopian focal goals of international law was due in large part to the primacy of the State, and it seems apparent that the UN suffers from the same frailty that the League had suffered from.

The first part of this chapter considers the influence that the aims of emancipatory idealism have had on the creation of the UN and the transition from the classical system to the modern international legal system. The second part of the chapter focuses on the principal organ of the UN, the Security Council and State interaction with it. Assessing the work of the Security Council brings the detrimental nature of State primacy in international law into greater focus. States play an integral role in the operation of the Security Council, which consequently creates opportunities for States to influence its work with their own realist objectives. It is in these situations that it seems States have undermined utopian focal goals of international law to seek out their own benefit. Such exploration

[5] M. Koskenniemi. *The Gentle Civilizer of Nations: The Rise and Fall of International Law 1870–1960*, (2004), 330.

[6] H. Kelsen, *Völkerrechstslehre*, (1995), at 278–283.

of the Security Council strengthens the argument that States prioritise their domestic duty over their international duty, which is to the detriment of achieving utopian focal goals. I illustrate the way in which States have undermined utopian focal goals, by analysing the tools the Security Council possess to maintain international peace and security, and then examining the manner in which the more influential States have interacted with the Security Council.

5.2 A New Era for International Law-the United Nations and Universalism

The failings and successes of the League was the springboard from which the UN system was drafted. What emerged from the Second World War bore little resemblance to any of the alternative models that circulated. One of the central attractions to the new system of international law was the inclusion of the United States and USSR. The other significant development was the establishment of the Security Council, which reinstated the Concert of Powers model where the central legal powers of the UN body resided. With chapter VII of the UN charter, powers were given to the Security Council to deal with 'threats to peace, breach of the peace, or act of aggression.'[7] With the permanent five members (United States, UK, USSR, China and France) of the Security Council it was the idea that this international organisation would be able to be more proactive in ensuring peace for the international community, with the primary objective of preventing another large-scale conflict. In the closing days of the Second World War, representatives of fifty nations met in San Francisco to establish the UN as a permanent peacetime organisation, with the United States, UK and France leading the talks. Jan Smuts delivered some rather romantic words to the representatives eager for a new path towards peace: '"For the human race," he declared, "the hour has struck. Mankind has arrived at the crisis of its fate, the fate of its future as a civilised world."'[8] Victory in the war must be crowned by 'a halt to the pilgrimage of death.'[9] The League was seen as 'politically toxic' and for this reason

[7] UN Charter, (1945), Article 39.

[8] Mazower, *supra* note 1, at 28.

[9] *Ibid*, at 28.

was considered a failure.[10] With the UN, a more apolitical approach was taken, and trust was given to the judgment and impartiality of lawyers in order to make the legal tradition more empirical and positivist. It was a direct response to the idealist framework of the League, for there was support for a more rigorous framework, which did not depend solely on a utopian ideology that would hopefully ensure that States would react to potential outbreaks of conflict. In order for the purpose of international law to be protected a more proactive system was officiated that would protect individuals and communities actively.

Nonetheless, utopian focal goals had a significant influence on the accelerated phase of development undertaken within the international legal system following the end of the Second World War. The aims of emancipatory idealism can be identified in this new phase of international law, 'which transformed the previous mere coordination of sovereign States into a system of cooperation and mutual benefit.'[11] Incidentally, through the establishment of the UN, trends towards the creation of the international community become most apparent.[12] The creation of such a worldwide organisation, with its extensive powers, was a decisive factor with the number of independent States growing to an unprecedented figure of 168. These States were bound by common links resulting from their membership in the United Nations, whose activities, along with those of other international organisations, gave birth to further obligations.[13] Manfred Lachs argued that with the UN ushered in an era of greater interdependence, giving legitimacy to the claim that an international community had been formed.[14] Affirming the existence of an international community also recognises the collective interests of those members belonging to the international community. It is in this push towards the international community that the influence of utopian focal goals can be identified. The emergence of the international community was connected with 'two other basic concepts of international law- *ius*

[10] *Ibid*, at 28.

[11] R. Wolfrum, 'International Law of Cooperation', (1995) 2 *Max Planck Encyclopaedia of Public International Law* 1242, 1242–1247.

[12] M. Lachs, 'Legal Framework of an International Community,' (1992) 6 *Emory International Law Review* 329, at 332.

[13] *Ibid*. See also R. L. Bindschedler, 'Illusion und Wirklichkeit: Gegenwart und Zukunft des Volkerrechts', (1958) 8 *Jahrbuch Int'l Recht* 1.

[14] Ibid., 335.

cogens and international public order- both referring to principles and rules of international law with a higher legal status than the other parts of international law.'[15] Such developments, alongside the proliferation of international organisations, signified international law's shift from coexistence to cooperation of States, not only to achieve international peace and security but also to further social and economic goals.

This shift was particularly apparent with international law's greater recognition of the individual's position in the legal system. Such recognition signified the introduction of individual justice in the international legal system typified by the development of international law directly affecting the individual. For example, there had been a failing in protecting the rights and life of minorities within the Nazi regime, which the UN model of international law attempted to rectify. The League's regime of protection of the minority had failed in the face of mass Jewish persecution and with its inability to reprimand Germany, allowing for other states to follow their steps, starting with Poland, who both ceased to carry out their formal obligations towards the protection of their minorities and then boycotted the League's programme of minority protection. This all represented a concerted effort to reduce Jews in particular to second-class status and forcing them to leave. By 1937, Europe was facing a refugee crisis of proportions unparalleled since the end of the First World War. The new system of law needed to apply some attention to the protection of individuals and to truly project liberal ideals in relation to such an entity. The first sign of this was to establish genocide as a crime. In the words of French prosecutor Champetier de Ribes in his concluding speech before the International Military Tribunal at Nuremberg:

> This is a crime so monstrous, so undreamt of in history throughout the Christian era up to the birth of Hitlerism, that the term 'genocide' has had to be coined to define it.[16]

[15] P. Malanczuk, *Akehurst's Modern Introduction to International Law*, (1997), at 30–31. See also G. Jaenicke, 'International Public Order', (1995) 2 *Max Planck Encyclopaedia of Public International Law* 1348, 1348–1351.

[16] Trial of the major war Criminals before the International Criminal before the International Military Tribunal, Nuremberg, 14 November 1945–1 October 1946 531 (1947).

Polish lawyer, Raphael Lemkin coined the term in his book when discussing the destruction of natural or ethnic groups. Lemkin insisted that genocide needed to be seen as a whole as it was a crime that comprised of different acts of persecution and destruction. The Hague Regulations of 1907 had already classified the illegality of some these acts of persecution. However, the Germans had introduced others as well, 'which collectively made the nineteenth century assumption that war was waged against sovereigns and armies, and not against civilians, outdated.'[17] Lemkin argued that the issue of genocide needed to be resolved immediately rather than later so that such atrocities and acts of persecution are prohibited. The events that unfolded during the war with the mass persecution of Jews, and the Chinese at the hand of Japanese forces, affirmed the necessity for certain safeguards for individuals and communities. Lemkin proposed that the new UN model would be a more stringent version of the League with substantial legal precedents protecting individuals and communities. His work on genocide came to fruition at the end of 1946. In the first General Assembly meeting, Lemkin managed to get a genocide resolution placed on the agenda, with support from Indian and South American delegates. The Genocide Convention was adopted by the General Assembly of the UN in 1948. It became one of the most widely accepted international human rights instruments with 112 ratifications by states parties and three signatures by 1993.[18] It is also widely recognised that the crime of genocide is part of customary international law. The jurisprudence of the International Court of Justice further considers the prohibition of genocide as *ius cogens* from which no derogation is permitted.[19]

Further to the cause of protecting individuals and communities from persecution, the UN Declaration of Human Rights was voted through in 1948, sparking the human rights movement. With this opened the doors for various human rights instruments, such as the ICCPR and ICESCR and Europe's development of human rights through the ECHR and the EU. This represents a significant turn in the attention of international law, as individual justice became a more prominent theme for the system,

[17] Ibid., 126.

[18] P. Akhavan, 'Enforcement of the Genocide Convention: A Challenge to Civilisation', (1995) 8.1 *Harvard Human Rights Journal* 229, at 230.

[19] Ibid., at 230.

extending existing conventions that tended to focus solely on the peaceful relations of states.

This change in focus turned attention towards protecting all members of the international community from the various dangers of conflict and modes of oppression. It seemed that with the UN system, utopian focal goals of international law were thrust further into the spotlight. The notion that the State was not the sole subject of international law, came to prominence with the emergence of human rights and individual justice, as in order to protect the international community from civilizational decline more safeguards were needed and such safeguards should not just be for States. Critical theorists such as Habermas and Linklater would tend to support the prominence of human rights for the sake of emancipation, as they protect the inclusionary ability of all members of the international community. As for Hegel, the realisation of knowledge and freedom is lost in the midst of war and oppression and consequently the development of concepts of human rights, human dignity and human security aid the progression of civilisation. From the backdrop of war, the aims and theory behind emancipatory idealism can be noticed in the advancement of international law in this particular phase of its development. The moral and political degeneration that occurred during the war was a great cause for concern for the international community. Ultimately, such analysis of the developments of the United Nations during its embryonic stages validates the first hypothesis of the project. The focus on individual justice in the United Nations model of international law, demonstrates how the central aims of emancipatory idealism helped shape international law following a large-scale crisis.

5.3 Security Council and Maintaining International Peace and Security

Although the establishment of the UN Security Council can also be considered as further illustration of utopian focal goals playing a significant role in the development of international law, such focus on this specific UN organ is to demonstrate the validity of the second hypothesis. The Security Council plays a pivotal role in establishing international peace and security in the contemporary international legal system As Article 24.1 of the UN Charter asserts, the Security Council's 'primary responsibility for the maintenance of international peace and security.'[20] Chapter VII of the Charter awards the Security Council the tools to act accordingly with respect to threats to peace, breaches of the peace, and acts of aggression it is evident the role this organ plays in international law.[21] Subsequently, it is through this lens that those focused on achieving emancipatory idealism examine the work of the Security Council. The Security Council was an evolutionary development of the role the Council played for the League of Nations.[22] Chapter 4 highlights the failings of the Council for it was an organ that 'met infrequently and was notoriously slow to respond in times of crisis. It was an organisation infused with the spirit of consensualism, where compliance was an option, sanctions not compulsory and the Covenant ambiguous regarding the authorisation of the use of force.'[23] Hence, when the meeting to form the UN took place in San Francisco in 1945, the intentions of the drafters were to establish an executive organ that had a wider remit and would be a longer-lasting system of general security than its predecessor.[24] With the inclusion of five permanent members, the vision was to establish responsibility upon such specific Member-States to lead operations to ensure international peace and security,[25] whether it was through the use of force or through non-aggressive measures such as the use of sanctions. This was a move to make the Security Council more proactive in dealing with threats to international peace and security, unlike the League's Council, which did not necessarily maintain a similar enforcement mechanism.[26]

For those focused on achieving utopian goals of international law this was a positive move forward by the drafters of the Security Council and the UN as a whole. With five permanent Security Council Member-States leading the work, it created a greater opportunity for achieving

[20] UN Charter (1945) Article 24.1.

[21] UN Charter (1945) Chapter VII.

[22] L. Goodrich, 'From the League of Nations to the United Nations', (1947) 1.1 *International Organization* 3, at 10.

[23] P. Nadin, *UN Security Council Reform* (2016), 7.

[24] M. Glennon, 'Why the Security Council Failed', (2003) 82.3 *Foreign Affairs* 16, at 16.

[25] D. Bourantonis, *The History and Politics of the UN Security Council Reform*, (2005), 3.

[26] Nadin, *supra* note 23, at 10.

the aims of emancipatory idealism. If substantial powers for the Security Council could be adopted in order to combat threats to international peace and security, the protection of individuals and a community of individuals could be ensured. Moreover, such an evolution in the Security Council's ***modus operandi*** could prevent the kind of civilizational degeneration the drafters has witnessed prior to San Francisco meeting in 1945. However, much relied upon the p-5 members and the application of their responsibility to lead the work towards ensuring international peace and security. If the Member-States utilised their position to achieve emancipatory idealism, the Security Council would become an effective mechanism for protecting individuals from modes of oppression and violence that create socio-political instability. However, if such influential Member-States exploited their position in the work of the Security Council, it would undermine utopian focal goals of international law. Furthermore, it would raise questions as to whether such an organ is in fact successful in combating threats to peace, breaches of peace and acts of aggression. This in itself raises alarms for those seeking to achieve emancipatory idealism, as the achievement of such a focal goal starkly relies upon the realist interest of the more influential Member-States.

5.4 Security Council Composition

Before covering how influential Member-States approached the Security Council, it is necessary to explore the composition of the Security Council. A descriptive analysis of the instruments the Security Council possesses to deal with threats to international peace and security allows this chapter to illustrate the potential possessed by the Security Council to achieve the central aims of emancipatory idealism.

Within the Charter, Chapters V, VI, VII, and VIII lay down the guidelines under which the Security Council operates. Chapter V details its composition, voting procedure, functions and powers. Chapter VI calls for Member-States to use alternative methods of dispute resolution in instances where there is an escalation of a dispute. Chapter VII, as mentioned above, allows the Security Council to determine threats to international peace and security and adopt measures to act upon any threat by way of either non-military or military means. Finally, Chapter VIII sets the rules for UN interaction with regional organisations and affirms that only the Security Council possesses the right to authorise use of force. In order to understand the Security Council's work to ensure that the central aim of emancipatory idealism is achieved, particular interest is set upon the Council's power originating from Chapter VII.

5.4.1 Article 39

Article 39 allows the Security Council to 'determine the existence of any threat to the peace, breach of the peace, or act of aggression.'[27] The discretion to determine when to act awards the Security Council a broad remit, which has led scholars to disagree on the Council's scope to utilise such powers. The contentious issue incumbent in such disagreements lies in whether such discretion is subject to limitation:

> Some authors claim that both types of action (the action of deciding when to act and how to act) fall within the absolute discretion of the Security Council.[28] Others argue that the decision as to when the Security Council should intervene in terms of Article 39 lies purely within its discretion,[29] but that general international law, in particular *ius cogens*, as well as the purposes and principles of the United Nations would pose limits to the type of action that may be taken by the Security Council.[30] Yet others argue the exact opposite and state that once the Security Council is acting in terms of Article 39, there are no limits as to what it can do. However, whether it has passed the threshold constituted by Article 39 is something that can be measured by means of judicial criteria.[31,32]

[27] UN Charter, (1945), Article 39.

[28] G.H. Oosthuizen, 'Playing the Devil's Advocate: The United Nations Security Council Is Unbound by Law', (1999) 12 *Leiden Journal of International Law* 549; & I. Österdahl, *Threat to the Peace* (1998), at 98.

[29] H. Kelsen, *The Law of the United Nations* (1950), at 730; B. Conforti,' The Legal Effect of Non-Compliance with Rules of Procedure in the UN General Assembly and the Security Council', (1969) 63 *American Journal of International Law* 479.

[30] T.D. Gill, 'Legal and Some Political Limitations on the Power of the UN Security Council to Exercise its Enforcement Powers under Chapter VII of the Charter', (1995) 26 *Netherlands Yearbook of International Law* 33, at 60.

[31] B. Martenczuk. 'The Security Council, the International Court and Judicial Review: What Lessons from Lockerbie?' (1999) 10 *EJIL* 517, at 538.

[32] E. De Wet, *The Chapter VII Powers of the United Nations Security Council*, (2004), at 133–134.

Opinions seem to differ as to whether the Council has absolute discretion in terms of how to act, which is discussed in greater depth below when analysing Articles 40, 41 and 42. The main focus of this section is to understand the scope of Article 39. The positions taken on the limitations of Article 39 differ based upon whether the Security Council should have absolute discretion or if such determination should be made based on substantive legal criteria.[33]

Supporters of unlimited Security Council discretion under Article 39 pose several points of justification for such a position. Firstly, as there is no definition as to what is termed as a 'threat to peace,' 'breach of peace' or 'act of aggression in the Charter,' the responsibility should be placed upon the Security Council and its members to determine such events based on 'factual findings and the weighing up of political considerations which could be measured by legal criteria.'[34] Moreover, the right to determine threats to international peace and security is political in nature. This is 'underscored by the lack of any obligation on the part of the Security Council to decide whether a given situation falls within the terms of Article 39 and whether to take any enforcement action when it has made such a determination.'[35] The most concerning argument, especially for those that focus on emancipatory idealism, 'the voting (veto) power attributed to the five permanent members in Article 27(3) of the Charter would be a reflection of the political nature of an Article 39 determination.'[36] The politicisation of Article 39 becomes problematic for it provides space for Member-States—in this instance the permanent five members—to instil their realist agenda into the work of the Security Council.

Opponents to such a position reject such arguments on several grounds. Although the terms stipulated in Article 39 in relation to threats to international peace and security are vague, this does not subsequently infer that such terms are left to the discretion of the Security Council. Indeed, the *travaux préparatoires* indicate that the Security Council maintained the authority 'to decide freely when a threat to the peace, a breach

[33] M. Selkirk, 'Judge, Jury and Executioner? Analysing the Nature of the Security Council's Authority under Article 39 of the UN Charter', (2003) 9 *Auckland University Law Review* 1101, at 1102.

[34] De Wet, *supra* note 32, at 135.

[35] Ibid., at 136.

[36] Ibid., at 135.

of the peace or an act of aggression existed.'[37] They are legal terms and therefore require interpretation from those that are well rehearsed in the legal tradition and language. Erika De Wet stresses that 'the mere fact that Article 39 distinguishes between three criteria that trigger binding resolutions of the Security Council, implies that it does not have an unbound discretion.'[38] Moreover, some work has been done to develop a definition of aggression. The General Assembly's resolution 3314 establishes aggression as the 'use of an armed force by a State against the sovereignty, territorial integrity or political independence of another State, or in any other manner inconsistent with the Charter of the United Nations, as set out in this Definition.'[39] Several articles are supplied in the resolution that covers the definition of aggression and how to deal with such a term legally. Subsequently, the argument that the terms stipulated in Article 39 are vague does not fully apply as some work has been done to reconcile such a problem.

The points of legal analysis incumbent within Article 39 cannot therefore be overridden completely by political consideration. If such provisions were deployed in such a manner, it would disrupt the balance of competencies in the Charter. This in particular alludes to Article 24.2, which appears to establish some sort of limitation[40]: 'in discharging [its, inter alia, Chapter VII] duties the Security Council shall act in accordance with the purposes and principles of the United Nations.'[41] Furthermore, the Security Council's powers to impose binding sanctions and order other measures for the maintenance of international peace and security are exercised under the provisions established in Chapter VII of the Charter. Yet the Security Council's Chapter VI powers, which deal with the peaceful settlement of disputes, are non-binding. Nevertheless, such a distinction between Chapter VI and VII would become obsolete if the Security Council at any given time were free to declare the provisions of Chapter VII applicable.

[37] J. Frowein, 'Article 39', in B. Simma (ed.), *The Charter of United Nations*, (1994), at 607.

[38] De Wet, *supra* note 32, at 136. See also Barbara Lorinser, *Bindende Resolutionen des Sicherheitsrates* 39 (Baden-Baden, Nomos, 1996) and Andreas Stein, *Der Sicherheitsrat der Vereinten Nationen und die Rule of Law* 27 (Baden-Baden, Nomos, 1999).

[39] GA Resolution 3314.

[40] Selkirk, *supra* note 33, at 1104.

[41] UN Charter, (1945), 24.2.

Regardless of the position critics of the Security Council take in regard to this issue, the Charter has awarded the Security Council an important responsibility. Determining a threat to international peace and security allows the Security Council to take steps to deal with such events if required, whether through the use of economic sanctions or other measures prescribed in Chapter VI of the Charter. The application of such an article is therefore crucial in ensuring that the central aim of emancipatory idealism is achieved when potential violations or disruptions to such utopian goals of international law arise.

5.4.2 Article 40, 41 and 42

Once the Security Council has confirmed the existence of a threat to international peace and security, there are three articles in Chapter VII of the Charter that specify the measures the Security Council can take to deal with such threats. Article 40 permits the Security Council to develop provisional measures that do not aggravate hostilities.[42] This can be for example the suspension of hostilities, troop withdrawal or the conclusion of or adherence to a truce. Article 41 allows for non-military coercive measures,[43] whilst Article 42 authorises the use of force to deal with threats to international peace and security.[44]

The Security Council seemingly has a wide degree of discretion when utilising these articles once it has been established under Article 39 that there is a threat to international peace and security. The Charter does not specify that Article 40 must be utilised first before making use of Article 41 and so on, nor does it say that once a threat to international peace and security has been determined that the Security Council is obligated to intervene. On a more substantive basis, the Security Council is able to deviate from customary international law or treaty law when adopting enforcement measures to deal with threats to peace and security.[45] For example, enforcement measures that establish a trade embargo

[42] UN Charter, (1945), Article 40.

[43] UN Charter, (1945), Article 41.

[44] UN Charter, (1945), Article 42.

[45] De Wet, *supra* note 32, at 182 and D. Akande, 'The International Court of Justice and the Security Council: Is there Room for Judicial Control of Decisions of the Political Organs of the United Nations?' (1997) 46.2 *International and Comparative Law Quarterly* 309, at 320.

potentially incur an impact upon the legal rights of both those States or entities against for which the measures have been arranged for, and those that have trade relations with them. For the sake of successfully ensuring the restoration of international peace and security, the Security Council has the discretion to supersede customary and treaty law. Such powers originate from within the Charter as Article 103 delineates that 'in the event of a conflict between the obligations of the Members of the United Nations under the present Charter and their obligations under any other international agreement, their obligations under the present Charter shall prevail.'[46] This covers Security Council resolutions, or a binding decision made under its Chapter VII powers when dealing with threats to international peace and security that contravene customary and treaty law.

However, it would be inaccurate to present the Security Council with an unlimited remit to adopt enforcement measures and supersede existing international law if necessary. There are some limitations as to how far Security Council enforcement measures can go. A prime example of such a limitation is the peremptory norms of international law, also known as *ius cogens*. Under the Vienna Convention on Law of Treaties, 'a treaty is void if, at any time of its conclusion, it conflicts with a peremptory norm of international law.'[47] As the Charter is a treaty, it must conform to such rules, and consequently, the Security Council is obligated to utilise Chapter VII powers without violating *ius cogens* norms. Counter arguments to such a view are that as the VCLT established such a principle after the UN Charter, the limitations *ius cogens* norms create upon the Security Council are not applicable. With this line of argument, it is then permissible that 'States could instrumentalise the collective security system in order to engage in slavery, apartheid or even genocide, provided that the requisite majority in the Security Council can be secured.'[48] However, the general consensus amongst most critics of international law concludes that *ius cogens* norms bind States acting individually as well as collectively within the UN. Tzanakopoulos advanced such an argument, reasserting the maxim *nemo plus juris transferre potest quam ipse habet*: if States cannot escape the operation of *jus cogens*, they certainly cannot

[46] UN Charter, (1945), Article 103.

[47] Vienna Convention on the Law of Treaties, (1969), Article 53.

[48] De Wet, *supra* note 32, at 190.

create an international organisation which is unbound by it.[49] Thus, the Charter must be interpreted in a manner that remains in harmony with the peremptory norms that existed at the time of its entry into force and based on peremptory norms that emerged subsequently.[50] If the harmony between the two does not exist, such interpretations of the Charter would leave it to be considered void.[51] Such an understanding of the limitations of the Charter would logically see Security Council resolutions conflicting with *jus cogens* as void. In fact, such a matter was discussed in Judge Lauterpacht's separate opinion in *Bosnian Genocide (Provisional Measures)*. Lauterpacht argued that Security Council resolution 713 (1991), which had established an arms embargo on Yugoslavia,[52] had prevented Bosnia-Herzegovina to fight back strongly against the better equipped Serbian forces, and effectively prevent genocide.[53] Lauterpacht advanced the notion that:

> Viewed in this light, the Security Council resolution can be seen as having in effect called on Members of the United Nations, albeit unknowingly and assuredly unwillingly, to become in some degree supporters of the genocidal activity of the Serbs and in this manner and to that extent to act contrary to a rule of *jus cogens*.[54]

In the light of such an unintended outcome of Security Council resolution 713, Lauterpacht suggested that one possible legal consequence would be that paragraph 6 of the resolution 'would cease to be valid in its operation against Bosnia-Herzegovina; and that Members of the United Nations then became free to disregard it.'[55] Incidentally, such a need for harmony between the Charter and peremptory norms illustrates that the Security

[49] A. Tzanakopoulos, *Disobeying the Security Council- Countermeasures Against Wrongful Sanctions*, (2010), at 71.

[50] Ibid., at 70.

[51] Ibid.

[52] UN Security Council Resolution 713, UN Doc/S/RES/713, (25 September 1991).

[53] *Application of the Convention on Prevention of Genocide and Punishment of the Crime of Genocide (Bosnia and Herzegovina v. Serbia)*, Provisional Measures, Judgement of 20 March 1993, [1993] ICJ Rep. 407, at 441 (Judge ad hoc Lauterpacht, Separate Opinion).

[54] Ibid.

[55] Ibid.

Council is restricted by *ius cogens* because such norms are a result of the common values of the international community as a whole.[56]

There lacks clarity as to which norms belong to *ius cogens*. Scholars of international law have identified a principal set of norms that fall within such a bracket. Such norms include the prohibition of the unilateral use of force, the right to self-defence, the prohibition of genocide, the prohibition of the violation of basic norms of international humanitarian law, the prohibition of racial discrimination and slavery and the right to self-determination. Erika De Wet even suggests that the right to a fair trial during criminal proceedings and the right to life also can be considered as elements of *ius cogens*.[57]

The second limit to the Security Council has already been mentioned above in relation to Article 39 of the Charter, and it is in regard to the principles and purposes of the Charter. Article 24.2 states that when attempting to maintain international peace and security, the Security Council 'should act in accordance with the Purposes and Principles of the United Nations.'[58] The purposes and principles stem from Articles 1 and 2. The purposes are the primary goal of peace and security (Article 1.1); respect for the self-determination of peoples (Article 1.2); and solving socio-economic and humanitarian problems and the promotion of human rights (Article 1.3).[59] The principles of the United Nations are the sovereign equality of Member-States (Article 2.1); the maintenance of *pacta sunt servanda*, which is the obligation to act in good faith (Article 2.2); the obligation of members to settle disputes through peaceful means (Article 2.3); the prohibition of Member-States from the threat or use of force (Article 2.4), the obligation of Member-States to assist the UN in the actions it takes in accordance with the Charter (Article 2.5); the obligation of the organisation to ensure that non-members act in accordance with the purposes and principles of the UN (Article 2.6); and the obligation of the organisation not to intervene in the domestic jurisdiction of members (Article 2.7).[60]

[56] Tzanakopolous, *supra note* 49, at 71. See also Draft Articles on the Responsibility of States for Internationally Wrongful Acts Commentary (2001), at 122(4).

[57] De Wet, *supra* note 32, at 191.

[58] UN Charter (1945) Article 24.2.

[59] UN Charter, (1945), Article 1.

[60] UN Charter, (1945), Article 2.

Article 24.2 ensures that the Security Council balances its primary goal of maintaining international peace and security with the requirement of acting in accordance with Articles 1 and 2 of the Charter.[61] Subsequently, the Security Council cannot achieve its primary goal at the complete expense of the exhaustive list of Articles 1 and 2. For those focused on emancipatory idealism as a focal goal of international law, this is a positive limit upon Security Council discretion. Much of what Articles 1 and 2 of the Charter contain establish the protection of individuals and a community of individuals. These purposes and principles strive to ensure the inclusion of all communities of individuals and continue the civilisational development that is an intrinsic facet of emancipatory idealism. Although the Security Council's primary goal is one that would be encouraged by those who focus on emancipatory idealism, if international peace and security is established at the cost of the purposes and principles of the Charter, it is a troublesome predicament for the utopian goals of international law.

For example, maintaining international peace and security at the expense of self-determination, basic human rights or norms of international humanitarian law, will not ensure the protection of individuals from acts of violence or oppression. Rather than the Security Council achieving the central aims of emancipatory idealism by utilising its Chapter VII powers, it instead is undermining them. Similarly, for the principles underlined in Article 2, these provisions ensure the protection of individuals or a community of individuals from the fears that those focused on achieving emancipatory idealism have in order to ensure civilizational development. Whether it is the prohibition on the threat or use of force or the obligation to settle disputes through peaceful means, these are principles that encourage the achievement of the utopian goals of international law.

However, it must be stated that specific principles, such as Articles 2.1 and 2.7, could be limited by enforcement measures adopted under Chapter VII of the Charter. This is based on the argument that regardless of the existence of principles within the Charter that limit enforcement measures established through either Articles 40, 41 or 42, the Security Council must balance its primary goals with its obligations under

[61] R.B. Lillich, 'The Role of Security Council in Protecting Human Rights in Crisis Situations: UN Humanitarian Intervention in the Post-Cold War World', (1995) 3 *Tulane Journal of International and Comparative Law* 1, at 3.

Articles 1 and 2.[62] Instances will arise where the balance is necessarily and legitimately tipped in the favour of the Security Council's primary goal of maintaining peace and security at the expense of Articles 2.1 and 2.7. Within the post-1945 world, 'grave and systematic violations of human rights and international humanitarian law cannot be regarded as purely internal matters anymore,'[63] and therefore, some scope must be permitted for the Security Council to act effectively in order to maintain peace and security. The question and concern for those analysing international law with the focus of achieving emancipatory idealism is how far does the balance tip in the favour of maintaining peace and security before it is detrimental to such utopian goals? If there is such scope for the Security Council, the concern is whether Member-States may misappropriate such powers. Instead of maintaining international peace and security, Member-States may use a Security Council mandate to justify intervention that would not normally be permissible under international law. A key example would be the Iraq War in 2003.

Administrative and procedural developments have also created a mechanism for reviewing and limiting the scope of the Security Council, especially in terms of the UN sanctions regime. Concerns arose in the late 1990s regarding the Security Council sanctions regime and the 'devastating humanitarian impact of blanket sanctions against States.'[64] A great concern regarding the sanctions regime—which became apparent with the sanctions regime against Iraq—was that the impact of sanctions was not only felt by States; but also the 'innocent and often oppressed civilian populations.'[65] In order to counteract this issue, the Security Council decided to start targeting sanctions measures against relevant

[62] D. Whittle, 'The Limits of Legality and the United Nations Security Council: Applying the Extra-Legal Measures Model to Chapter VII Action', (2015) 26.3 *EJIL* 671, at 673.

[63] De Wet, *supra* note 32, at 194.

[64] D. Hovell, The Power of Process: The Value of Due Process in Security Council Sanctions Decision-Making, (2016), 11.

[65] *Ibid.* See also R. Geiss, 'Humanitarian Safeguards in Economic Sanctions Regimes: A Call for Automatic Suspension Clauses, Periodic Monitoring, and Follow-up Assessment of Long-Term Effects' (2005) 18 *Harvard Human Rights Journal* 167 & M. Reisman, 'Assessing the Lawfulness of Nonmilitary Enforcement: The Case of Economic Sanctions', (1995) 89 *American Society of International Law Proceedings* 350, at 351.

individuals, entities, and products, rather than against States.[66] This was the introduction of a system where a list of individuals against which specific sanctions measures was imposed by Security Council resolutions. However, the issue with such an approach was that 'the transformation was not accompanied by any procedural reform to protect the rights of those included on sanctions blacklists.'[67] Thus listed individuals experienced a comprehensive freezing of their assets around the globe, and the denial of international travel, visas, and educational opportunities for the blacklisted individual and their families.[68]

Such repercussion of the Security Council's policy shift advanced the claims for procedural reforms. This was highlighted with the establishment of the 1267 Sanctions Committee in 1999. However, criticisms have been made in terms of its procedural framework being 'woefully deficient, particularly in terms of listing, notification, reason-giving, and de-listing procedures.'[69] A central reason to such failings is that the priority for winning the war against terror superseded the need for due process. This is illustrated by the 'fact that there is no real evidentiary burden that proposals must meet. For over five years, the only criteria for listing an individual, group, or entity was on the basis of an "association with" Osama Bin Laden, Al Qaeda, or the Taliban.'[70] Moreover, individuals would be listed without providing them with a right to a hearing. Member-States have often defended the denial of the right to a hearing on the basis that '[t]hose facts and that evidence, once classified as confidential or secret by the State which made the Sanctions Committee aware of them, are not, obviously, communicated to [the individual], any more

[66] UN Security Council resolution 1127, UN Doc S/RES/1127, (28 August 1997); UN Security Council resolution 1173, UN Doc S/RES/1173, (12 June 1998). At the height of the UNITA sanctions regime, 157 individuals were subject to asset freezes and travel bans.

[67] Hovell, *supra* note 64, at 12.

[68] International Commission of Jurists, *Assessing Damage, Urging Action: Report of the Eminent Jurists Panel on Terrorism: Counter-Terrorism and Human Rights*, (2009), at 117.

[69] Hovell, *supra* note 64, at 14.

[70] Ibid., at 15.

than they are to the Member States of the United Nations to which the Security Council's resolutions are addressed.'[71]

Additionally, there was no requirement for the Committee or Member-States to notify listed individuals or entities about their inclusion on the list, nor to provide them with reasons for the listing. This position was defended on the grounds 'maintain[ing] an element of surprise in listings in order to prevent the flight of individuals and assets, and the destruction of documents.'[72] However, provisions had subsequently been made for retrospective notification of listings. Security Council resolution 1526 (2004) included a voluntary request to notify individuals and entities of their listing, but mandatory notification requirements were not introduced until 2008. Resolution 1822 provided that, in relation to future listings, the Secretariat must notify the State of nationality and residence of listed individuals or entities within one week of the listing. The Committee itself only assumed a direct obligation to notify individuals in December 2009.

Issues also persisted in regard to States and other bodies having little opportunity to learn why they had been added to the list.[73] Such an approach was justified by 'the need to protect secret intelligence material and sources, from which the names are usually derived, and by the desire to include suspected bad actors on the list as soon as possible.'[74] However, by 2005, the Security Council required States to provide a statement of case describing the basis of any listing proposal.[75] In 2006 and 2012, the Security Council provided further procedural reform, asserting that the statement of case 'should provide as much detail as possible on the bases for the listing, including: (i) specific findings demonstrating the association or activities alleged; (ii) the nature of the

[71] Joined Cases T-306/01 and T-315/01 Kadi v Council and Commission [2005] ECR II-0000, at 276.

[72] T. Biersteker & S. Eckert, *Strengthening Targeted Sanctions Through Fair and Clear Procedures*, (2006), at 7.

[73] 'Ninth Report of the Analytical Support and Sanctions Monitoring Team Submitted Pursuant to Resolution 1822 (2008) Concerning Al-Qaida and the Taliban and Associated Individuals and Entities' (13 May 2009) UN Doc S/2009/245, para 47.

[74] E. Rosand, 'Panel Discussion on UN Terrorist Designations and Sanctions: A Fair Process and Effective Regime?' (Center for Strategic and International Studies, Washington DC, 5 June 2008).

[75] UN Security Council resolution 1617 (29 July 2005) UN Doc S/RES/1617, para 4.

information [e.g. intelligence, law enforcement, judicial, media, admissions by subject, etc.]; and (iii) supporting evidence or documents that can be supplied.'[76]

The most contentious issue was the de-listing procedure, demonstrated by the p-5's reluctance for reform on this matter. Individuals typically had no direct access to the Sanctions Committee to challenge their listings. Initially, the listed individuals or entities depended on the agreement of their State of nationality or residence to take up their case on their behalf, usually through diplomatic negotiations with the designating State. If States were unwilling to take up cases on behalf of listed individuals, such individuals had no access to the Sanctions Committee. Eventually, the Committee introduced formal intermediaries through which individuals could petition the Committee. The Security Council established the 'focal point,' which was an initiative intended to serve as a non-State-based forum to which designated individuals or entities could submit a request for de-listing. However, this was considered an inadequate development, merely seen as a 'glorified post-box.'[77]

In fact, there seemed to be widespread dissatisfaction with the procedural developments advanced by the Security Council in regard to the sanctions decision-making. Both the UN High Commissioner for Human Rights and the UN Special Rapporteur on human rights and counter-terrorism 'have determined that the 1267 sanctions regime falls short of internationally recognised standards of due process because there is no recourse to independent judicial or quasi-judicial review either of a decision to list or denial of a request to de-list.'[78] In order to remedy such criticisms, the Security Council adopted resolution 1904 (2009), establishing the Office of the Ombudsperson.[79] Although it was not a form of judicial review over the sanctions regime, the Ombudsperson fulfilled

[76] A. Ciampi, 'Security Council Targeted Sanctions and Human Rights' in B. Fassbender (ed), *Securing Human Rights?: Achievements and Challenges of the UN Security Council*, (2011), at 107.

[77] Hovell, *supra* note 64, at 20.

[78] Ibid., at 24. See also 'Report of the United Nations High Commissioner for Human Rights on the Protection of Human Rights and Fundamental Freedoms while Countering Terrorism' (15 December 2010) UN Doc A/HRC/16/50, para 21; & 'Report of the Special Rapporteur on the Promotion and Protection of Human Rights and Fundamental Freedoms while Countering Terrorism' (2 August 2010) UN Doc A/65/258, paras 56–57.

[79] UN Security Council resolution 1904 (17 December 2009) UN Doc S/RES/1904.

a fact-finding or inquisitorial role. The Ombudsperson would undergo a lengthy period of fact gathering before preparing a comprehensive report outlining the information they had obtained and laying out the principal arguments concerning the de-listing request. If the Ombudsperson recommended de-listing, the individual or entity will be removed from the list unless, within sixty days, the Committee decides by consensus to maintain the listing. Although the Ombudsperson had produced results and received some supports, criticisms remained. The central arguments were that 'the Ombudsperson is "not a court." This seems to be shorthand for the dual criticism that the Ombudsperson is not sufficiently independent of the Security Council and no power to bind the Sanctions Committee.'[80] For these critics of the Ombudsperson, it was vital that sanctions regime underwent a form of judicial review, in order to determine the legal validity of Security Council decisions.

Through the push towards judicial review, substantial procedural developments occurred through domestic and regional courts upholding challenges to the sanctions regime. The most significant case being *Kadi*, where the Court of First Instance assumed a power to review the validity of the Council's decision to list Mr. Kadi under international law. In *Kadi II*, the ECJ held that 'the improvements' (of which the Ombudsperson procedure was the most notable) did not provide the listed individuals with 'the guarantee of effective judicial procedure.'[81] This confirmed the views expressed by the European Court of Human Rights and the EU General Court that the Ombudsperson 'cannot be equated with the provision of an effective judicial procedure for review of decisions of the Sanctions Committee.'[82] Additionally, the Swiss Parliament adopted a motion in March 2010, in which it intended to refuse to apply sanctions to any listed individual 'who had not been given judicial access after three years, was unable to appeal his or her listing before a judicial body,

[80] Hovell, *supra* note 64, at 29.

[81] *European Commission v Kadi* (2013) EU ECJ, at 133.

[82] Case T-85/09 *Kadi v European Commission* (2010) EUECJ, at 28. See also *Nada v Switzerland* (2012) ECHR 169, at 209–214; *Al-Dulimi and Montana v Switzerland* (App No 580/08), ECHR, 26 November 2013, at 119; Case T-85/*09 Kadi v European Commission* (2010) EU ECJ, at 128.

and had not had any further accusations made against him or her.'[83] This signalled a noteworthy procedural development that had created some limitations to the Security Council sanctions decision-making.

Irrespective of such substantive limits to Security Council discretion in establishing enforcement measures with the application of either Article 40, 41 or 42, the discretion it has is still wide.[84] The Security Council has a number of methods through which it can maintain international peace and security once a threat to international peace has been determined. However, what is also clear is the reliance the operation of the Security Council has upon the contribution of States, in particular the permanent five members.[85] Though there are several mechanisms for the Security Council to implement in order to maintain international peace and security, and indeed, these mechanisms have the potential to help achieve utopian focal goals, the use of such mechanisms is plagued by the realist agenda Member-States bring to the work of the Security Council when dealing with threats to international peace and security.

5.5 Member-States and the Use of Chapter VII Powers

The analysis conducted above of Article 39–42 contributes towards the argument that States, specifically the more influential States in the international sphere, shape the activity of Security Council. The reasons for such a phenomenon are several. The first of which has been discussed above as the political nature of the application of Chapter VII provisions allows for Member-States to influence its proceedings. However, the delegation of Chapter VII powers to Member-States has more structural origins than just the politicisation of Chapter VII Powers.

[83] Hovell, *supra* note 64, at 25. See also Rapport de la Commission de Politique Extérieure du Parlement Suisse, 'Les Fondements de Notre Ordre Juridique Court-Circuités par l'ONU' (2010), translated in Council of Europe Parliamentary Assembly, Committee of Legal Affairs and Human Rights, 'Compatibility of UN Security Council and EU [terrorist] Black Lists with European Convention on Human Rights requirements' (7 December 2010), at 6.

[84] Lillich, *supra* note 61, at 5.

[85] Ibid., at 4–5.

5.5.1 The Security Council and Military Enforcement Measures

It seems that the drafters of the Charter had always intended for UN Member-States to contribute forces when military enforcement mechanisms were required to maintain or restore international peace and security.[86] With the UN unable to develop a fully functioning military force of its own, relying upon Member-States to partially help fulfil such a role on an ad hoc basis was paramount to ensuring such an objective.[87] Article 43 is where the Charter has asserted such a provision, specifying that:

> All Members of the United Nations, in order to contribute to the maintenance of international peace and security, undertake to make available to the Security Council, on its call and in accordance with a special agreement or, armed forces, assistance, and facilities, including rights of passage, necessary for the purpose of maintaining international peace and security.[88]

This is an important precedent to analyse for Member-States' forces are carrying out military enforcement actions on behalf of the Security Council. This in itself bears substantial repercussions to the effective operation of the Security Council's primary task both on a practical and political level.[89]

However, Member-States are not exercising command and control over such actions; such a responsibility lies with the Military Staff Committee. The Military Staff Committee's responsibility and role is stipulated in Articles 46 and 47 of the Charter, as well as in the General Principles Governing the Organisation of the Armed Forces, which suggests that 'supreme direction of the military operations shall be exclusively in the hands of the UN and that the commanders of the national contingents shall take their operational orders from the UN, not from

[86] I. Hurd, 'Legitimacy, Power, and the Symbolic Life of the UN Security Council', (2002) *Global Governance* 35, at 35.

[87] E. Grove, 'UN Armed Forces and the Military Staff Committee: A Look Back', (1993) 17.4 *International Security* 172, at 177.

[88] UN Charter (1945) Article 43.1.

[89] See E. Grove, *supra* note 87, for details on the discussions amongst the Permanent Members in regard to the contributing forces to the Security Council, highlighting the obstacles that arose from such a setup.

their national governments.'[90] The intention for such a mechanism was to allow national contingents to 'subject to their own regulations and obey their own national commander who would take commands from a UN Force Commander who was to be under the control of Military Staff Committee.'[91] Furthermore, the Security Council would exercise overall command through the Military Staff Committee. This, in theory, prevents Member-States from misappropriating such military operations as a cover to fulfil their own realist goals and to go beyond the Council's stipulated objectives. Such provisions assert that when Member-States agree to contribute forces for the Council's military operations, not on the basis of its own *modus operandi,* but on the Council's objectives and strategized plan of action. This goes as far as 'requiring the Council to specify the level of the use of force to be undertaken.'[92]

Despite establishing such a mechanism 'the lack of effective functioning of the Military Staff Committee has seen the Council delegate the power of command and control to UN Member-States who have volunteered their forces to carry out military enforcement action.'[93] This subsequently means that the Council has delegated to Member-States the competence to carry out military enforcement action under their own command and control. As nowhere in the Charter is the delegation of such powers prohibited, it does open up the possibility for such a cause of action. On the other hand, there is 'no provision in the Charter which provides in express terms for a delegation by the Council of its Chapter VII powers to UN Member-States. Neither is there such a reference in the *travaux preparatoires* of the Charter.'[94] The Council's decision on the matter was taken on the basis of pragmatism. When military operations are required to ensure the maintenance or restoration of international peace and security, if such powers of command and control are not delegated, the Council would be unable to deal with such matters. Thus, to ensure the effectiveness of the Council, the delegation of such powers is a

[90] D. Sarooshi, *The United Nations and the Development of Collective Security- The Delegation of the UN Security Council of its Chapter VII Powers,* (2000), 142–143. See also F. Seyersted, *United Nations Forces* (1966), 32.

[91] Ibid., at 142. See also 'Report of the Military Staff Committee to the Security Council', S/336, SCOR Special Supplement (1947), No.1., Article 36–40.

[92] Ibid., at 159.

[93] Ibid., at 142–143.

[94] Ibid. at 149.

practical necessity. Sarooshi goes to some detail to argue that the Council does possess the competence to delegate such Chapter VII powers. His argument is that such competencies are in accordance with the object and purpose of Article 42, as such a 'delegation of Chapter VII powers may be necessary for the attainment of the Council's primary function: the maintenance or restoration of international peace security.'[95]

This is a significant position for the Member-States to play in the work of the Security Council. However, there are still restrictions that remain, regardless of such delegation of powers. The first, discussed briefly above, is that if Member-States accept to carry out Security Council operations, they agree to conduct such operations only for the achievement of the Council's substantiated objective. Similarly, if Chapter VII powers are delegated to Member-States, then such powers must also be exercised under the same framework of achieving Security Council objectives. Furthermore, if there has been a delegation of powers to Member-States, the Council is obligated to supervise the exercise of delegated powers. 'The aim of supervision by the Council is twofold: to determine when the Council's stated objective has been attained; and to ensure the delegated powers are being exercised in an appropriate manner, that is for the attainment of the Council's stated objective.'[96] Additionally, the Council imposes upon Member-States exercising Chapter VII powers to report on the progress of the operation on a regular basis.

Sarooshi explains that one of the central reasons for establishing such a reporting mechanism is due to Articles 51 and 54 of the Charter. Article 54 establishes that regional organisations that use force in order to maintain international peace and security must report back to the Security Council.[97] This provision is to ensure that the Council has the necessary information to be able to exercise overall control and authority effectively over the 'regional arrangement or agency.' Sarooshi asserts that, 'the purpose of Article 54 is applicable to the exercise of delegated power of Chapter VII since the action taken is the same objective: the maintenance of international peace and security.'[98] Moreover, Article 51 also

[95] Ibid. at Pg 148. See also F. Kirgis, 'The Security Council's First Fifty Years' (1995) 89 *AJIL* 506, at 521.

[96] Ibid. at 160.

[97] UN Charter, (1945), Article 54.

[98] Sarooshi, *supra* note 90, at 191.

affirms Member-States' obligation to report back to the Security Council if they have exercised their right to individual or collective self-defence. The assertion is that the object and purpose of such a provision is 'to ensure the responsibility of the Council for the maintenance of international peace and security is preserved.'[99] This would seem to suggest that even if a State is lawfully exercising its right to individual or collective self-defence without the overall control and authority of the Council, regular reporting to the Council is still required. The rationale behind such a requirement is to ensure that the Security Council can continue on its role as the 'guardian of international peace and security.' Therefore, it would seem that even if Member-States are exercising delegated powers, under such a rationale States are required nonetheless to report back to the Security Council.

Indeed, there are strict guidelines to ensure that the delegation of Chapter VII powers to Member-States is not misused, however, it highlights a persistent theme of how important the State is in international law. The ability of the Security Council to act as the guardian of peace and security is reliant upon the Member-States that the organ is composed of.[100] Therefore, as much as the provisions of the Charter attempt to extract the realist objectives of States when maintaining international peace and security it is unable to escape such a predicament. With the requirement to delegate Chapter VII powers to Member-States, the possibility of maintaining international peace and security through military enforcement is reliant upon the willingness of Member-States. Yet, Member-States tend to only contribute to such operations if a realist objective can be achieved.[101]

For those focused on achieving emancipatory idealism, this is a troublesome predicament, as this could leave individuals and communities vulnerable to modes of oppression. If States do not see a realist gain for contributing to military enforcement operations to ensure the protection of individuals and communities, international peace and security may be

[99] D. Grieg, 'Self-Defence and the Security Council: What Does Article 51 Require?' (1991) 40 *ICLQ* 336, at 391.

[100] V. Gowlland-Debbas, 'Security Council Enforcement Action and Issues of State Responsibility,' (1994) 43.1 *The International and Comparative Law Quarterly* 55, at 63.

[101] Glennon, *supra* note 24, at 25.

compromised.[102] For those who focus on emancipatory idealism as a focal goal of international law, this could result in precisely what should be prevented, a stunt in societal and technological development. However, this is not the only facet of the Security Council that could compromise international peace and security for the sake of Member-States seeking out their self-interest.

5.5.2 *The P-5 Members and Veto Powers*

A facet of the Security Council that has been most scrutinised by academics and practitioners alike is the veto powers of the permanent five members of the Council. This has historically been sighted as one of the central obstacles as to why the executive organ has failed to maintain international peace and security effectively on a consistent basis.

When the Charter was drafted, it became apparent that the rigid structure of the Council was established to ensure 'not all fifteen members [of the Security Council] were considered equal.' Chapter V of the Charter goes some way to establish this goal as Article 23.1 affirms that China, France, Russia, United States and UK are permanent members of the Security Council. Moreover, Article 27.3 ensures that the p-5 members maintain veto powers, even though it is not expressly stated so in the provision.[103] There are positive and negative effects to adopting such a framework. Tending first to the positive effects, one of the major flaws of the League of Nations was its failure to maintain a sense of continuity. 'The League Council was a veritable revolving door, with permanent members withdrawing from the organisation whenever their actions were condemned.'[104] However, with the UN Charter the goal was to override such a failing by ensuring that there were five permanent members that

[102] M. Koskenniemi, 'The Place of Law in Collective Security', (1996) 17.2 *Michigan Journal of International Law* 455, at 460.

[103] Article 27(3) of the UN Charter: '*Decisions of the Security Council on all matters shall be made by an affirmative vote of nine members including the concurring votes of the permanent members; provided that, in decisions under Chapter VI, and under paragraph 3 of Article 52, a party to a dispute shall abstain from voting.*

[104] Nadin, *supra* note 23, at 9.

would lead the matters of the Council with greater authority.[105] Furthermore, it ensured a level of continuity that was missing from the League's Council.

The negative effects to the establishment to such a framework however have become more apparent over the lifespan of the executive organ. An integral issue is that 'the composition of the Security Council, as well as its voting procedure does not reflect the changes to the international system since 1945.'[106] The issue of equal representation has come under a significant degree of criticism. 'Non-aligned and developing countries' brought this matter up first in 1979, and it is an issue that continues to be a popular debate. With two European countries, and no African or Latin American states holding permanent membership, the call for reform seems justified.[107] More so, it is the manner in which the p-5 have utilised their veto powers and their position that has raised greater concern for the maintenance of international peace and security. With realist interests at the heart of their interaction with international law, the repercussions are troublesome as John Quigley suggest:

> Member states, and particularly the major powers, have not been willing to subordinate their actions to the organisation and have insisted on retaining the free hand that the authorisation technique affords. These states have, in effect, blackmailed the United Nations into accepting authorisation. Their implicit message to the organisation has been that it either accept its authorisation or stand idly by in the face of threats to peace... The Western powers, enjoy predominance in the Security Council, are in a position to secure the adoption of resolutions giving themselves a free hand to use military force.[108]

The concern is that States are willing to sacrifice the goal of international peace and security in order to advance their self-interested

[105] Selkirk, *supra* note 33, at 1103.

[106] Malanczuk, *supra* note 15, at 376.

[107] S. Tharoor, 'Security Council Reform: Past, Present and Future', (2011) 25.4 *Ethics & International Affairs* 397, at 397–400.

[108] J. Quigley, 'The "Privatisation" of Security Council Enforcement Action: A Threat to Multilateralism' (1996) 17.2 *Michigan Journal of International Law* 249, at 283.

ambitions.[109] For those focused on emancipatory idealism such a situation is concerning, for it leaves utopian goals vulnerable. If Member-States are willing to maintain international peace and security if only for the sake of their realist ambitions, then the Security Council has fallen short of achieving the aims of emancipatory idealism as a utopian focal goal. Several critics such as Koskenniemi have raised this point:

> Why Libya, but not Israel? Why the Council's passivity during most of the eight-year Iran-Iraq war? Why has the Council's reaction in Africa been markedly less vigorous and effective than in the Gulf? Why the discrepancy between the Council's forceful attack on Iraq (an Islamic country) and its timidity to defend the Muslims of Bosnia-Herzegovina? The choice of targets, as well as the manner of reacting, has certainly not been automatic. The argument is made that the Council has not reflected the collective interests of the United Nations as a whole, but only the special interests and factual predominance of the United States and its Western allies within the Council.[110]

The selective nature of the Security Council's decision to intervene in breaches to international peace and security shifts away from emancipatory idealism. This tends to leave individuals or a community of individuals vulnerable to modes of oppression, if there is not an incentive for the permanent members to intervene. The current form of the Security Council makes it difficult to provide collective security for all in the twenty-first century.[111] Instead, it allows the Security Council to nurture realist goals of the more influential States within the legal system.[112] This in itself is a dangerous path to follow, because if Member-States see Security Council intervention in a humanitarian crisis in direct conflict with their own interest, they are willing to veto support for such resolutions. This in turn is blockading the full achievement of emancipatory idealism as a utopian focal goal of international law. Emancipatory idealism seeks to ensure the protection of all individuals or community of individuals from

[109] Bourantonis, *supra* note 25, at 5.

[110] M. Koskenniemi, *The Politics of International Law*, (2011) at 85.

[111] Y.Z. Blum, 'Proposals for UN Security Council Reform', (2005) 99 *AJIL* 632, at 632.

[112] Bourantonis, *supra* note 25, at 6.

modes of oppression. However, this rather selective approach adopted by members of the Security Council does little to realise such aims.

An example of such a tension is China's response to providing aid for Macedonia through the Security Council. When the matter was brought before the Security Council, China vetoed any resolution to help the people of Macedonia.[113] China had based its reasoning not on the basis of necessary peacekeeping measures but rather on the basis that Macedonia had established ties with Taiwan,[114] a State that China believed was part of its territory. China stated that, 'The situation in [Macedonia] had apparently stabilized in the past few years, and its relations with neighbouring countries had improved,'[115] which is contrary to on-field reports from UNPREDEP that stressed the instability inherent within the Macedonian territory.[116] Their decision was not based on the need to protect individuals but on a necessity to uphold their political position.

5.6 The Security Council in Action

It is essential to explore the successes and failures of the Security Council, as it is able to highlight the contribution Member-States have made and the realist influences they bring into the work of the UN organ. Realist approaches to international law have persisted to influence the work of the UN.[117] This is apparent when examining the Security Council has or has not opted to utilise the instruments it possesses to deal with threats to international peace and security.

There were occasions in which such a realist approach coincided with the utopian focal goals to work towards maintaining international peace and security. The decade following the end of the Cold War is a prime example of such an occurrence. The start of the 1990s incurred a seismic

[113] E. Stamnes, 'Critical Security Studies and the United Nations Preventative Deployment in Macedonia', (2007) 11 *International Peacekeeping* 161, at 169.

[114] UN doc. S/1999/201; UN doc. SC/6648. See also https://www.securitycouncilreport.org/un-documents/document/s1999201.php accessed 19 June 2019.

[115] UN SC press release on China's veto on Macedonia: http://www.un.org/Depts/DPKO/Missions/unpred_p.htm accessed 25 November 2017.

[116] UNPREDEP report:http://www.un.org/Depts/DPKO/Missions/unpred_p.htm accessed 25 November 2017.

[117] C. Reus-Smit, 'The Politics of International Law' in C. Reus-Smit (ed.) in *The Politics of International Law*, (2004) at 15–16.

shift not only in the work of the Security Council but also in the use of international law.[118] With the breakup of the Soviet Union, the United States moved into a new and central position with regard to the maintenance of international peace and security. Rosalyn Higgins was quick to point out this shift in the international community:

> Since the end of the Cold War there has been a marked decline in the unilateral use of force by the United States outside the United Nations. Since the coincidence of its own objectives and those of the United Nations in the Iraq invasion Kuwait, the advantage has been seen in the United States of making the United Nations the centre of foreign policy. The disappearance of the old, hostile Soviet Union has made the Security Council a more comfortable environment. There has been a substantial common interest in peace and security matters between the United States, France and the United Kingdom, with much common ground also with the Russian Federation. China remains uneasy but does not feel strongly enough to veto.[119]

The climate at the start of the 90 s was a healthy one for the Security Council to operate within. The newfound cooperation amongst the permanent five members allowed for a surge in Security Council activity. By 1989, only 646 resolutions had been passed during a period of forty-three years. However, by 1999, the number of resolutions passed had risen to 1284. It seemed that the end of the Cold War ushered in a period where the Security Council would be able to make full use of Chapter VII powers, 'not only to repel external aggression, but also to pursue quite different goals, such as to intervene militarily in internal conflicts for humanitarian reasons and even to enforce democracy.'[120] There was a general sense of collaboration amongst the more influential Member-States to ensure international peace and security.[121] Thus, Security Council proactivity started when the use of force was authorised

[118] Grove, *supra* note 87, at 172.

[119] R. Higgins, 'Peace, Security, Achievements and Failures', (1995) 6 *EJIL* 445, at 449.

[120] Malanczuk, *supra* note 15, at 426.

[121] J. Boulden, 'Double Standards, Distance and Disengagement: Collective Legitimization in the Post-Cold War Security Council' (2006) 37.3 *Security Dialogue* 409, at 412.

to deal with the Iraqi invasion of Kuwaiti territory.[122] With the success of such missions, there was a sudden surge in peacekeeping missions with operations in Somalia, Rwanda, Bosnia, Sierra Leone and Haiti for example.

On the one hand for those seeking to achieve utopian focal goals of international law this is a moment to champion yet concerns still remained in regard to whether the self-interest of States would undermine such objectives. Certainly, it is a positive indication that the most influential States of the international legal system expressed their dedication to ensuring international peace and security.[123] An even more positive proposition is the desire to intervene militarily in internal conflicts for humanitarian reasons. This indicated a move away from the traditional model of international law that was State centric, to a system tending to individual justice and preventing the sociopolitical and economic breakdowns that could potentially destabilise whole regions. This encapsulated the prime objectives of emancipatory idealism. The dedication of the most influential Member-States was leading the international legal system and the international community in a direction where the utopian goals were in a position of being achieved.

Yet the achievement of such utopian focal goals could in general only be realised with one integral caveat intact.[124] The Member-States (the permanent five members in particular) could not allow their realist goals to undermine utopian goals of international law when the two came into conflict during the work of the Council. The League of Nations and the Security Council's first forty years had already demonstrated the

[122] Lillich, *supra* note 61, at 5.

[123] Bourantonis, *supra* note 25, at 27.

[124] The operation in Somalia would be the exception to this proposition. The humanitarian intervention in Somalia though had the support of the United States, who led the military operation to protect the delivery of humanitarian relief, was a failure but not because of a lack of commitment from Member-States. First of all, as there was no working government it was difficult to establish any semblance of control once the crisis had been neutralised. Instead, this meant that the political climate of Somalia would prove to be more unstable. Secondly, the reactionary expansion of the UN mandate from providing humanitarian relief to use force in order to establish a secure environment in Somalia and 'assist in rebuilding the economy and social and political institutions of the country' was problematic. Several other States criticised such an expansion of the UN mandate as the presence of heavy military forces was seemingly worsening the situation. Ultimately, the Security Council had entered into this humanitarian crisis with a lack of effective planning.

detrimental nature of such tensions in respect to achieving emancipatory idealism as a focal goal of international law. It is here that the various degrees of success of each mission could be assessed. For example, in regard to military intervention in Iraq, the operations were successful as there was a full commitment from the likes of the United States, UK and France to ensure peace and security within the region.[125] UK argued the legitimacy of intervention in Iraq stating that 'we believe that international intervention without the invitation of the country concerned can be justified in cases of extreme humanitarian need. This is why we were prepared to commit British forces to Operation Haven, mounted by the coalition in response to the refugee crisis involving the Iraqi Kurds. The deployment of these forces was entirely consistent with the objectives of SCR 688.'[126]

On the other hand, in regard to the Rwandan Genocide when the Security Council authorised the enlargement of UNAMIR by sending of 5500 troops.[127] Most Member-States were unwilling to supply such a number of troops with only Ethiopia showing any commitment to do so. Such measures had been adopted after the Security Council realised that size of UNAMIR and its mandate was insufficient in dealing with the grave violation of core human rights principles. Eventually, France offered to intervene in Rwanda, which paved the way for SC resolution 929. The Security Council authorised France and other willing Member-States to use 'all necessary means' in order to protect the civilian population in Rwanda. However, much of the damage had already been inflicted and the Rwandan Genocide, whilst French-led forces were accused of being bias in protecting Hutu civilians living amongst the genocidaires who had committed much of the atrocities against the Tutsi population. Rwanda remains a heavy reminder of the consequences of undermining emancipatory idealism as a utopian focal goal.

The issue of Member-States' self-interest persisted in the Security Council's failings to deal effectively with breaches of international peace and security. This was a key reason to NATO's illegal intervention in Kosovo as the Security Council had become deadlocked by Russia and

[125] G. Nolte, 'The Different Functions of the Security Council with respect to Humanitarian Law' in V. Lowe, A. Roberts, J. Welsh & D. Zaum (eds.), *The United Nations Security Council and the Evolution of Thought and Practice since 1945*, (2010), at 538.

[126] G. Marston, 'UK Materials on International Law', (1992) 63 *BYIL* 615, at 624.

[127] UN Security Council Resolution 918 (17th May 1994) UN Doc/S/RES/918).

China's veto on the matter. Natasha Kuhrt summarises the position both Russia and China hold, thus further revealing the problematic consequences such a position may have on achieving the central aims of emancipatory idealism:

> Both Russia and China hold a restrictionist view of the Charter, which sees sovereignty as ranking higher than human rights. In terms of enlargement of the scope that constitutes a threat to international peace and security, China has tended to resist this trend more than Russia. Russia has made it clear that any intervention in response to threats of an international nature must be authorised by the UNSC and that the interpretation of such "threats" must not go beyond the framework set out in Chapter VII of the Charter.[128]

To further stress how the realist ambitions undermine utopian focal goals, China's rejection of the third pillar of the Responsibility to Protect doctrine stems from the belief that the 'maintenance of sovereignty and territory has been regarded as its ruling ethos and source of legitimacy, as well as how it relates to vitally important interests. In this regard, China's ambivalence towards the third pillar because it may serve as an excuse to intervene in the internal business of China.'[129] With China having a history of ethnic separatist movements, intervention based on humanitarian grounds could trigger the violation of its sovereign territory.[130] Russia similarly holds the position that the sovereignty of State is of prime importance and intervention which places Article 2(4) in risk of violation is unfavourable. For these reasons, China and Russia 'appeared ready to veto any call for UN intervention [in Kosovo], as well as any mandate that conferred upon NATO or any other such entity the right.'[131] The argument put forward against intervention in Kosovo was that without Security Council explicit authorisation, NATO could not intervene militarily. The Security Council was deadlocked and thus the

[128] N. Kuhrt, 'Russia, The Responsibility to Protect and Intervention' in D. Fiott, & J. Koops (eds.), *The Responsibility to Protect and the Third Pillar,* (2015), 97 at 99.

[129] P. Wang, 'China and the Third Pillar' in D. Fiott, & J. Koops (eds.), *The Responsibility to Protect and the Third Pillar* (2015), 78 at 89.

[130] Ibid., at 79.

[131] R. Falk, 'Kosovo, World Order, and the Future of International Law', (1999) 93.4 *AJIL* 847–857.

Albanian majority in Kosovo was still placed in danger, as well as the Serbian minority from Kosovan rebels. The framework of the UN's international legal system was failing to protect a community of individuals. With the Milošević government's policies 'involving fundamental denials of human rights' and the potential for ethnic cleansing, there was strong justification for intervention.

Regardless of the Security Council deadlock on the matter of humanitarian intervention in Kosovo, the general consensus within Europe and the United States was that something needed to be done, 'or else the Bosnian ordeal would be catastrophically reproduced with damaging consequences for the future of Europe and the credibility of the transatlantic alliance with the United States.'[132] NATO consequently decided to carry out *Operation Allied Force* in March 1999 without Security Council authorisation. Regardless of the political motivations, such an operation was a violation of Article 2(4), Article 24 (on the primacy of the Security Council) and Article 53 (on the need for Security Council authorisation or enforcement action by regional organisations) of the Charter. Those within the Security Council supporting NATO's actions stressed the need for intervention on the basis of preventing large-scale violations of fundamental human rights principles and the furtherance of the aims of the international community. Although the Security Council adopted resolution 1244 'to endorse the agreement between the parties on the principles of a political solution to end the Kosovo crisis' as a way of retrospective legal affirmation of NATO action, it highlighted States undermining the utopian goals of international law. The general consensus is that NATO's actions in Kosovo were legitimate yet illegal. This indicates that occasions may arise where in order to achieve emancipatory idealism a violation of the Charter may be required. However, such situations are only arising because the Security Council is failing to ensure international peace and security. With States harbouring their self-interest when assessing the need for intervention, it underlines the failures of the Security Council to respond effectively when required.

Within the twenty-first century, this problem has persisted to handicap the Security Council in achieving utopian goals of international law. It is important to analyse the effect invasion of Iraq in 2003 had upon the international community, for Aidan Hehir notes that:

[132] Ibid, at 849.

> In many respects, the invasion of Iraq has undermined much of the nascent optimism about humanitarian intervention. The dissonance caused by the invasion and the seemingly cynical use of humanitarian rhetoric constituted a significant setback for the pro-intervention agenda, which appeared so promising after Operation Allied Force and the publication of "The Responsibility to Protect."[133]

Within the current decade, there is greater reservation for humanitarian intervention following the United States and UK military efforts in Iraq. The enthusiasm prevalent within the end of the previous century had weakened. Thomas Weiss rued the damage done to the humanitarian cause, citing the 'poisonous' atmosphere in the General Assembly as evidence of the regression caused by Iraq. States have become less inclined to intervene and situations have arisen such as Sri Lanka in 2005 and 2009, where no action was taken to intervene in the civil war amidst the killing of civilians on a systematic scale. Following a re-escalation of violence in 2005 between the Singhalese Sri Lankan government and the Liberation Tigers of Tamil Eelam (LTTE), UN reports suggest that 'there could have been as many as 40,000 civilian deaths.'[134] The report also asserted that 'without clear Security Council support, the UN felt it could not play a lead role and made no attempt to implement a comprehensive strategy.'[135]

The conflict between Israel and Palestine has similarly suffered from such roadblocks. After many decades of conflict, the Security Council has come under constant criticism for its inability to effectively deal with the dispute. Scholars such as Ramesh Thakur 'have regarded the Security Council's interjections into the Palestinian-Israeli conflict as slight or completely irrelevant.'[136] The lack of effective Security Council interjection stems from US support of Israel. Such support has led to the blocking of any veto resolution countering Israeli interest. This has

[133] A. Hehir, 'Humanitarian Intervention: Past, Present and Future', (2006) 6 *Political Studies Review* 327, at 328.

[134] Report of the Secretary-General's Internal Review Panel on the United Nations action in Sri Lanka, (November 2012), at 14, para 34. https://www.un.org/News/dh/infocus/Sri_Lanka/The_Internal_Review_Panel_report_on_Sri_Lanka.pdf accessed 15 May 2019.

[135] Ibid., at 9, para18.

[136] R. Thakur, 'Law, Legitimacy and the United Nations' in R. Falk, M. Juergensmeyer, & V. Popovski (eds.), *Legality and Legitimacy in Global Affairs*, (2011), at 45–71.

been the case regardless the ICJ's advisory opinion in 2004 establishing that 'the construction of the wall being built by Israel, the occupying Power, in the Occupied Palestinian Territory, including in and around East Jerusalem, and its associated regime, are contrary to international law.'[137] The General Assembly has also supported the ICJ's finding with UNGA Resolution ES-10/15, acknowledging the duty of Israel and all UN Member-States 'to comply with their legal obligations as mentioned in the advisory opinion.' Also, the General Assembly's applied pressure with UNGA resolution 67/19 in 2012 where the decision was made to 'accord to Palestine non-member observer State status in the United Nations,'[138] and also to 'reaffirm the right of the Palestinian people to self-determination and to independence in the Palestinian territory occupied since 1967.'[139] With Israeli breaches of international law having been recognised and the Palestinian people's right to self-determination being blocked, the deadlock in the Security Council to adequately deal with the situation grows increasingly troublesome. The violations of international law occurring in the Palestine-Israel conflict that has been left unattended further exemplify the undermining of the utopian goals of international law. It all the more asserts the problematic nature of Member-States' conduct in the operation of the Security Council and the position they have in the workings of international law.

The most recent example of such a situation is with Syria. Human Rights Watch has reported that 'the death toll from the conflict as of February 2016 was 470,000' with '6.1 million internally displaced people and 4.8 million seeking refuge abroad.'[140] Various reports suggest gross violations of international law by all parties to the conflict spanning from the targeting of civilians to the use of incendiary weapons, cluster munitions, and chemical weapons. UN special envoy for Syria, Staffan de

[137] *Legal Consequences of the Construction of a Wall in the Occupied Palestinian Territory*, Advisory Opinion of 9 July 2004, [2004], ICJ Rep. 136, 69 at para163.

[138] United Nations General Assembly Resolution 67/19, (29 November 2012) UN Doc A/Res/67/19.

[139] Ibid.

[140] https://www.hrw.org/world-report/2017/country-chapters/syria accessed 25 November 2017.

Mistura, has determined the Syrian Civil War to be 'the worst humanitarian tragedy since World War II.'[141] However, with Russian support of the Syrian government through military intervention, any meaningful Security Council intervention has been blocked. The lack of will displayed by the remaining members of the Security Council to effectively deal with the Civil War in a timely manner has also contributed to the most significant undermining of emancipatory idealism in recent times. It further highlights the repercussions of not protecting individuals or a community of individuals from modes of oppression. The sociological, political and economic stability of the region has been shaken and their opportunity to contribute to civilizational development has been prevented.

In fact, the failure to effectively deal with the humanitarian crisis in Syria and also Yemen represents a deeper crisis within the Security Council and the current world order. The United States under the Trump administration has often been criticised for its disengagement from globalism.[142] The United States has in recent years done its utmost to 'undermine international institutions and resign from global leadership.'[143] A clear example of such a phenomenon is US targeted strikes in Syria in 2017 and 2018. Without Security Council authorisation and no clear justification for exercising self-defence, be it through the Charter or international law, such targeted strikes are a clear violation of the prohibition on the use of force. More concerning is that justifications for such strikes refer very little to international law, and in particular why such an attack creates an exception to Article 2(4) of the Charter. Instead, justifications were made on the basis of 'establishing a strong deterrent against the production, spread, and use of chemical weapons,'[144] and protectionist rhetoric.[145] Such conduct represents at best a general distancing from legal system, at worst a disregard for international law. Couple such

[141] http://www.aljazeera.com/programmes/upfront/2016/09/failed-syria-160923192457782.html accessed 25 November 2017.

[142] H. Koh. *The Trump Administration and International Law*, (2018), at 5.

[143] *Ibid*. See also S. Von Einsiedal & D. Malone, 'Security Council' in T.G. Weiss & S. Daws (eds.), *Oxford Handbook on the United Nations*, (2018), 149.

[144] Ibid., at 129.

[145] Jen Kirby, Read Trump's Statement on Syria Strike: "They Are Crimes of a Monster," Vox, Apr. 13, 2018, https://www.vox.com/2018/4/13/17236862/syria-strike-donald-trump-chemical-attack-statement: Trump restated his objective as 'doing what is necessary to protect American people.'.

a cutback from world affairs with the poor outcomes of its military interventions over the past two decades, and the result has been the US more reluctant to initiate humanitarian intervention.[146] Moreover, Russia and China's reservations on the aspect of humanitarian intervention have only hardened since intervention in Libya. Such intervention was regarded as 'mandate overreach,' when Security Council authorisation to use force against the *de jure* government of a UN member state for the purpose of protecting civilians,[147] had been interpreted as authorising military attacks against the regime assets in Tripoli.[148] This has consequently ushered in a phase in the Security Council timeline where legal humanitarian intervention has become less likely. The return of 'power tensions'[149] amongst the permanent five members has therefore restricted the Security Council's capacity to maintain international peace and security. Thus, for the emancipatory idealists the current power tensions that plague the Security Council is of urgent concern. For the Security Council's such inability to intervene in just humanitarian causes—which is a result of States prioritising their domestic duty over their duty to the international community—leaves individuals and groups of individuals vulnerable to the gravest modes of oppression.

5.7 Conclusion—The Security Council, Emancipatory Idealism & the Dual Duties of States

Analysing the Security Council, whether it is its responses to threats to international peace and security or the tools they possess to deal with such threats, goes some way to highlight why the primacy of the State in the international legal system is problematic for those focused on utopian focal goals.[150] Such analysis fleshes out the relationship between States and utopian focal goals, indicating the readiness of States to undermine them. The Security Council's failure to deal with threats to international

[146] Jeffrey Goldberg, 'The Obama Doctrine,' *The Atlantic*, April 2016.

[147] A.J. Bellamy & P.D. Williams, 'Libya,' in S. Von Einsiedel, D.M. Malone & B.S. Ugarte (eds.), *The UN Security Council in the 21st Century*, (2016), 699–716.

[148] S. Von Einsiedal & D. Malone, 'Security Council' in T.G. Weiss & S. Daws (eds.), *Oxford Handbook on the United Nations*, (2018), 149.

[149] Ibid., at 141.

[150] Boulden, *supra* note 121, at 412.

peace and security successfully, whether it be Rwanda, Sri Lanka or Syria, shows that the success of the Security Council is far too reliant upon Member-States. Primacy of the State in the work of the Security Council brings the sort of politicisation that is not conducive for achieving the aims of emancipatory idealism.

Moreover, the Security Council has the potential to ensure threats to international peace and security are effectively dealt with and to achieve emancipatory idealism as a utopian focal goal of international law. The powers it possesses under the Charter are adequate safeguards that can ensure individuals or communities of individuals are protected from modes of oppression if utilised effectively. The capacity is there to achieve utopian focal goals, yet the effective utilisation of such powers is dependent upon the will of States.[151] Analysing the work of the Security Council shows that though there are legitimate cases to utilise such powers, Member-States and in most cases the permanent members, have on occasions obstructed the Security Council's ability to ensure that individuals or a community of individuals are protected from modes of oppression. What is more concerning is the realist impulse that tends to motivate Member-States undermining utopian focal goals, as the overall impact of such decisions has little benefit for the international community as a whole. Such actions are taken in order to 'help ensure acceptance of their policies.'[152] If we return to China's veto of extending the UNPREDEP mission in Macedonia, it becomes clear that this action was not based on whether Macedonia required such assistance, but instead was based on a political decision that would protect their interests in international relations; to invalidate Macedonia's recognition of Taiwan as a separate State. Similar instances can be recited when addressing the dispute in Kosovo or between Israel and Palestine. Decisions not to intervene were made on the realist grounds of specific States protecting their own political interest. This further demonstrates that when States' dual duties are in tension, they tend to prioritise its domestic duty over its international duty. The arguments advanced by Schmitt and Foucault are strengthened by State conduct in the Security Council. States are working

[151] Reus-Smit, *supra* note 116, at 17–18.

[152] N. Krisch, 'The Security Council and the Great Powers' in V. Lowe, A. Roberts, J. Welsh & D. Zaum (eds.), *The United Nations Security Council and the Evolution of Thought and Practice Since 1945*, (2010), at 152.

towards tending to the needs of its populace, for it is in their very composition to do so. Biopolitics gives explanation for States injecting their realist goals when interacting with the Security Council. States act in this manner for they are the 'managers of life,'[153] more specifically the managers of the lives that they govern over. It is the State's primary responsibility to ensure the survival of its citizens, and to look out for its best interest.[154] Schmitt adopts a similar position, advocating a strong State to ensure order, peace and security within its region.[155]

However, there are further limits to the ability of the Security Council to maintain international peace and security. The reliance upon States to contribute military forces creates another level of dependence the Security Council has upon the will of States. Following Goldsmith and Posner's argument that States shall only use international law to justify their actions 'no matter how transparently self-interested their actions are,'[156] States still use the Security Council to instil their realist agenda. States only contribute military forces in the name of international security when it fulfils the more influential States' internal benefits. Recounting the problems that faced UNAMIR when dealing with the Rwandan Genocide for example, underlines the reliance upon Member-States to contribute forces to UN peacekeeping operations has handicapped the capacity for the Security Council to effectively deal with threats to international peace and security. With Belgium pulling out their troops and the US showing a level of hesitancy to contribute to the UNAMIR operations, the repercussions were severe.[157] In the decades since, peacekeeping operations have been increasing based on troop contributions from developing nations, who retain the national incentive to gain resources and equipment associated with participating in UN missions.

A greater concern is misappropriating the instruments the Security Council possesses to legitimise intervention which otherwise would be deemed illegal under international law. The US invasion of Iraq in 2003

[153] M. Foucault *Society Must be Defended*, (2003), at 241.

[154] Ibid.

[155] C. Schmitt, *Concept of the Political* (2007) at 27.

[156] J. Goldsmith & E. Posner, *The Limits of International Law*, (2005), at 169.

[157] M.N. Barnett, 'The UN Security Council, Indifference, and Genocide in Rwanda', (1997) 12.4 *Cultural Anthropology* 551, at 558.

was indicative of such a concern with US interpretation of relevant Security Council resolutions and the claim on the possible extension on the right of self-defence raising such alarms. Perhaps this is the most concerning facet of the primacy of the State in the work of the Security Council. The very tools used to ensure international peace and security can be utilised for an illegitimate intervention. It must be added that the revival of Security Council resolution 686 through SC resolution 1441 in order to justify intervention in Iraq is somewhat of a unique situation. However, it reveals the scope for Member-States to justify illegitimate use of force through the Security Council.[158] It also raises the argument that 'the Council has not reflected the collective interests of United Nations members as a whole, but only the special interests and factual predominance of the United States and its Western allies within the Council.'[159] In the light of such arguments, concerns arise with 'the Great Powers constantly trying to expand their privileges through changes in the informal operation of the Council.'[160] It seems that such expansion of powers is not necessarily to ensure the utopian focal goals are achieved, but rather to fulfil the special interests of the Member-States who have a more influential position in the Security Council. The concern for those focused on achieving emancipatory idealism is that such expansion of powers will be used to undermine utopian focal goals, which is an argument that can be raised when analysing US and UK efforts to legitimise the Iraqi invasion in 2003 through the Security Council.

Calls for reform have been put forward; however, any substantial advancements to curtail the impact of the more influential States have not yet occurred. Balance is required, with greater representation of the international community being necessary and the dominance of the permanent five members in the work of the Security Council deeply problematic.[161] The more influential Member-States enjoy a fruitful position where they are able to align their national interests with the work of the Security Council. It is for this reason precisely that the reform advocated is hard to foresee. The expectation is that the more influential States release the level

[158] 'Attorney General's Advice on the Iraq War Iraq: Resolution 1441' (2005) 54.3 *International and Comparative Law Quarterly* 767.

[159] M. Koskenniemi, *supra* note 110, at 460–461.

[160] Krisch, *supra* note 152, at 152.

[161] Ibid.

of control they hold within the work of the Security Council. However, such States would be unwilling to jeopardise their nationalist interest for the sake of nurturing an environment better suited for achieving utopian focal goals.[162] Thus, the veto powers that the permanent five members enjoy have continued to undermine the potential for the emancipatory idealism to be achieved within the international legal system.

It is apparent that the Security Council is dominated by the power politics of the more influential States, handicapping the ability for the Security Council to ensure that utopian focal goals are achieved. It is necessary at this point to return to the origins of both the League of Nations and the UN. The reason for establishing an international legal system in the twentieth and twenty-first century was to ensure large-scale crises would not cause the levels of political, economic and sociological destabilisation that can have the potential to destabilize the wider region. When drafting both international organisations, nations came together so that the levels of violence witnessed during the two world wars would not repeat itself. Analysing the Security Council seems to suggest that States are not always working towards such goals. Instead, such analysis proves the second hypothesis of the project which is that the primacy of the State in the international legal system can be problematic for those focused on achieving emancipatory idealism. States, instead, use the international legal system to further their own agendas undermining utopian focal goals if it does not further their interest. States are willing to undermine such focal goals; by showing a level of unwillingness to deal with threats to international peace and security and by justifying intervention that would previously be deemed illegal under international law, as shown by the Iraq War.

History indicates that the repercussions of such conduct have been directly detrimental to achieving the aims of emancipatory idealism. The Security Council on many occasions failed to protect individuals or communities of individuals from modes of oppression, and the reason for such failure has on many occasions been the result of the conduct of the Member-States. This further substantiates the position that the achievement of emancipatory idealism as a utopian focal goal of international law is heavily reliant upon States and in particular the more influential States. Moreover, such analysis validates the problematic nature of States being the primary object and subject of the international legal system, for it is apparent that States exhibit a level of readiness to undermine utopian focal goals if it furthers their own interests.

[162] Nadin, *supra* note 23, at 66.

CHAPTER 6

Conclusion: Utopianism and State Primacy in International Law

The endeavour of this project is to demonstrate the validity of two hypotheses. First, that utopianism plays an important role in the development of not only international law but also in ensuring that all individuals or community of individuals are protected from modes of oppression. Second, that the position that States enjoy in international law, as the primary objects and subjects of the international legal system, has been a central reason as to why the League of Nations and the United Nations failed to achieve utopian focal goals of international law.

By introducing emancipatory idealism, one of the central aims of the project was also to give a detailed justification as to why utopian concepts such as human dignity, human security and human rights for example, must be ensured for all individuals and communities of individuals. Where these utopian concepts could not on their own give a justification as to why they must be pursued, by using Hegelian philosophy and critical theory to argue that every individual and communities of individuals have the potential to contribute to the advancement of civilisation, emancipatory idealism has contributed in this manner. Thus, for utopians seeking to achieve emancipatory idealism, international law is primarily about the prosperity of civilisation. For such civilisational prosperity to occur the protection of all individuals and communities of individuals from modes

D. Mawar, *States Undermining International Law*,
Philosophy, Public Policy, and Transnational Law,
https://doi.org/10.1007/978-3-030-64789-6_6

of oppression must be ensured. Such utopian aspirations for international law move the system away from its classical positivist traditions espoused by the likes of Oppenheim, Verdross and Weil, who contend that international law is primarily about States.[1] Instead, attempting to achieve utopian focal goals of international law drives the international legal system towards the social idealist projects of Phillip Allott and Anne Peters. Indeed, emancipatory idealism shares Allott's sentiments that international law should be utilised for humanity's prosperity and survival.[2]

Chapter 2 demonstrated how important utopianism and utopian focal goals are to international law, in developing not only the legal system, but also the international community by protecting all individuals and communities of individuals. This was done in two ways. Firstly, by showing how influential utopian focal goals have been to the most accelerated and important phases of development the international legal system has undergone, it affirms that such influences are of paramount importance to the positive advancements made in international law. The second way was by introducing emancipatory idealism as the utopian focal goal of international law. By developing this concept, which better explains the idealist progression of international law and fully encapsulates the key merits of utopianism, emancipatory idealism establishes precisely why utopianism is so important to international law and the international community. Emancipatory idealism establishes the intrinsic worth of every individual and community. It supports the need to realise all social and political goods and to prevent suffering and injustices. This is due to every individual's capacity to contribute to civilisational development, both on a technological and sociological level. Emancipatory idealism, as a utopian focal goal of international law, conclusively justifies the need for utopian advancements in the international legal system.

Furthermore, by introducing emancipatory idealism in Chapter 2, the project was also able to develop the first hypothesis. In fact, delving into

[1] See P. Weil, 'Towards Relative Normativity in International Law?' (1983) 77.3 *The American Journal of International Law* 413; A.V. Verdross, 'On the Concept of International Law', (1949) 43.3 *American Journal of International Law* 435; L. Oppenheim, 'The Science of International Law: Its Task and Method', (1908) 2.2 *American Journal of International Law* 313.

[2] P. Allott, *The Health of Nations: The Society and Law Beyond the State*, (2002), at 387, para 18.30.

the creation of the League and the UN played an integral role in proving the first hypothesis of the project. Such historical analysis demonstrates that utopian focal goals have been a key element in the development of international law following a large-scale crisis. It is the influence of the utopian focal goals of international law that has helped drive the creation of both the League and the UN, plus the creation of a multitude of legal sources that provide individuals and communities of individuals with the necessary safeguards to live freely from suffering and injustice. Moreover, utopian focal goals also played a role in the transformation the international legal system underwent during post-large-scale crisis phases of the twentieth century. International law's history suggests that when there is political, social and economic destabilisation on a macro-level, utopianism has its greatest influence on the development of international law. Other factors must be taken into consideration, such as the need to quickly remedy the upheaval suffered by the international community following a large-scale crisis or the realist objectives of States to push forward international legislation that would better protect their own populace. But nonetheless, the analysis conducted in Chapter 2 indicates that key elements of utopianism are apparent in these accelerated phases of development. Indeed, achieving the realisation of all social and political goods, and that no further suffering or injustices occur seems to be a vital goal during some of the most significant developments in international law. Thus, Chapter 2 shows that utopian focal goals have in fact influenced the development of international law when advancements are most needed.

In order to prove such a hypothesis Chapters 4 and 5 analysed the creation of the League and UN to highlight how the aims of emancipatory idealism (which is to protect all individuals and communities of individual from modes of oppression) helped shape these two models of international law. Chapter 4 analyses the creation of the League, showing how international law transitioned from the Westphalian non-institutionalised legal system to an institutionalised system of international law. 'Although most histories of the field stress the importance of various nineteenth-century European institutional innovations, they express little doubt that the modern international institution was born with the League of Nations in the aftermath of the First World War,'[3] as the League

[3] D. Kennedy, 'The Move to Institutions', (1987) 8.8 *Cardozo Law Review* 841, at 841–842.

provided a structured framework for achieving international peace and security. Furthermore, buoyed by the dedicated and concerted efforts of its Member-States to ensure that the international organisation was a success, several conflicts were prevented from becoming larger problems, legislature was introduced such as the Locarno Treaties and the Kellogg-Briand Pact, and there was a concerted effort towards achieving disarmament, a movement that has not been seen since. Such analysis also highlighted a key factor for achieving utopian focal goals, State commitment to achieving such focal goals. During the first ten years of the League, States had a vested interest for it to succeed. However, once realist objectives diverged from utopian focal goals, States' commitment to the League waned, paving the road for the Second World War.

Similar analysis was undertaken in Chapter 5 to prove the first hypothesis of the project. By analysing the creation of the United Nations, the influence of utopian goals of international law can be identified when the legal system transformed the previous mere coordination of sovereign states into a system of cooperation and mutual benefit.[4] The UN model of international law also introduced the concept of an 'international legal community.'[5] Furthermore, this period sparked the individual justice movement in international law, as the individual was better recognised as a subject of the legal system. Such a movement was realised with the Universal Declaration of Human Rights, which in itself was the origin of international human rights law, the Genocide Convention, developments in international humanitarian law and subsequent other conventions and treaties focused on protecting individuals thereafter. Additionally, the United Nations model also witnessed a proliferation of international organisations, dealing with diverse matters on various levels of international society. Such developments in the international legal system highlight the focus placed on protecting individuals and communities of individuals, as international law continued to expand in scope.

However, Chapters 4 and 5's evaluation of the relationship between States and utopianism highlight that States can often be a barrier to achieving utopian focal goals, as suggested by the second hypothesis of

[4] R. Wolfrum, 'International Law of Cooperation', (2005) 2 *EPIL* 1242, 1242–1247.

[5] M. Lachs, 'Legal Framework of an International Community', (1992) 6 *Emory International Law Review* 329, 329–337.

the project. Analysing the League and the UN shows that States only seek to achieve utopian focal goals if they align with their realist interests. Such analysis consequently strengthens the argument that States, as the primary objects and subjects of international law, must be questioned if the focus is on achieving utopian focal goals. Moreover, it shows that if there is a tension between a State's dual duties, it tends to prioritise its domestic duty over its international duty.

Though the historical analysis of international law revealed that States as the primary object and subject of international law is problematic for those seeking to achieve utopian focal goals, additional philosophical analysis of the nature of the State conducted in Chapter 3 further cemented such an argument. Carl Schmitt and Michel Foucault demonstrate that when faced with the need to prioritise either its international or domestic responsibilities, States tend to opt for the latter over the former. Both Schmitt and Foucault's insistence that the State is solely responsible for the protection of its own populace explains why it is that they are more likely to undermine utopian focal goals of international law.[6] The international responsibilities that States now possess are relatively new, emerging only in the last hundred or so years, whereas the States' domestic responsibility is far more established over a considerably longer period of time.

Moreover, Hans Kelsen's attempts to introduce a more scientific tradition of international law further demonstrated the problematic nature of the primacy of the State in international law. Kelsen had advocated for an international legal system that was more empirical in nature; however, it would do little to counteract the problems pertaining State primacy.[7] Kelsen proposed such a model of international law so as to drive out non-legal elements and prevent States from incorporating their realist motives within the international legal framework.[8] This was to ensure that States would not ignore their international responsibilities and follow the legality already established, and consequently ensure that utopian focal goals are achieved. However, Kelsen's model of international law failed to overcome the primacy of the State. International law still originated from the

[6] See C. Schmitt, *Concept of the Political*, (2007); M. Foucault, *Society Must be Defended* (2003).

[7] H. Kelsen, *Das Problem der Souveränität*, (1960).

[8] H. Kelsen, *Pure Theory of Law*, (1992), at 134–139.

will of the State and with the ambiguous nature of several international legal sources. This permitted for plenty of space to bend international law to match their specific agendas, allowing States to continue to prioritise their domestic responsibilities at the expense of utopian focal goals.

Alongside the political and legal philosophers, international lawyers have similarly argued that States tend to interact with the international legal system in order to ensure the protection of its domestic territory. Analysing the writings of Goldsmith and Posner, the Chayeses and Thomas Franck has provided further support for the argument that States often prioritise their domestic duty over their international duty, which is problematic for those seeking to achieve utopian focal goals of international law. Whether it is the managerial model proposed by the Chayeses, Franck's fairness in international law concept or Goldsmith and Posner's position on State's utilising international law is that it is a means to an end. These theories on the State have helped establish the second hypothesis of the project, which is proven by analysing the failure of both the League and the UN to achieve utopian focal goals.

When examining the collapse of the League, and the manner in which States dismantled the international organisations ability to ensure international peace and security Franck's theories are particularly resonant. If we look at Germany, Italy and Japan's lack of compliance with the international legal system, Franck's suggestion that State perceptions regarding the legitimacy of rules are dependent upon whether they fall in line with principles of fair process hold true.[9] The fact that international law limited such States' goals of expansion led these particular States to disobey international law for the benefits exceeded the costs.[10] Moreover, the failure of Britain and France as the (hesitant) leaders of the League was another key factor to the failure of the League and can be explained by the Chayeses argument that compliance to international law is based on efficiency, national interest and regime norms.[11] The fact that efficiency and national interest emboldened France and Britain to secretly hold talks with Italy, which derailed the League's efforts to deal with the Abyssinian crisis, or their initial leniency to Germany's lebensraum policy, highlights State prioritisation of their domestic duty over their international duty. Such

[9] T. Franck, *Fairness in International Law and Institutions*, (1995), at 7.

[10] Ibid., at 7.

[11] A. Chayes & A.H. Chayes, *The New Sovereign*, (1995), at 1–28.

events reveal the prioritisation of a State's domestic duty for France and Britain sought to gain Italy's favour and alliance during the Abyssinian crisis rather than ensure that Italy were held accountable for their violations of international law.[12] Similar claims could be made in regard to appeasing Germany during their hostile foreign policy in the 1930s. For France and Britain, it was more efficient and in their national interest to gain the favour of the likes of Italy and Germany than supporting the League in its mission to ensure international peace and security.

Analysing the Security Council further strengthens the hypothesis that the State's primary position is problematic for those seeking to achieve utopian focal goals of international law. How the Security Council Member-States use (or do not use) the executive organ's powers supports Goldsmith and Posner's claim that States' legal and moral rhetoric are disguises or pretexts for actions motivated by a desire for power.[13] Returning to US invasion of Iraq in 2003 is indicative of such a claim. The revival of Security Council resolution 686 through SC resolution 1441 in order to justify intervention in Iraq is somewhat of a unique situation; however, it reveals the scope for Member-States to justify illegitimate use of force through the Security Council.[14] It raises the argument that, 'the Council has not reflected the collective interests of United Nations members as a whole, but only the special interests and factual predominance of the United States and its Western allies within the Council.'[15] It highlights the Security Council's failure to achieve utopian focal goals for States use the international legal system to further their own interests, jeopardising the needs of the international community. These examples support Schmitt and Foucault's theories about the State, and the fact that the State is designed to serve its populace first and foremost. It reveals the inherent nature of the State to act in a way that would not endanger the duty it has to its domestic environment, ensuring its own survival and prosperity.

Consequently, by establishing the importance of utopianism in insssssssssternational law and demonstrating that the inherent nature of

[12] F.P. Walters, *The History of the League of Nations*, (1969), at 678.

[13] J. Goldsmith & E. Posner, *The Limits of International Law*, (2005), at 170.

[14] 'Attorney General's Advice on the Iraq War Iraq: Resolution 1441' (2005) 54.3 *International and Comparative Law Quarterly* 767.

[15] M. Koskenniemi, 'The Place of Law in Collective Security', (1996) 17.2 *Michigan Journal of International Law* 455, at 460–461.

the State is to tend to its domestic duty over its international duty, strengthens the argument that the State's position as primary subjects and objects of international law is problematic. Exploring the history of international law, in particular the rise of and fall of the League and the issues that beseech the UN Security Council demonstrates the strength of such an argument. With Chapter 2 establishing the importance of utopianism, Chapters 4–5 revealed that the greatest barriers to achieving utopian focal goals are States. These chapters subsequently showed that States undermine utopian focal goals, and as a consequence are responsible for much of the suffering and injustices that have occurred in the international community in the twentieth and twenty-first centuries.

Having researched both utopianism and State primacy in international law, some topics covered within the project have the potential for more extensive research. A particular area prime for future research is the further analysis of emancipatory idealism. This project does not necessarily prove the key tenets of emancipatory idealism; that if individuals and communities of individuals are safe from modes of oppression, they are better placed to contribute to civilisational development on a technological and sociological level. However, a case study to prove the key elements of emancipatory idealism can be particularly fruitful in strengthening the argument that utopianism plays a key role in international law. Therefore, if further research can be conducted in order to demonstrate a correlation with a stable political, sociological and economic environment and civilisational development, such research can further support the importance emancipatory idealism places upon the protection of individuals and communities.

A second avenue for future research is the more detailed analysis of how international law responds to large-scale crisis. Analysing the history of international at these specific points helps to develop a clearer picture of the nature of international law. Furthermore, such analysis helps to understand how international law may develop in the future, and what are the catalysts for the legal system's most accelerated phases of development.

Thus, exploring the history of international law in the twentieth and twenty-first centuries has helped to unravel the significant influence of utopianism on the international legal system. Examining both the League of Nations and the United Nations indicates that utopianism has been most influential following a large-scale crisis such as the two World Wars and the various international crises that occurred during the 90s. Additionally, such analysis also draws attention to the problematic nature of the position States enjoy in international law as primary subjects and objects of the international legal system. Therefore, proving the importance of utopianism in international law and understanding some of the obstacles such an ideology faces, has helped to outline the ways in which the legal system can be structured in order to realise social and political goods and prevent suffering and injustice.

The manufacturer's authorised representative in the EU is Springer Nature Customer Service Centre GmbH, Europaplatz 3, 69115 Heidelberg, Germany. If you have any concerns regarding our products, please contact ProductSafety@springernature.com

Printed and bound by CPI Group (UK) Ltd, Croydon, CR0 4YY
30/09/2026
02225702-0007